CONTENTS

SOUS VIDE BREAKFAST RECIPES

Cinnamon Toast

Preparation time: 10 minutes
Cooking time: 1 hour
Servings: 4
Ingredients:
- ½ teaspoon cinnamon powder
- 1 tablespoon brown sugar
- ¼ cup ghee, melted
- 4 bread slices
- 2 eggs, whisked

Directions:
1.   In a bowl, mix the eggs with the cinnamon, sugar and the ghee and whisk.
2.   Dip the bread slices in this mix, place them in a sous vide bag, seal it, introduce in your sous vide machine and cook them at 147 degrees F for 1 hour.
3.   Serve right away for breakfast.

Nutrition:
calories 172
fat 4
fiber 5
carbs 12
protein 5

Eggs Cheesy Mix

Preparation time: 10 minutes
Cooking time: 1 hour
Servings: 4
Ingredients:
- 4 eggs, whisked
- 1 tablespoon chives, chopped
- Salt and black pepper to the taste
- ½ cup heavy cream
- ½ cup mozzarella, shredded

Directions:
1.   In a bowl, mix the cream with the eggs and the other ingredients, whisk well and pour this into a sous vide bag.
2.   Seal the bag, cook the eggs at 170 degrees F for 1 hour and serve them for breakfast.

Nutrition:
calories 188
fat 4
fiber 7
carbs 12
protein 4

Shallot Scramble

Preparation time: 10 minutes
Cooking time: 1 hour
Servings: 4
Ingredients:
- Salt and black pepper to the taste
- ½ cup mozzarella, shredded
- 2 tablespoons heavy cream
- 4 eggs, whisked
- ½ cup shallots, chopped
- 1 tablespoon chives, chopped

Directions:
1.   In a bowl, mix the eggs with the shallots and the other ingredients, whisk well and pour into a sous vide bag.
2.   Seal the bag, cook at 160 degrees F for 1 hour and serve for breakfast.

Nutrition:
calories 200
fat 3
fiber 6
carbs 12
protein 4

Eggs and Ham

Preparation time: 10 minutes
Cooking time: 1 hour
Servings: 4
Ingredients:
- ½ cup heavy cream
- Salt and black pepper to the taste
- ½ teaspoon chili powder
- ½ cup bacon, chopped
- 4 eggs, whisked

Directions:
1.   In a bowl, mix the eggs with the bacon and the other ingredients, whisk and pour into a sous vide bag.
2.   Seal the bag, submerge in preheated water oven and cook at 170 degrees F for 1 hour.
3.   Divide the mix between plates and serve.

Nutrition:
calories 162
fat 3
fiber 6
carbs 12
protein 5

Eggs Mix with Crab

Preparation time: 10 minutes
Cooking time: 25 minutes
Servings: 2
Ingredients:
Salt and black pepper to the taste
- 1 tablespoon chives, chopped
- 2 tablespoons cream cheese
- 1 tablespoon crabmeat
- 2 eggs, whisked
- 1 tablespoon butter, melted

Directions:
1.   Put eggs whisked with the butter, crabmeat and the other ingredients in 2 sous vide bags, submerge in your sous vide machine and cook them for 25 minutes at 167 degrees F.
2.   Divide between plates and serve.

Nutrition:

calories 172
fat 4
fiber 6
carbs 12
protein 5

Lime Coconut Jars

Preparation time: 10 minutes
Cooking time: 3 hours
Servings: 6
Ingredients:
- 1 tablespoon brown sugar
- ½ tablespoon heavy cream
- ½ tablespoon lime juice
- 1-quart almond milk, heated
- ½ cup coconut cream
- ½ tablespoon lime zest, grated

Directions:
1. In a bowl, combine the milk with the cream and the other ingredients, whisk well, pour into canning jars, put the lid on, introduce in your sous vide machine and cook for 3 hours and 120 degrees F.
2. Serve for breakfast.

Nutrition:
calories 134
fat 4
fiber 4
carbs 6
protein 3

Coconut Berry Mix

Preparation time: 10 minutes
Cooking time: 20 minutes
Servings: 2
Ingredients:
- 2 tablespoons sugar
- ½ teaspoon vanilla extract
- Juice of 1 lemon
- 1 cup blackberries
- 1 cup heavy cream
- 2 tablespoons coconut flakes

Directions:
1. In a bowl mix the berries with the cream and the other ingredients, toss, divide in canning jars, put the lid on, introduce in your sous vide machine and cook at 147 degrees F for 20 minutes.
2. Divide into bowls and serve for breakfast.

Nutrition:
calories 152
fat 3
fiber 3
carbs 6
protein 4

Parmesan Eggs

Preparation time: 10 minutes
Cooking time: 35 minutes
Servings: 4
Ingredients:
- ½ cup parmesan, grated
- Salt and black pepper to the taste
- 2 scallions, chopped
- 4 eggs
- 2 tablespoons chives, chopped
- ½ teaspoon sweet paprika
- ½ teaspoon cumin, ground

Directions:
1. Crack each egg in a sous vide bag, season with the chives, paprika and the other ingredients, seal the bags, submerge in the water oven and cook at 150 degrees F for 35 minutes.
2. Divide between plates and serve for breakfast.

Nutrition:
calories 162
fat 3
fiber 6
carbs 12
protein 5

Scrambled Eggs

Preparation time: 10 minutes
Cooking time: 30 minutes
Servings: 2
Ingredients:
- teaspoon cumin, ground
- Salt and black pepper to the taste
- 1 tablespoon chives, chopped
- 4 eggs, whisked
- ½ teaspoon rosemary, dried
- ½ teaspoon sweet paprika
- ½ teaspoon chili powder

Directions:
1. In a bowl, mix the eggs with the paprika, rosemary and the other ingredients, whisk, transfer to a sous vide bag, seal it, introduce in your sous vide machine and cook at 160 degrees F for 30 minutes.
2. Divide between plates and serve for breakfast.

Nutrition:
calories 200
fat 3
fiber 6
carbs 12
protein 5

Pesto Eggs

Preparation time: 10 minutes
Cooking time: 30 minutes
Servings: 2
Ingredients:
- 1 tomato, cubed
- 2 tablespoons basil pesto
- 4 eggs
- Salt and black pepper to the taste
- ½ teaspoon hot paprika

Directions:

1.	Place the eggs in your sous vide bath, cook at 150 degrees F for 30 minutes and crack them on plates
2.	Divide the pesto, tomato and sprinkle the paprika on each egg and serve for breakfast.
Nutrition:
calories 177
fat 3
fiber 6
carbs 8
protein 7

Spinach Scramble

Preparation time: 10 minutes
Cooking time: 20 minutes
Servings: 2
Ingredients:
- ½ teaspoon rosemary, dried
- 4 eggs
- 1-ounce spinach, chopped
- Salt and black pepper to the taste
- 1 tablespoon parmesan, grated
- 1 tablespoon chives, minced
- A pinch of red pepper flakes, crushed

Directions:
1.	In a bowl, mix eggs with salt, pepper, parmesan and the other ingredients, whisk, pour into a sous vide bag, introduce in your sous vide machine and cook at 140 degrees F for 20 minutes.
2.	Divide between plates and serve for breakfast.
Nutrition:
calories 211
fat 3
fiber 6
carbs 8
protein 2

Herbed Ricotta Cheese

Preparation time: 10 minutes
Cooking time: 40 minutes
Servings: 12
Ingredients:
- 3 tablespoons chives, chopped
- 1 tablespoon oregano, chopped
- 1 tablespoon parsley, chopped
- 3 quarts almond milk
- 1 cup white vinegar

Directions:
1.	Put the milk in a big sous vide bag, remove most of the air, seal, submerge in bath water and cook in your sous vide machine for 40 minutes at 172 degrees F.
2.	Add the vinegar, and the other ingredients, stir, open the bag, collect the curd, drain for a couple of hours and serve for breakfast.
Nutrition:
calories 132
fat 3

fiber 3
carbs 7
protein 7

Cinnamon Rice Pudding

Preparation time: 10 minutes
Cooking time: 40 minutes
Servings: 4
Ingredients:
- 1 teaspoon cinnamon powder
- ½ teaspoon vanilla extract
- 1 cup white rice
- 2 cups almond milk
- 3 tablespoons sugar

Directions:
1.	In a sous vide pouch, mix the rice with the milk and the other ingredients, whisk, seal, submerge in your sous vide machine and cook at 180 degrees F for 40 minutes.
2.	Divide the rice pudding into bowls and serve.
Nutrition:
calories 141
fat 2
fiber 6
carbs 7
protein 5

Spinach and Eggs Mix with Asparagus

Preparation time: 10 minutes
Cooking time: 50 minutes
Servings: 4
Ingredients:
- Cooking spray
- 1 teaspoon smoked paprika
- Salt and black pepper to the taste
- 1 teaspoon chives, chopped
- 2 asparagus spears, chopped
- 4 eggs whisked
- ¼ cup parmesan, grated
- ½ cup heavy cream

Directions:
1.	Grease 4 ramekins with the cooking spray, and divide the eggs mixed with the asparagus and the other ingredients in each.
2.	Preheat your water oven, place ramekins inside, cover them with tin foil and cook everything at 180 degrees F for 50 minutes.
3.	Serve for breakfast.
Nutrition:
calories 211
fat 3
fiber 6
carbs 8
protein 5

Coconut Eggs

Preparation time: 10 minutes
Cooking time: 40 minutes

Servings: 4
Ingredients:
* ½ teaspoon nutmeg, ground
* 3 tablespoons sugar
* 2 tablespoons coconut milk
* 4 eggs, whisked
* 1 cup coconut cream

Directions:
1. In a bowl, mix the eggs with the cream and the other ingredients, whisk and divide into 4 ramekins.
2. Put the ramekins in the water oven, add water halfway, and cook at 140 degrees F for 40 minutes.
3. Serve for breakfast right away.

Nutrition:
calories 165
fat 3
fiber 8
carbs 12
protein 6

Mix Pepper Eggs

Preparation time: 10 minutes
Cooking time: 40 minutes
Servings: 4
Ingredients:
* 1 red onion, chopped
* 8 eggs, whisked
* Salt and black pepper to the taste
* 1 tomato, cubed
* ¼ teaspoon chili powder
* 1 tablespoon cilantro, chopped
* 1 tablespoon butter, melted
* 1 red bell pepper, chopped
* 1 green bell pepper, chopped

Directions:
1. Heat up a pan with the butter over medium heat, add the onion, pepper and the other ingredients except the eggs, toss, cook for 10 minutes and take off the heat.
2. In a bowl, mix the eggs with salt, pepper and the sautéed ingredients and whisk.
3. Pour this mix into a ziplock bag, seal, submerge in the preheated water oven and cook at 167 degrees F for 30 minutes.
4. Divide between plates and serve for breakfast.

Nutrition:
calories 250
fat 12
fiber 5
carbs 12
protein 7

Sausage Ramekins

Preparation time: 10 minutes
Cooking time: 40 minutes
Servings: 4

Ingredients:
* Salt and black pepper to the taste
* 1 red bell pepper, chopped
* 2 spring onions, chopped
* 1 tablespoon chives, chopped
* 1 tablespoon parsley, chopped
* ½ teaspoon sweet paprika
* Cooking spray
* 2 sausage links, chopped
* 6 eggs, whisked

Directions:
1. Grease 4 ramekins with the cooking spray and divide the eggs mixed with the sausage, pepper and the other ingredients in each.
2. Carefully place ramekins in the preheated water oven and cook at 170 degrees F for 40 minutes.
3. Serve for breakfast right away.

Nutrition:
calories 240
fat 6
fiber 4
carbs 12
protein 14

Green Beans and Mushrooms with Eggs

Preparation time: 10 minutes
Cooking time: 30 minutes
Servings: 2
Ingredients:
* 1 red onion, chopped
* ½ teaspoon sweet paprika
* Salt and black pepper to the taste
* 1 tablespoon avocado oil, melted
* 4 eggs, whisked
* 1 cup green beans, chopped
* ½ cup mushrooms, sliced

Directions:
1. Heat up a pan with the oil over medium heat, add the onion, mushrooms and the other ingredients except the eggs, toss and sauté for 5 minutes.
2. In a bowl, mix eggs with sautéed mushroom mix and whisk.
3. Pour this into a sous vide bag, seal, submerge in the water oven and cook at 167 degrees F for 25 minutes.
4. Divide between plates and serve for breakfast.

Nutrition:
calories 260
fat 13
fiber 6
carbs 15
protein 8

Cream Cheese and Spinach Eggs

Preparation time: 10 minutes
Cooking time: 30 minutes
Servings: 4

Ingredients:
- 2 garlic cloves, minced
- ½ teaspoon coriander, ground
- Salt and black pepper to the taste
- 2 tablespoons parmesan, grated
- 1 cup baby spinach, torn
- ½ cup cream cheese, soft
- 4 eggs, whisked

Directions:
1.	In a bowl, mix the eggs with the spinach, cheese and the other ingredients and whisk well.
2.	Pour this into a sous vide bag, seal, submerge in the water oven and cook at 170 degrees F for 30 minutes.
3.	Divide the whole mix between plates and serve.

Nutrition:
calories 248
fat 4
fiber 1
carbs 7
protein 18

Avocado and Eggs Mix with Smoked Salmon

Preparation time: 10 minutes
Cooking time: 30 minutes
Servings: 4
Ingredients:
- Salt and black pepper to the taste
- 4 ounces smoked salmon, skinless, boneless and flaked
- 1 teaspoon garlic powder
- Salt and black pepper to the taste
- 1 tablespoon lemon juice
- 1 tablespoon lemon zest, grated
- 4 eggs, whisked
- 1 avocado, peeled, pitted and cubed
- 1 tablespoon spring onions, chopped

Directions:
1.	In a bowl, mix the eggs with the spring onions, avocado and the other ingredients, whisk well, transfer to a ziplock bag, seal, submerge in the water oven and cook at 165 degrees F for 30 minutes.
2.	Divide everything between plates and serve.

Nutrition:
calories 220
fat 10
fiber 2
carbs 15
protein 8

Lime Eggs, Tomato and Avocado Mix

Preparation time: 10 minutes
Cooking time: 30 minutes
Servings: 4
Ingredients:
- 1 tablespoon lime zest, grated
- 4 eggs, whisked

- Salt and black pepper to the taste
- 1 tablespoon chives, chopped
- 2 avocados, pitted, peeled and cubed
- ½ cup tomatoes, cubed
- ½ teaspoon rosemary, dried
- ½ teaspoon chili powder

Directions:
1.	In a bowl, mix the eggs with the avocados, tomatoes and the other ingredients, toss well,, pour into a sous vide bag, seal, introduce in your sous vide water oven and cook at 165 degrees F for 30 minutes.
2.	Divide between plates and serve for breakfast.

Nutrition:
calories 250
fat 6
fiber 7
carbs 13
protein 15

Zucchini and Eggs

Preparation time: 10 minutes
Cooking time: 40 minutes
Servings: 4
Ingredients:
- ½ teaspoon chili powder
- Salt and black pepper to the taste
- ½ teaspoon garlic powder
- ½ teaspoon basil, dried
- 8 eggs, whisked
- 2 zucchinis, grated
- ½ teaspoon rosemary, dried

Directions:
1.	In a bowl, mix the eggs with the zucchinis and the other ingredients, and whisk well.
2.	Transfer this to a sous vide bag, seal, submerge in the water oven and cook at 170 degrees F for 40 minutes.
3.	Divide between plates and serve for breakfast.

Nutrition:
calories 240
fat 15
fiber 2
carbs 13
protein 17

Ground Beef and Eggs Ramekins

Preparation time: 10 minutes
Cooking time: 30 minutes
Servings: 4
Ingredients:
- 8 eggs, whisked
- ½ teaspoon chili powder
- 1 yellow onion, chopped
- 1 cup baby spinach, torn
- Salt and black pepper to the taste
- 1 pound beef stew meat, ground
- 1 tablespoon olive oil

- 4 mushrooms, sliced

Directions:

1. Heat up a pan with the oil over medium heat, add the mushrooms and the onion and sauté for 5 minutes.
2. Add the meat, brown for another 5 minutes and take off the heat.
3. Divide the mix into 4 ramekins, add the eggs and the remaining ingredients as well, put the ramekins in the water oven, add water halfway and cook at 167 degrees F for 20 minutes.
4. Divide between plates and serve right away.

Nutrition:

calories 245
fat 7
fiber 6
carbs 14
protein 22

Tomato Ramekins

Preparation time: 10 minutes
Cooking time: 40 minutes
Servings: 6
Ingredients:

- 2 tablespoons parsley, chopped
- 8 eggs, whisked
- 2 tablespoons parmesan, grated
- ½ teaspoon coriander, ground
- 1 cup cherry tomatoes, cubed
- Salt and black pepper to the taste
- ½ teaspoon chili powder

Directions:

1. In a bowl, mix the eggs with the tomatoes and the other ingredients and whisk well.
2. Pour this mix into ramekins, introduce them into your sous vide water oven, add water halfway and cook at 174 degrees F for 40 minutes.
3. Divide between plates and serve for breakfast.

Nutrition:

calories 340
fat 13
fiber 3
carbs 12
protein 17

Coconut Leeks Mix

Preparation time: 10 minutes
Cooking time: 40 minutes
Servings: 4
Ingredients:

- ½ teaspoon cumin, ground
- 1 tablespoon chives, chopped
- Salt and black pepper to the taste
- ¼ teaspoon garlic powder
- 2 leeks, chopped
- 8 eggs, whisked
- ¼ cup coconut milk
- ½ teaspoon rosemary, dried

Directions:

1. In a bowl, mix the eggs with the leeks, milk and the other ingredients, whisk well and divide into 4 ramekins.
2. Place them in your sous vide machine, add water halfway and cook at 176 degrees F for 40 minutes.
3. Divide between plates and serve for breakfast.

Nutrition:

calories 340
fat 12
fiber 3
carbs 8
protein 13

Almond Oats

Preparation time: 10 minutes
Cooking time: 2 hours
Servings: 2
Ingredients:

- ½ teaspoon vanilla extract
- ½ cup almond milk
- ¾ cup coconut cream
- 1 teaspoon cinnamon powder
- 1 cup old fashioned oats
- ½ cup almonds, ground

Directions:

1. In a ziplock bag, mix the oats with the cream, milk and the other ingredients, toss, seal the bag, submerge in the water oven and cook at 180 degrees F for 2 hours.
2. Divide into bowls and serve.

Nutrition:

calories 260
fat 12
fiber 4
carbs 8
protein 16

Lemon Eggs

Preparation time: 10 minutes
Cooking time: 20 minutes
Servings: 4
Ingredients:

- Salt and black pepper to the taste
- 4 eggs, whisked
- 2 teaspoons lemon thyme, chopped
- ½ cup chives, chopped
- Juice of 1 lemon

Directions:

1. In a sous vide bag, mix the eggs with the lemon thyme, chives and the other ingredients, whisk and seal the bag.
2. Submerge the bag into the water oven and cook at 167 degrees F for 20 minutes.
3. Divide between plates and serve for breakfast.

Nutrition:

calories 203
fat 7
fiber 2
carbs 11
protein 8

Oregano Scramble

Preparation time: 10 minutes
Cooking time: 20 minutes
Servings: 4
Ingredients:
- 2 tablespoons parmesan cheese, grated
- ½ teaspoon sweet paprika
- Salt and black pepper to the taste
- ½ cup heavy cream
- 8 eggs, whisked
- 1 tablespoon oregano, chopped
- 2 tablespoons butter, melted

Directions:
1. In a bowl, mix the eggs with the oregano, butter and the other ingredients, whisk well, pour into a ziplock bag, introduce in your sous vide machine in the water oven and cook at 167 degrees F for 20 minutes.
2. Divide the mix between plates and serve.

Nutrition:
calories 160
fat 3
fiber 2
carbs 6
protein 10

Bacon and Radish Scramble

Preparation time: 10 minutes
Cooking time: 30 minutes
Servings: 2
Ingredients:
- Salt and black pepper to the taste
- 1 yellow onion, chopped
- 1 tablespoon chives, chopped
- ½ cup bacon, chopped
- ½ cup radish, chopped
- 8 eggs, whisked

Directions:
1. In a bowl, mix the eggs with the radishes and the other ingredients, whisk, pour into a ziplock bag, seal, introduce in your sous vide machine and cook at 170 degrees F for 30 minutes.
2. Divide everything between plates and serve.

Nutrition:
calories 240
fat 7
fiber 3
carbs 12
protein 8

Salad with Brussels Sprouts

Preparation time: 10 minutes
Cooking time: 30 minutes

Servings: 4
Ingredients:
- ½ cup black olives, pitted and halved
- 2 shallots, minced
- 12 ounces Brussels sprouts, halved
- 2 ounces bacon, cooked and chopped
- 1 tablespoon balsamic vinegar
- Salt and black pepper to the taste
- 1 tablespoon olive oil
- 1 cup cherry tomatoes, halved

Directions:
1. In a sous vide bag, mix the sprouts with the tomatoes and the other ingredients, toss, seal, introduce in your sous vide machine and cook at 170 degrees F for 30 minutes.
2. Divide into bowls and serve for breakfast.

Nutrition:
calories 240
fat 7
fiber 4
carbs 12
protein 12

Seeds Porridge

Preparation time: 3 minutes
Cooking time: 1 hour
Servings: 2
Ingredients:
- ½ cup heavy cream
- ½ teaspoon cinnamon powder
- 1 tablespoon sugar
- ¾ teaspoon vanilla extract
- 1 cup almond milk
- 2 tablespoons flax seeds
- 1 tablespoon sunflower seeds

Directions:
1. In a sous vide bag, mix the almond milk with the seeds and the other ingredients, seal the bag, introduce in your sous vide machine and cook at 180 degrees F for 1 hour
2. Divide the porridge into bowls and serve for breakfast.

Nutrition:
calories 230
fat 12
fiber 7
carbs 12
protein 13

Cinnamon Eggs

Preparation time: 10 minutes
Cooking time: 30 minutes
Servings: 2
Ingredients:
- 1/3 cup heavy cream
- ½ teaspoon cinnamon powder
- 4 eggs, whisked
- 1 teaspoon ginger powder
- 2 tablespoons sugar

Directions:
1.   In a sous vide bag, combine the eggs with the sugar and the other ingredients, seal, introduce in your sous vide machine and cook at 167 degrees F for 30 minutes.
2.   Divide into bowls and serve.
Nutrition:
calories 240
fat 12
fiber 6
carbs 12
protein 14

Chicken and Eggs

Preparation time: 10 minutes
Cooking time: 30 minutes
Servings: 2
Ingredients:
- 4 eggs, whisked
- 1 avocado, peeled, pitted and cubed
- Salt and black pepper to the taste
- 1 cup rotisserie chicken, cooked and shredded
- ½ cup black olives, pitted and halved
- 1 tomato, chopped

Directions:
1.   In a sous vide bag, combine the meat with the eggs and the other ingredients, toss, seal the bag, introduce in your sous vide machine and cook at 170 degrees F for 30 minutes.
2.   Divide between plates and serve.
Nutrition:
calories 260
fat 6
fiber 6
carbs 12
protein 25

Chia Eggs and Lime

Preparation time: 10 minutes
Cooking time: 20 minutes
Servings: 2
Ingredients:
- 1 tablespoon lime juice
- ½ cup heavy cream
- 1 teaspoon sweet paprika
- Salt and black pepper to the taste
- 4 eggs, whisked
- 1 tablespoon chia seeds

Directions:
1.   In a sous vide bag, combine the eggs with the chia seeds and the other ingredients, toss, seal, introduce in your sous vide machine and cook in the water oven at 167 degrees F for 20 minutes.
2.   Divide the mix between plates and serve.
Nutrition:
calories 260
fat 12
fiber 6

carbs 14
protein 14

Broccoli Eggs

Preparation time: 10 minutes
Cooking time: 30 minutes
Servings: 4
Ingredients:
- Salt and black pepper to the taste
- 4 eggs, whisked
- 2 garlic cloves, minced
- 1 tablespoon chives, chopped
- ½ cup heavy cream
- 1 cup broccoli florets
- ½ teaspoon sweet paprika
- ½ teaspoon coriander, ground

Directions:
1.   In a sous vide bag, combine the eggs with the broccoli, paprika and the other ingredients, toss, seal, introduce in your sous vide machine and cook at 175 degrees F for 30 minutes.
2.   Divide everything between plates and serve for breakfast.
Nutrition:
calories 230
fat 3
fiber 3
carbs 6
protein 10

Ginger Tomatoes Eggs

Preparation time: 10 minutes
Cooking time: 40 minutes
Servings: 4
Ingredients:
- A drizzle of olive oil
- 1 red onion, chopped
- Salt and black pepper to the taste
- A pinch of red pepper, crushed
- 1 garlic clove, minced
- 1 tablespoon chives, chopped
- 1 cup cherry tomatoes, cubed
- 1 tablespoon ginger, grated
- 4 eggs, whisked

Directions:
1.   Heat up a pan with the oil over medium heat, add the ginger, onion and the other ingredients except the eggs, stir and cook for 10 minutes.
2.   In a bowl, combine the eggs with the ginger mix, stir, pour this into a sous vide bag, seal, submerge in the water oven and cook at 170 degrees F for 30 minutes.
3.   Divide everything between plates and serve for breakfast.
Nutrition:
calories 210
fat 6
fiber 4
carbs 15

protein 12

Bok Choy and Veggies Bowls

Preparation time: 10 minutes
Cooking time: 30 minutes
Servings: 4
Ingredients:
- 1 cup white mushrooms, halved
- 1 cup cherry tomatoes, halved
- 1 cup kalamata olives, pitted and halved
- Salt and black pepper to the taste
- ½ tablespoon red pepper flakes
- 1 red onion, chopped
- 1 bunch bok choy, chopped
- A drizzle of olive oil
- 2 tablespoons balsamic vinegar
- 2 tablespoons Worcestershire sauce
- 2 tablespoons chives, chopped

Directions:
1. Heat up a pan with the oil over medium heat, add the mushrooms and onion and sauté for 10 minutes.
2. In a sous vide bag, mix the bok choy with the tomatoes, mushroom mix and the remaining ingredients, seal, introduce in your sous vide machine and cook at 170 degrees F for 20 minutes.
3. Divide the whole mix into bowls and serve for breakfast.
Nutrition:
calories 100
fat 3
fiber 1
carbs 2
protein 6

Bok Choy and Eggs

Preparation time: 10 minutes
Cooking time: 20 minutes
Servings: 2
Ingredients:
- ½ teaspoon chili powder
- 2 bunches bok choy, chopped
- 2 bacon slices, chopped
- Salt and black pepper to the taste
- A drizzle of avocado oil
- 2 garlic cloves, minced
- 4 eggs, whisked
- ½ teaspoon turmeric powder

Directions:
1. In a sous vide bag, combine the eggs with the bok choy and the other ingredients, toss, seal, submerge in the water bath and cook at 170 degrees F for 20 minutes.
2. Divide between plates and serve for breakfast
Nutrition:
calories 120
fat 1
fiber 2

carbs 6
protein 6

Greens and Eggs

Preparation time: 10 minutes
Cooking time: 20 minutes
Servings: 4
Ingredients:
- 1 tablespoon lime juice
- 8 eggs, whisked
- ½ teaspoon chili powder
- Salt and black pepper to the taste
- 1 cup baby spinach
- 1 cup collard greens, chopped
- ¼ cup spring onions, chopped

Directions:
1. In a sous vide bag, combine the greens with the eggs and the other ingredients, seal the bag, introduce in your sous vide machine and cook at 170 degrees F for 20 minutes.
2. Divide between plates and serve for breakfast.
Nutrition:
calories 170
fat 8
fiber 1
carbs 7
protein 7

Eggs and Asparagus

Preparation time: 10 minutes
Cooking time: 25 minutes
Servings: 4
Ingredients:
- 4 eggs, whisked
- ½ teaspoon sweet paprika
- ½ teaspoon chili powder
- 1 cup cheddar cheese, grated
- ¼ cup red onion, chopped
- 1 pound asparagus spears, chopped
- Salt and black pepper to the taste

Directions:
1. In a sous vide bag, combine the eggs with the eggs and the other ingredients, toss, seal, introduce in your sous vide machine and cook at 168 degrees F for 20 minutes.
2. Divide between plates and serve for breakfast.
Nutrition:
calories 200
fat 12
fiber 2
carbs 7
protein 14

Zucchini Bowls

Preparation time: 10 minutes
Cooking time: 30 minutes
Servings: 4

Ingredients:
- 1 tablespoon butter, melted
- 1 teaspoon oregano, dried
- 2 spring onions, chopped
- 1 ounce parmesan, grated
- ¼ cup heavy cream
- 2 zucchinis, cubed
- 4 eggs, whisked
- Salt and black pepper to the taste

Directions:
1. Heat up a pan with butter over medium-high heat, add the spring onions and the zucchinis and sauté for 5 minutes.
2. In a sous vide bag, combine the eggs with the zucchinis and the other ingredients, seal the bag, introduce in your sous vide machine and cook at 180 degrees F for 25 minutes.
3. Divide into bowls and serve for breakfast.

Nutrition:
calories 200
fat 4
fiber 2
carbs 6
protein 8

Tomato Sausage Salad

Preparation time: 10 minutes
Cooking time: 40 minutes
Servings: 4
Ingredients:
- 1 tablespoon avocado oil
- 1 cup kalamata olives, pitted and halved
- 2 tablespoons lemon juice
- 2 tablespoons basil pesto
- Salt and black pepper to the taste
- 2 pork sausage links, sliced
- 1 cup cherry tomatoes, halved
- 1 cup baby spinach

Directions:
1. In a sous vide bag, mix the sausage slices with the tomatoes, spinach and the other ingredients, seal the bag, submerge in the water bath, cook at 180 degrees F for 40 minutes, divide into bowls and serve for breakfast.

Nutrition:
calories 250
fat 12
fiber 3
carbs 12
protein 18

Mushrooms Mix and Sausages

Preparation time: 10 minutes
Cooking time: 40 minutes
Servings: 4
Ingredients:
- 1 cup cherry tomatoes, halved
- Salt and black pepper to the taste
- 2 sweet onions, chopped

- 1 tablespoon balsamic vinegar
- A drizzle of olive oil
- 1 cup Italian pork sausage, chopped
- 1 cup white mushrooms, halved
- 1 cup baby spinach

Directions:
1. Heat up a pan with the oil over medium-high heat, add the sausage, mushrooms and the onions and sauté for 10 minutes.
2. Put the mix in a sous vide bag, add the rest of the ingredients, seal the bag, submerge in the water oven and cook at 160 degrees F for 30 minutes.
3. Divide the mix plates and serve for breakfast.

Nutrition:
calories 230
fat 12
fiber 1
carbs 13
protein 9

Kale, Eggs and Sausage

Preparation time: 10 minutes
Cooking time: 45 minutes
Servings: 4
Ingredients:
- eggs, whisked
- ½ cup red bell pepper, chopped
- Salt and black pepper to the taste
- ½ cup kale, chopped
- 1 teaspoon garlic, minced
- ¼ cup red hot chili pepper, chopped
- 1 tablespoon chives, chopped
- 1 red onion, chopped
- A drizzle of olive oil
- 1 cup Italian pork sausage, sliced
- 1 cup kale, torn

Directions:
1. Heat up a pan with the oil over medium-high heat, add onion, kale and sausage, stir and cook for 10 minutes.
2. Transfer this to a sous vide bag, add the rest of the ingredients, stir, seal the bag, submerge in the water bath and cook at 180 degrees F for 35 minutes.
3. Divide everything between plates and serve.

Nutrition:
calories 200
fat 4
fiber 6
carbs 12
protein 12

Eggs, Sun-dried Tomatoes Mix and Cheese

Preparation time: 10 minutes
Cooking time: 45 minutes
Servings: 4
Ingredients:
- ½ cup sun-dried tomatoes, thinly sliced
- Salt and black pepper to the taste

- ½ cup cheddar cheese, grated
- A pinch of red pepper flakes
- A handful parsley, chopped
- 8 eggs, whisked
- A drizzle of avocado oil
- 1 yellow onion, sliced

Directions:

1. Heat up a pan with the oil over medium heat, add the onion and tomatoes, cook for 5 minutes and take off the heat.
2. In a sous vide machine, combine the eggs with the onion and tomato mix and the other ingredients, seal, submerge in the water bath, cook at 187 degrees F for 40 minutes, divide between plates and serve for breakfast.

Nutrition:

calories 200,
fat 5
fiber 3
carbs 12
protein 14

Shrimp, Eggs and Mushrooms

Preparation time: 10 minutes
Cooking time: 30 minutes
Servings: 4
Ingredients:

- 3 spring onions, chopped
- ½ teaspoon coriander, ground
- ½ teaspoon turmeric powder
- 4 bacon slices, chopped
- Salt and black pepper to the taste
- ½ cup coconut cream
- 1 cup mushrooms, sliced
- 4 eggs, whisked
- 1 cup shrimp, peeled and deveined

Directions:

1. In a sous vide bag, combine the eggs with the mushrooms, shrimp and the other ingredients, seal, introduce in a sous vide machine and cook at 140 degrees F for 30 minutes.
2. Divide between plates and serve for breakfast.

Nutrition:

calories 340
fat 23
fiber 1
carbs 14
protein 17

Enchilada Eggs Mix

Preparation time: 10 minutes
Cooking time: 30 minutes
Servings: 4
Ingredients:

- 1 avocado, peeled, pitted and cubed
- ½ cup kalamata olives, pitted and sliced
- 1 tomato, chopped
- ½ cup red onion, chopped

- 1 tablespoon chives, chopped
- ½ cup enchilada sauce
- Salt and black pepper to the taste
- 8 eggs, whisked

Directions:

1. In a sous vide bag, combine the eggs with the sauce, avocado and the other ingredients, toss, seal, introduce in your sous vide machine and cook at 180 degrees F for 30 minutes.
2. Divide between plates and serve.

Nutrition:

calories 250
fat 32
fiber 4
carbs 7
protein 12

Olives Bowls and Italian Squash

Preparation time: 10 minutes
Cooking time: 40 minutes
Servings: 4
Ingredients:

- Salt and black pepper to the taste
- ½ cup tomatoes, chopped
- 2 garlic cloves, minced
- ½ teaspoon Italian seasoning
- 3 ounces Italian salami, chopped
- 1 tablespoon oregano, chopped
- 1 tablespoon butter, melted
- 1 butternut squash, peeled and cubed
- 4 eggs, whisked
- 1 cup black olives, pitted and cubed

Directions:

1. In a sous vide bag, mix the squash with the melted butter, eggs and the other ingredients, toss, seal, introduce in your sous vide machine and cook at 170 degrees F for 40 minutes.
2. Divide everything between plates and serve.

Nutrition:

calories 263
fat 23
fiber 4
carbs 12
protein 15

Prosciutto and Zucchini Eggs

Preparation time: 10 minutes
Cooking time: 30 minutes
Servings: 4
Ingredients:

- ½ teaspoon rosemary, dried
- 2 zucchinis, cubed
- Salt and black pepper to the taste
- ¼ cup chives, chopped
- 8 eggs, whisked
- 4 prosciutto slices, chopped
- 1 teaspoon sweet paprika

Directions:

1.		In a sous vide bag, mix the eggs with the prosciutto, paprika and the other ingredients, seal, introduce in the sous vide machine and cook at 170 degrees F for 30 minutes.
2.		Divide between plates and serve for breakfast.
Nutrition:
calories 200
fat 3
fiber 6
carbs 13
protein 10

Green Beans, Eggs and Kale

Preparation time: 10 minutes
Cooking time: 35 minutes
Servings: 4
Ingredients:
* ½ teaspoon sweet paprika
* ½ teaspoon ginger, ground
* A pinch of salt and black pepper
* 1 tablespoon parmesan, grated
* 8 eggs, whisked
* 1 cup green beans, trimmed and roughly sliced
* 1 cup baby kale, chopped

Directions:
1.		In a sous vide bag, combine the eggs with the kale, green beans and the other ingredients, toss, seal, submerge in the water oven and cook at 170 degrees F for 35 minutes.
2.		Divide between plates serve for breakfast.
Nutrition:
calories 200
fat 4
fiber 6
carbs 8
protein 5

Oregano Eggs

Preparation time: 10 minutes
Cooking time: 30 minutes
Servings: 2
Ingredients:
* A pinch of salt and black pepper
* 1 tablespoon oregano, chopped
* ½ teaspoon chili powder
* ½ teaspoon sweet paprika
* 1 red bell pepper, chopped
* 2 shallots, chopped
* 4 eggs, whisked

Directions:
1.		In a bowl, mix the eggs with the pepper, shallots and the other ingredients, whisk and pour into a sous vide bag.
2.		Seal the bag, submerge in the water oven and cook at 170 degrees F for 30 minutes.
3.		Divide between plates and serve.
Nutrition:

calories 331
fat 17.7
fiber 8.7
carbs 43.1
protein 7

Quinoa and Berries Bowls

Preparation time: 10 minutes
Cooking time: 30 minutes
Servings: 4
Ingredients:
* ½ cup strawberries, halved
* 2 tablespoons sugar
* 1 teaspoon vanilla extract
* 1 cup quinoa
* 2 cups almond milk
* ½ cup blueberries

Directions:
1.		In a sous vide bag, mix the quinoa with the milk and the other ingredients, whisk and seal the bag.
2.		Submerge in preheated water oven and cook at 170 degrees F for 30 minutes.
3.		Divide the mix into bowls and serve.
Nutrition:
calories 217
fat 10
fiber 5
carbs 15
protein 14

Eggplant Bowls

Preparation time: 10 minutes
Cooking time: 25 minutes
Servings: 2
Ingredients:
* ½ teaspoon basil, dried
* 1 tablespoon oregano, chopped
* A pinch of salt and black pepper
* 1 tablespoon chives, chopped
* 2 spring onions, chopped
* 1 pound eggplants, cubed
* 8 eggs, whisked
* 1 cup baby spinach

Directions:
1.		In a bowl mix the eggs with the basil, oregano and the other ingredients, whisk and pour into a ziplock bag.
2.		Seal the bag, submerge in the water oven and cook at 170 degrees F for 25 minutes.
3.		Divide into bowls and serve.
Nutrition:
calories 223
fat 12
fiber 5
carbs 15
protein 5

Banana Oatmeal

Preparation time: 10 minutes
Cooking time: 25 minutes
Servings: 4
Ingredients:
- 2 bananas, peeled and mashed
- ½ teaspoon vanilla extract
- ½ teaspoon nutmeg, ground
- 1 cup old fashioned oats
- 2 cups almond milk

Directions:
1. In a sous vide bag, mix the oats with the milk and the other ingredients, whisk, seal the bag, submerge in the water oven and cook at 167 degrees F for 25 minutes.
2. Divide the oatmeal into bowls and serve.

Nutrition:
calories 371
fat 12
fiber 2
carbs 5
protein 5

Cheddar Eggs

Preparation time: 10 minutes
Cooking time: 30 minutes
Servings: 4
Ingredients:
- 2 spring onions, chopped
- ½ teaspoon sweet paprika
- A pinch of salt and black pepper
- 2 tablespoons chives, chopped
- 8 eggs, whisked
- ½ cup almond milk
- ½ cup cheddar cheese, shredded

Directions:
1. In a bowl, mix the eggs with the milk and the other ingredients, whisk and divide into 4 ramekins.
2. Put the ramekins in the water oven and cook at 165 degrees F for 25 minutes.
3. Serve for breakfast.

Nutrition:
calories 367
fat 13
fiber 3
carbs 15
protein 12

Spinach Frittata

Preparation time: 5 minutes
Cooking time: 30 minutes
Servings: 4
Ingredients:
- ½ teaspoon sweet paprika
- A pinch of salt and black pepper
- ½ cup heavy cream
- 8 eggs, whisked
- 1 cup baby spinach
- 2 spring onions, chopped

Directions:
1. In a bowl, mix the eggs with the spinach and the other ingredients, whisk and pour into a ziplock bag.
2. Seal the bag, submerge in the water oven and cook at 168 degrees F for 30 minutes.
3. Serve for breakfast.

Nutrition:
calories 253
fat 4.9
fiber 2
carbs 26.4
protein 23.6

Mushroom Oatmeal

Preparation time: 10 minutes
Cooking time: 30 minutes
Servings: 4
Ingredients:
- ½ teaspoon cumin, ground
- 1 red chili, minced
- A pinch of salt and black pepper
- 1 carrot, peeled and grated
- ½ pound mushrooms, sliced
- 1 cup steel cut oats
- 2 cups coconut milk

Directions:
1. In a ziplock bag, mix the oats with the mushrooms and the other ingredients, whisk and seal the bag.
2. Submerge in the water oven and cook at 170 degrees F for 30 minutes.
3. Divide into bowls and serve.

Nutrition:
calories 342
fat 12
fiber 5
carbs 16
protein 15

Strawberry Bowls

Preparation time: 10 minutes
Cooking time: 25 minutes
Servings: 4
Ingredients:
- ¼ teaspoon raw honey
- ½ tablespoon lime juice
- 2 teaspoons vanilla extract
- 1 cup strawberries
- 1 cup coconut milk

Directions:
1. In a sous vide bag, mix the berries with the honey and the other ingredients, toss gently, seal the bag and cook in the water oven for 25 minutes at 117 degrees F.
2. Divide into bowls and serve for breakfast.

Nutrition:
calories 197
fat 2

fiber 3
carbs 36
protein 6

Sweet Potato Mix

Preparation time: 10 minutes
Cooking time: 30 minutes
Servings: 4
Ingredients:
- A pinch of salt and black pepper
- 3 tablespoons Greek yogurt
- 1 teaspoon oregano, dried
- 1 tablespoon chives, chopped
- ½ pound sweet potatoes, peeled, and cubed
- 4 eggs, whisked
- ½ teaspoon sweet paprika

Directions:
1. In a bowl, mix the sweet potatoes with the eggs and the other ingredients, whisk and pour everything into a ziplock bag.
2. Seal the bag, submerge in the water oven and cook at 165 degrees F for 30 minutes.
3. Divide the mix into bowls and serve.

Nutrition:
calories 438
fat 13
fiber 9
carbs 64
protein 26

Walnut and Berries Bowls

Preparation time: 10 minutes
Cooking time: 30 minutes
Servings: 4
Ingredients:
- 1 cup coconut cream
- 1 tablespoon raisins
- ½ teaspoon vanilla extract
- 1 cup walnuts, chopped
- ½ cup old fashioned oats
- 1 cup blackberries

Directions:
1. In a sous vide bag, mix the walnuts with the berries and the other ingredients, toss, seal the bag and cook in the water oven at 160 degrees F for 30 minutes.
2. Divide into bowls and serve.

Nutrition:
calories 224
fat 12
fiber 5
carbs 15
protein 5

Chives Avocado Quinoa

Preparation time: 10 minutes
Cooking time: 30 minutes
Servings: 4
Ingredients:
- ½ teaspoon coriander, ground
- ½ teaspoon chili powder
- A pinch of salt and black pepper
- 1 teaspoon chili powder
- ½ teaspoon sweet paprika
- 1 cup quinoa
- 2 cups veggie stock
- 1 avocado, peeled, pitted and cubed
- 1 tablespoon chives, chopped

Directions:
1. In a ziplock bag, mix the quinoa with the stock and the other ingredients, toss, seal the bag, submerge in the water oven and cook at 165 degrees F for 30 minutes.
2. Divide into bowls and serve for breakfast.

Nutrition:
calories 300
fat 12
fiber 6
carbs 16
protein 6

Tomato Salad and Balsamic Avocado

Preparation time: 10 minutes
Cooking time: 15 minutes
Servings: 4
Ingredients:
- 1 avocado, peeled, pitted and cubed
- 2 cucumbers, cubed
- 1 tablespoon balsamic vinegar
- A pinch of salt and black pepper
- 1 tablespoon chives, chopped
- ½ pound cherry tomatoes, halved
- 1 tablespoon avocado oil
- ½ teaspoon rosemary, dried
- ½ teaspoon chili powder

Directions:
1. In a sous vide bag, mix the tomatoes with the avocado oil, avocado and the other ingredients, toss, seal the bag and cook at 165 degrees F for 15 minutes.
2. Divide into bowls and serve for breakfast.

Nutrition:
calories 424
fat 23
fiber 12
carbs 42
protein 15

Apple Salad

Preparation time: 5 minutes
Cooking time: 20 minutes
Servings: 2
Ingredients:
- 1 teaspoon cinnamon powder
- 2 teaspoons raw honey
- 1 teaspoon vanilla extract
- ½ pound apples, cored and cut into wedges
- ¼ cup almond milk

Directions:
1.   In a sous vide bag, mix the apples with the milk and the other ingredients, toss, seal the bag, submerge in the water oven and cook at 165 degrees F for 20 minutes.
2.   Divide the salad into bowls and serve for breakfast.
Nutrition:
calories 305
fat 19
fiber 5
carbs 29
protein 8

Pesto Zucchini Ramekins

Preparation time: 10 minutes
Cooking time: 30 minutes
Servings: 4
Ingredients:
- 2 garlic cloves, minced
- 8 eggs, whisked
- ½ teaspoon oregano, dried
- ½ teaspoon chili powder
- A pinch of salt and black pepper
- 1 tablespoon dill, chopped
- Cooking spray
- 2 spring onions, chopped
- 2 tablespoons basil pesto
- ½ pound zucchinis, cubed

Directions:
1.   In a bowl, mix the eggs with the zucchinis and the other ingredients except the cooking spray and whisk well.
2.   Grease 4 ramekins with the cooking spray, divide the zucchini mix, put the ramekins in the water oven and cook at 170 degrees F for 30 minutes.
3.   Serve the mix for breakfast.
Nutrition:

calories 356
fat 29
fiber 2,
carbs 3,
protein 18

Chickpeas Breakfast Spread

Preparation time: 10 minutes
Cooking time: 20 minutes
Servings: 4
Ingredients:
- 1 tablespoon lemon juice
- 1 tablespoon lemon zest, grated
- 1 tablespoon tahini paste
- ¼ teaspoon sweet paprika
- A pinch of salt and black pepper
- 1 tablespoon chives, chopped
- 2 cups canned chickpeas, drained and rinsed
- 1 cup heavy cream
- 2 spring onions, chopped
- 1 tablespoon avocado oil

Directions:
1.   In a sous vide bag, mix the chickpeas with the cream, spring onions and the other ingredients except the oil and the tahini paste, seal the bag, submerge in the water oven and cook at 165 degrees F for 20 minutes.
2.   Transfer the mix to a blender, add the remaining ingredients, pulse well, divide into bowls and serve for breakfast.
Nutrition:
calories 203
fat 12
fiber 4
carbs 15
protein 4

SOUS VIDE LUNCH RECIPES

Lemon Shrimp and Avocado Bowls

Preparation time: 10 minutes
Cooking time: 20 minutes
Servings: 4
Ingredients:
- 1 cup baby spinach
- A pinch of salt and black pepper to the taste
- 2 tablespoons ghee, melted
- 1 pound shrimp, peeled and deveined
- Juice of ½ lemon
- 1 avocado, peeled, pitted and cubed

Directions:
1. In s sous vide bag, mix the shrimp with the lemon juice and the other ingredients, toss, seal the bag, put it into your sous vide machine and cook everything at 126 degrees F for 20 minutes.
2. Divide into bowls and serve for lunch.

Nutrition:
calories 211
fat 5
fiber 6
carbs 12
protein 6

Mustard Salmon Steaks

Preparation time: 10 minutes
Cooking time: 25 minutes
Servings: 4
Ingredients:
- 1 tablespoon lemon juice
- 1 teaspoon chives, chopped
- 2 tablespoons olive oil
- 4 salmon steaks, bones removed
- 2 tablespoons mustard
- Salt and black pepper to the taste

Directions:
1. In a bowl, mix the salmon with the mustard and the other ingredients, and toss well.
2. Transfer the salmon steaks to sous vide bags, seal them, submerge in your sous vide machine and cook at 130 degrees F for 25 minutes.
3. Divide steaks between plates and serve with a side salad.

Nutrition:
calories 221
fat 4
fiber 6
carbs 12
protein 5

Shrimp Salad

Preparation time: 10 minutes
Cooking time: 20 minutes
Servings: 2
Ingredients:
- 1 tablespoon olive oil

- 1 tablespoon lemon juice
- 1 tablespoon balsamic vinegar
- 1 tablespoon chives, chopped
- 1 pound shrimp, peeled and deveined
- 1 cup cherry tomatoes, halved
- 1 cup baby spinach
- 1 cup kalamata olives, pitted and halved

Directions:
1. In a sous vide bag, mix the shrimp with the tomatoes, spinach and the other ingredients, seal, submerge in the bath water and cook at 104 degrees F for 20 minutes.
2. Divide into bowls and serve for lunch.

Nutrition:
calories 152
fat 6
fiber 5
carbs 8
protein 5

Tomatoes and Balsamic Calamari

Preparation time: 10 minutes
Cooking time: 30 minutes
Servings: 2
Ingredients:
- 1 cup cherry tomatoes, halved
- 1 teaspoon chili powder
- 4 scallions, chopped
- ½ teaspoon balsamic vinegar
- A pinch of salt and black pepper
- 1 cup calamari rings
- ½ cup tomato sauce

Directions:
1. In a sous vide bag, mix the calamari rings with the tomatoes and the other ingredients, toss, seal the bag, submerge in the water bath and cook at 170 degrees F for 30 minutes.
2. Divide into bowls and serve for lunch.

Nutrition:
calories 152
fat 6
fiber 2
carbs 6
protein 5

BBQ Cod Mix

Preparation time: 10 minutes
Cooking time: 30 minutes
Servings: 2
Ingredients:
- 1 tablespoon olive oil
- 2 tablespoons BBQ sauce
- 1 tablespoon lime juice
- A pinch of salt and black pepper
- 1 pound cod fillets, boneless
- 1 tablespoon chives, chopped
- ½ teaspoon coriander, ground

Directions:
1.   In a bowl, mix the cod with the bbq sauce and the other ingredients, toss gently and transfer to a sous vide bag.
2.   Seal the bag, introduce in the preheated water oven and cook at 140 degrees F for 30 minutes.
3.   Divide between plates and serve for lunch.
Nutrition:
calories 200
fat 6
fiber 6
carbs 12
protein 6

Cod Salsa

Preparation time: 10 minutes
Cooking time: 30 minutes.
Servings: 2
Ingredients:
- ½ teaspoon sweet paprika
- 1 tablespoon rosemary, chopped
- ½ tablespoon olive oil
- Salt and black pepper to the taste
- 1 pound cod fillets, boneless and skinless
- 1 cup mild salsa
- ½ teaspoon red pepper flakes, crushed

Directions:
1.   In a sous vide bag, mix the fish with the salsa, pepper flakes and the other ingredients, seal the bag, submerge in the water oven and cook at 161 degrees F for 30 minutes.
2.   Divide between plates serve for lunch.
Nutrition:
calories 172
fat 4
fiber 6
carbs 8
protein 8

Salmon and Shrimp Bowls With Calamari

Preparation time: 10 minutes
Cooking time: 50 minutes
Servings: 4
Ingredients:
- 1 celery stalk, chopped
- 1 tablespoon black peppercorns
- 1 garlic clove, minced
- ¼ cup vinegar
- 1 shallot, chopped
- 1 teaspoon mustard
- Juice of 1 lime
- 1 teaspoon smoked paprika
- 1 tablespoon olive oil
- Salt and black pepper to the taste
- 1 carrot, peeled and sliced
- 1 cup calamari rings
- 1 cup smoked salmon, skinless, boneless and cut into strips
- 1 cup shrimp, peeled and deveined

Directions:
1.   In a sous vide bag, combine the carrot with the calamari and the other ingredients, toss, seal, submerge in the water oven and cook at 185 degrees F for 50 minutes.
2.   Divide into bowls and serve.
Nutrition:
calories 215
fat 4
fiber 8
carbs 12
protein 4

Mustard Salmon Mix

Preparation time: 10 minutes
Cooking time: 35 minutes
Servings: 4
Ingredients:
- 1 cup baby kale
- Salt and black pepper to the taste
- 1 tablespoon homemade mayonnaise
- Juice of 1 lemon
- Zest of 1 lemon, grated
- 2 scallions, chopped
- 2 tablespoons capers, chopped
- 2 tablespoons olive oil
- 1 pound salmon fillets, boneless and roughly cubed
- 2 tablespoons mustard
- 1 cup baby spinach

Directions:
1.   In a sous vide bag, combine the salmon with the spinach, mustard and the other ingredients, seal the bag, submerge in the water oven and cook at 170 degrees F for 35 minutes.
2.   Divide into bowls serve.
Nutrition:
calories 201
fat 3
fiber 6
carbs 8
protein 6

Creamy Calamari

Preparation time: 10 minutes
Cooking time: 30 minutes
Servings: 2
Ingredients:
- 1 cup corn
- 2 tablespoons olive oil
- Salt and black pepper to the taste
- 2 tablespoons chives, chopped
- 2 cups calamari rings
- 1 cup heavy cream
- 1 cup baby spinach
- 1 cup cherry tomatoes, halved

Directions:
1.   In a sous vide bag, mix the calamari rings with the spinach, cream and the other ingredients,

seal the bag, cook in the water bath at 180 degrees F
for 30 minutes, divide into bowls and serve.
Nutrition:
calories 199
fat 3
fiber 6
carbs 8
protein 7

Lime Lobster

Preparation time: 10 minutes
Cooking time: 30 minutes
Servings: 2
Ingredients:
- 1 teaspoon sweet paprika
- ½ teaspoon turmeric powder
- Juice of 1 lime
- Salt and black pepper to the taste
- 2 lobster tails
- 6 tablespoons butter, melted

Directions:
1.   In a sous vide bag, combine the lobster with
the melted butter and the other ingredients, toss, seal
the bag, introduce in the preheated water oven and
cook at 140 degrees F for 30 minutes.
2.   Divide the lobster tails and lime sauce
between plates and serve.
Nutrition:
calories 166
fat 3
fiber 6
carbs 8
protein 5

Shrimp, Chicken and Rice

Preparation time: 10 minutes
Cooking time: 1 hour
Servings: 4
Ingredients:
- 1 cup cherry tomatoes, halved
- ½ teaspoon chili powder
- 1 tablespoon Creole seasoning
- Salt and black pepper to the taste
- 1 green bell pepper, chopped
- 2 spring onions, chopped
- 3 garlic cloves, minced
- 1 tablespoon chives, chopped
- 1 pound chicken breast, skinless, boneless
and cubed
- 1 pound shrimp, peeled and deveined
- 1 cup wild rice
- 2 cups chicken stock

Directions:
1.   In a sous vide bag, mix the chicken with the
shrimp, rice and the other ingredients, seal the bag,
submerge in the water bath and cook at 180 degrees
F for 1 hour.
2.   Divide into bowls and serve.
Nutrition:

calories 243
fat 4
fiber 6
carbs 15
protein 5

Butter Shrimp and Vanilla

Preparation time: 10 minutes
Cooking time: 30 minutes
Servings: 2
Ingredients:
- A pinch of salt and black pepper
- 1 cup cherry tomatoes, halved
- 2 tablespoons butter, melted
- 1 tablespoon chives, chopped
- ½ teaspoon vanilla extract
- 1 pound shrimp, peeled and deveined
- ¼ teaspoon sweet paprika

Directions:
1.   In a sous vide bag combine the shrimp with
the vanilla, butter and the other ingredients, seal,
introduce in the preheated sous vide machine and
cook at 136 degrees F for 30 minutes.
2.   Divide into bowls and serve..
Nutrition:
calories 188
fat 3
fiber 7
carbs 9
protein 5

Blueberries Mix and Pork

Preparation time: 10 minutes
Cooking time: 2 hours
Servings: 2
Ingredients:
- A pinch of cayenne pepper
- 1 teaspoon cumin, ground
- 1 teaspoon fennel seeds, crushed
- 2 tablespoons soy sauce
- ½ cup blueberries
- 2 tablespoons stevia
- ½ teaspoon chili sauce
- 1 tablespoons chives, chopped
- 2 pounds pork roast, sliced
- 1 tablespoon olive oil
- Salt and black pepper to the taste
- 1 tablespoon cinnamon powder

Directions:
1.   In a sous vide bag, mix the roast with the oil,
cinnamon and the other ingredients, seal the bag,
cook in the water bath at 180 degrees F for 2 hours,
divide between plates and serve.
Nutrition:
calories 312
fat 5
fiber 7
carbs 16
protein 5

BBQ and Paprika Ribs

Preparation time: 10 minutes
Cooking time: 2 hours
Servings: 4
Ingredients:
- 2 tablespoons sweet paprika
- 2 tablespoons cumin, ground
- 2 tablespoons garlic powder
- 1 tablespoon chives, chopped
- 2 pounds baby back pork ribs
- 2 tablespoons olive oil
- 1 cup bbq sauce
- Salt and black pepper to the taste

Directions:
1. In a sous vide bag, mix the ribs with the oil, sauce and the other ingredients, toss, seal the bag, submerge in the water bath and cook at 180 degrees F for 2 hours.
2. Divide between plates and serve them with a side salad.

Nutrition:
calories 351
fat 6
fiber 7
carbs 9
protein 5

Sun dried Tomatoes and Herbed Pork

Preparation time: 10 minutes
Cooking time: 2 hours
Servings: 2
Ingredients:
- 1 tablespoon mustard
- Zest of 1 lime, grated
- ½ teaspoon cloves, crushed
- 1 teaspoon oregano, dried
- 1 teaspoon coriander, ground
- 1 teaspoon thyme, chopped
- 1 tablespoon chives, chopped
- 2 pounds pork roast, sliced
- 1 cup sun-dried tomatoes, chopped
- 2 tablespoons olive oil
- Juice of 1 lime

Directions:
1. In a large sous vide bag, combine the roast with the tomatoes, oil and the other ingredients, seal the bag, submerge in the sous vide machine and cook at 180 degrees F for 2 hours
2. Divide between plates and serve right away.

Nutrition:
calories 336
fat 6
fiber 6
carbs 16
protein 5

Buttery Pork Tenderloin

Preparation time: 10 minutes
Cooking time: 2 hours

Servings: 4
Ingredients:
- Juice of 1 lime
- 1 and ½ tablespoons Italian seasoning
- Salt and black pepper to the taste
- 2 tablespoons butter, melted
- 2 pounds pork tenderloin, sliced
- ½ teaspoon turmeric powder
- 1 teaspoon chili powder

Directions:
1. In a sous vide bag, combine the pork with the melted butter and the other ingredients, seal the bag, introduce it in the preheated water oven and cook at 135 degrees F for 2 hours.
2. Divide between plates and serve with a side salad.

Nutrition:
calories 321
fat 4
fiber 7
carbs 12
protein 5

Nutmeg Pork and Garlic

Preparation time: 10 minutes
Cooking time: 2 hours
Servings: 6
Ingredients:
- Juice of 1 lime
- Salt and black pepper to the taste
- 1 teaspoon rosemary, dried
- 2 bay leaves
- 1 tablespoon cilantro, chopped
- 2 pounds pork roast, sliced
- 4 garlic cloves, minced
- 1 teaspoon nutmeg, ground
- 2 tablespoons olive oil

Directions:
1. In a sous vide bag, combine the pork with the garlic, nutmeg and the other ingredients, seal, introduce them into your preheated water oven and cook at 180 degrees F for 2 hours.
2. Divide between plates and serve.

Nutrition:
calories 353
fat 7
fiber 8
carbs 15
protein 17

Thyme Pork and Carrots

Preparation time: 10 minutes
Cooking time: 3 hours
Servings: 4
Ingredients:
- ½ teaspoon coriander, ground
- 2 garlic cloves, minced
- 2 tablespoons olive oil
- 2 tablespoons black peppercorns

- Salt and black pepper to the taste
- 2 bay leaves
- ½ teaspoon smoked paprika
- Salt and black pepper to the taste
- 1 tablespoon mustard powder
- 2 pounds pork roast, sliced
- ½ pound carrots, peeled and sliced
- 1 tablespoon thyme, chopped
- 1 cup red wine
- ½ teaspoon sweet paprika

Directions:
1. In a large sous vide bag, combine the roast with the carrots, thyme and the other ingredients, seal, submerge in the water oven and cook at 190 degrees F for 3 hours
2. Divide between plates and serve.

Nutrition:
calories 400
fat 6
fiber 7
carbs 16
protein 22

Thyme Pork Chops

Preparation time: 10 minutes
Cooking time: 2 hours
Servings: 4
Ingredients:
- ½ teaspoon chili powder
- Salt and black pepper to the taste
- A drizzle of olive oil
- 4 pork chops, bone in
- 2 tablespoons thyme, chopped
- Juice of 1 lime

Directions:
1. In a sous vide bag, combine the pork chops with the thyme and the other ingredients, seal the bag, submerge in the preheated water oven and cook at 138 degrees F for 2 hours.
2. Divide between plates and serve.

Nutrition:
calories 312
fat 4
fiber 6
carbs 15
protein 17

Cherry Tomatoes Mix and Lamb Rack

Preparation time: 10 minutes
Cooking time: 2 hours
Servings: 4
Ingredients:
- ½ teaspoon rosemary, dried
- ½ bunch mint, chopped
- ½ cup olive oil
- 2 garlic cloves, minced
- 1 rack of lamb
- 1 cup cherry tomatoes, halved
- Salt and black pepper to the taste

Directions:
1. In a sous vide bag, combine the rack of lamb with the tomatoes and the other ingredients, seal the bag, submerge into your preheated water oven and cook at 150 degrees F for 2 hours.
2. Divide the mix between plates and serve.

Nutrition:
calories 276
fat 5
fiber 9
carbs 16
protein 20

Pomegranate Mix and Lamb

Preparation time: 10 minutes
Cooking time: 2 hours
Servings: 4
Ingredients:
- 2 tablespoons balsamic vinegar
- 2 rosemary springs, chopped
- Salt and black pepper to the taste
- 1 tablespoon butter, melted
- 1 cup pomegranate seeds
- 2 pounds lamb chops
- 2 cups pomegranate juice

Directions:
1. In sous vide bag, combine the lamb chops with the pomegranate seeds and the other ingredients, seal, introduce in the preheated water oven and cook at 160degrees F for 2 hours.
2. Divide everything between plates and serve.

Nutrition:
calories 300
fat 5
fiber 8
carbs 15
protein 20

Lamb, Leeks and Mushroom Mix

Preparation time: 10 minutes
Cooking time: 2 hours
Servings: 4
Ingredients:
- 2 tablespoons balsamic vinegar
- 2 tablespoons olive oil
- Salt and black pepper to the taste
- 1 cup coconut cream
- 1 tablespoon chives, chopped
- 2 pounds lamb chops
- 2 leeks, sliced
- 1 cup mushrooms, sliced

Directions:
1. In a sous vide bag, combine the lamb chops with the leeks and the other ingredients, seal the bag, submerge in the water bath, cook at 180 degrees F for 2 hours, divide between plates and serve.

Nutrition:
calories 311
fat 4,

fiber 7
carbs 18
protein 16

Coriander Leg of Lamb

Preparation time: 10 minutes
Cooking time: 8 hours
Servings: 4
Ingredients:
- 2 tablespoons olive oil
- Salt and black pepper to the taste
- 2 teaspoons smoked paprika
- 2 pounds leg of lamb, boneless
- 3 garlic cloves, minced
- 2 tablespoons coriander, chopped
- Juice of 1 lime

Directions:
1.   In a sous vide bag, combine the leg of lamb and the other ingredients, toss, seal, introduce in the preheated water oven and cook at 150 degrees F for 8 hours.
2.   Slice the meat, divide between plates, and serve.

Nutrition:
calories 277
fat 6
fiber 8
carbs 16
protein 17

Lamb Fillets and Olives

Preparation time: 10 minutes
Cooking time: 3 hours
Servings: 4
Ingredients:
- 2 cups green olives, pitted and sliced
- Juice of 1 orange
- 1 tablespoon capers
- 2 tablespoons balsamic vinegar
- 1 cup cherry tomatoes, halved
- 1 cup parsley, chopped
- 2 pounds lamb loin fillets
- Salt and black pepper to the taste
- 2 tablespoons olive oil

Directions:
1.   Divide the lamb fillets into 2 sous vide bags, add the oil, olives and the other ingredients, seal them, cook in the water oven at 160 degrees F for 3 hours, divide between plates and serve.

Nutrition:
calories 300
fat 6
fiber 8
carbs 17
protein 5

Rack of Lamb and Baby Cauliflower Mix

Preparation time: 10 minutes
Cooking time: 2 hours
Servings: 4
Ingredients:
- 2 leeks, sliced
- 3 baby cauliflowers, florets separated
- 1 red onion, sliced
- 2 tablespoons balsamic vinegar
- Salt and black pepper to the taste
- 1 pound rack of lamb
- Salt and black pepper to the taste
- 1 tablespoon rosemary, chopped
- 2 shallots chopped

Directions:
1.   In a sous vide bag, combine the rack of lamb with the rosemary and the other ingredients, seal the bag, submerge in the water bath, cook at 183 degrees F for 2 hours, divide between plates and serve.

Nutrition:
calories 282
fat 5
fiber 8
carbs 18
protein 12

Garlic and Peppercorns Lamb Chops

Preparation time: 10 minutes
Cooking time: 2 hours
Servings: 2
Ingredients:
- Juice of 1 lemon
- ½ teaspoon turmeric powder
- 1 teaspoon oregano, chopped
- 8 black peppercorns, crushed
- Salt and black pepper to the taste
- 2 pounds lamb chops
- 2 garlic cloves, minced
- 2 tablespoons olive oil

Directions:
1.   In a sous vide bag, combine the lamb chops with the garlic and the other ingredients, seal, submerge in the preheated water oven and cook at 132 degrees F for 2 hours.
2.   Divide between plates and serve.

Nutrition:
calories 300
fat 8
fiber 9
carbs 17
protein 14

Sage Cajun Turkey

Preparation time: 10 minutes
Cooking time: 2 hours
Servings: 4
Ingredients:
- A pinch of salt and black pepper
- 1 tablespoon black peppercorns
- 1 tablespoon sage, chopped
- ¼ cup chicken stock

- 2 pounds turkey breast, skinless, boneless and cut into strips
- 1 tablespoon Cajun seasoning
- 2 tablespoons balsamic vinegar

Directions:
1. In a sous vide bag, combine the turkey with the seasoning and the other ingredients, seal the bag, introduce into your preheated water oven and cook at 176 degrees F for 2 hours.
2. Divide between plates and serve with a side salad.

Nutrition:
calories 342
fat 7
fiber 9
carbs 17
protein 6

Ginger and Shallot Duck

Preparation time: 10 minutes
Cooking time: 2 hours and 30 minutes
Servings: 2
Ingredients:
- 2 curry leaves
- 1 cup shallot, chopped
- ½ teaspoon chili powder
- 2 teaspoons coriander powder
- ½ teaspoon garam masala
- 1 cup coconut milk
- 2 duck breasts, trimmed and some of the fat removed
- 1 teaspoon turmeric powder
- 1 tablespoon ginger paste
- 2 tablespoons olive oil

Directions:
1. In a sous vide bag, combine the duck with the turmeric, ginger and the other ingredients, seal, submerge it in the preheated water oven and cook at 140 degrees F for 2 hours and 30 minutes.
2. Divide duck breasts between plates, and serve.

Nutrition:
calories 300
fat 5
fiber 8
carbs 17
protein 13

Curry Chicken Thighs

Preparation time: 10 minutes
Cooking time: 1 hour and 30 minutes
Servings: 4
Ingredients:
- Salt and black pepper to the taste
- 1 teaspoon garlic powder
- 6 tablespoons butter, melted
- 2 tablespoons avocado oil
- 2 pounds chicken thighs, boneless and skinless

- 1 tablespoon yellow curry paste

Directions:
1. In a sous vide bag, combine the chicken with the oil, butter and the other ingredients, seal the bag, introduce in the preheated water oven and cook at 150 degrees F for 1 hour and 30 minutes.
2. Divide between plates and serve.

Nutrition:
calories 241
fat 6
fiber 8
carbs 9
protein 12

Provence Chicken Breast

Preparation time: 10 minutes
Cooking time: 3 hours
Servings: 2
Ingredients:
- 4 tablespoons butter, melted
- 1 tablespoon coriander, chopped
- 1 garlic clove, minced
- 1 teaspoon herbs de Provence
- 2 pounds chicken breasts, skinless and boneless
- Salt and black pepper to the taste
- Juice of 1 lime
- ½ teaspoon garam masala

Directions:
1. In a sous vide bag, combine the chicken with the lime juice and the other ingredients, toss, seal the bag, introduce in the preheated water oven and cook at 140 degrees F for 3 hours.
2. Divide between plates and serve with a side salad.

Nutrition:
calories 226
fat 7
fiber 9
carbs 12
protein 17

Turkey Breast and Cranberries

Preparation time: 10 minutes
Cooking time: 3 hours
Servings: 4
Ingredients:
- Salt and black pepper to the taste
- 2 tablespoons butter, melted
- ½ cup shallots, chopped
- ¼ cup red wine
- 1 pound turkey breast, skinless, boneless and sliced
- 1 cup cranberries
- 1 tablespoon sage, chopped

Directions:
1. In a large sous vide bag, combine the turkey with the cranberries and the other ingredients, toss,

seal the bag, submerge in the preheated water oven and cook at 156 degrees F for 3 hours.

2. Divide the turkey between plates and serve with the cranberries mix on top.

Nutrition: calories 272

fat 8

fiber 6

carbs 18

protein 11

Chili Chicken

Preparation time:10 minutes

Cooking time: 2 hours

Servings: 4

Ingredients:

- 1 yellow onion, quartered
- 2 tablespoons butter, melted
- 2 garlic cloves, minced
- Salt and black pepper to the taste
- 2 pounds chicken breasts, skinless and boneless
- ½ tablespoon chili sauce
- 1 red chili, minced

Directions:

1. In a sous vide bag, combine the chicken with the chili sauce and the other ingredients, seal the bag, submerge in the preheated water oven and cook the chicken at 146 degrees F for 2 hours.

2. Serve the chicken with a side salad.

Nutrition:

calories 221

fat 4

fiber 8

carbs 12

protein 6

Spring Onion and Soy Chicken

Preparation time: 10 minutes

Cooking time: 3 hours

Servings: 2

Ingredients:

- 1 tablespoon soy sauce
- Salt and black pepper to the taste
- 1 tablespoon parsley, chopped
- 1 bunch spring onions, roughly chopped
- 2 garlic cloves, minced
- 1 tablespoon avocado oil
- 2 pounds chicken breast, skinless, boneless and sliced

Directions:

1. In a sous vide bag, combine the chicken with the spring onions and the other ingredients, seal the bag, introduce in the preheated water oven and cook at 160 degrees F for 3 hours.

2. Divide between plates and serve.

Nutrition:

calories 201

fat 4

fiber 3

carbs 8

protein 6

Beet Cream Soup

Preparation time: 10 minutes

Cooking time: 1 hour

Servings: 8

Ingredients:

- ½ red cabbage head, shredded
- 2 quarts veggie stock
- ½ cup chives, chopped
- 3 tablespoons red vinegar
- Salt and black pepper to the taste
- 1 pound beets, peeled and cubed
- 1 red onion, sliced
- 4 carrots, chopped
- ½ tablespoon rosemary, chopped

Directions:

1. In a sous vide bag, mix the beets with the carrots, onion and the rest of the ingredients, toss, seal the bag, submerge in the water oven and cook at 182 degrees F for 1 hour.

2. Transfer this to a blender, pulse well, divide into bowls and serve.

Nutrition:

calories 191

fat 3

fiber 7

carbs 8

protein 5

Chicken Soup

Preparation time: 10 minutes

Cooking time: 2 hours

Servings: 4

Ingredients:

- ½ cup carrots, chopped
- 1 red onion, chopped
- ½ teaspoon garlic powder
- Salt and black pepper to the taste
- 1 tablespoon olive oil
- 1-quart chicken stock
- 1 red bell pepper, chopped
- 1 green bell pepper, chopped
- 2 cups rotisserie chicken, skinless, boneless and shredded

Directions:

1. In a big sous vide bag, combine the chicken with the carrots and the other ingredients except the stock, toss well, seal the bag, introduce in the preheated water oven and cook at 182 degrees F for 1 hour and 30 minutes.

2. Transfer the mix to a pot, add the stock, bring to a simmer, cook for 30 minutes over medium heat, divide into bowls and serve.

Nutrition:

calories 200

fat 4

fiber 6

Cauliflower Soup

Preparation time: 10 minutes
Cooking time: 1 hour
Servings: 4
Ingredients:

- ½ teaspoon turmeric powder
- 1 tablespoon chives, chopped
- A drizzle of olive oil
- 1 cauliflower head, florets separated
- 2 spring onions, chopped
- 4 cups chicken stock
- 4 garlic cloves, minced
- Salt and black pepper to the taste

Directions:,
1. In a sous vide bag, combine the cauliflower with the spring onions, and the other ingredients except the stock, toss, seal the bag, submerge in the preheated water oven and cook at 190 degrees F for 1 hour.
2. Transfer the veggies to a blender, add the stock, pulse well, divide into bowls and serve.

Nutrition:
calories 211
fat 5
fiber 7
carbs 12
protein 4

Zucchini Cream

Preparation time: 10 minutes
Cooking time: 1 hour
Servings: 6
Ingredients:

- ½ teaspoon turmeric powder
- 1 yellow onion, chopped
- 1 garlic clove, minced
- 3 cups veggie stock
- 2 cups coconut cream
- 1 pound zucchinis, roughly cubed
- A pinch of salt and black pepper
- 2 tablespoons butter, melted
- ½ teaspoon curry powder

Directions:
1. In a sous vide bag, combine the zucchinis with the butter and the other ingredients except the stock and the cream, seal the bag, submerge in the water bath, cook at 170 degrees F for 1 hour, transfer to a blender, add the rest of the ingredients, pulse well, divide into bowls and serve.

Nutrition:
calories 199
fat 3
fiber 6
carbs 8
protein 6

Roasted Pork and Apples

Preparation time: 10 minutes
Cooking time: 4 hours
Servings: 6
Ingredients:

- 2 cups apples, cored and cut into wedges
- 2 pounds pork roast, sliced
- Salt and black pepper to the taste
- A drizzle of olive oil
- 1 cup red wine
- 1 tablespoon lemon zest, grated
- 1 tablespoon lemon juice

Directions:
1. In a sous vide bag, combine the pork with the wine and the other ingredients, seal it, submerge in the preheated water oven in your sous vide machine and cook at 155 degrees F for 4 hours.
2. Divide between plates and serve.

Nutrition:
calories 356
fat 14
fiber 4
carbs 16
protein 25

Pork Chops and Mushrooms

Preparation time: 10 minutes
Cooking time: 3 hours
Servings: 4
Ingredients:

- 1 teaspoon rosemary, chopped
- 1 teaspoon nutmeg
- 1 tablespoon balsamic vinegar
- ½ cup red wine
- 1 cup mushrooms, sliced
- 2 pounds pork chops
- 1 teaspoon garlic powder

Directions:
1. in a sous vide bag, combine the pork chops with the mushrooms and the other ingredients, seal it, submerge in the preheated water oven and cook them at 1780 degrees F for 3 hours.
2. Divide pork chops between plates, and serve.

Nutrition:
calories 370
fat 10
fiber 1
carbs 14
protein 30

Lemony and Parsley Beef

Preparation time: 10 minutes
Cooking time: 3 hours
Servings: 4
Ingredients:

- Zest of 1 lemon, grated
- Salt and black pepper to the taste
- A pinch of lemon pepper

- 6 garlic cloves, minced
- 2 tablespoons parsley, chopped
- 1 tablespoons olive oil
- 2 pounds beef stew meat, cubed
- 1 cup beef stock
- Juice of ½ lemon

Directions:

1. In a sous vide bag, mix the beef with the oil, stock and the other ingredients, seal the bag, submerge in the water oven and cook at 160 degrees F for 3 hours.
2. Divide the mix between plates and serve with a side salad.

Nutrition:
calories 366
fat 25
fiber 1
carbs 14
protein 40

Cranberry Beef

Preparation time: 10 minutes
Cooking time: 3 hours
Servings: 4
Ingredients:

- ½ teaspoon onion powder
- ½ teaspoon garlic powder
- ½ teaspoon ginger powder
- ½ cup cranberries
- 2 garlic cloves, minced
- Juice of 1 lime
- 1 tablespoon avocado oil
- 2 pounds beef steaks
- Salt and black pepper to the taste

Directions:

1. In a sous vide bag, combine the steaks with the oil, onion powder and the other ingredients, toss, seal the bag, submerge it in the preheated water oven and cook at 170 degrees F for 3 hours.
2. Divide between plates and serve with a side salad.

Nutrition:
calories 430
fat 23
fiber 2
carbs 15
protein 45

Maple Pork Chops

Preparation time: 10 minutes
Cooking time: 6 hours
Servings: 4
Ingredients:

- Juice and zest of 1 lime
- Salt and black pepper to the taste
- ½ teaspoon rosemary, dried
- 3 scallions, chopped
- 2 tablespoons maple syrup
- 2 pounds pork chops

Directions:

1. In 2 sous vide bags, combine the pork chops with the scallions, maple syrup and the other ingredients, seal the bag, submerge in the preheated water oven and cook them at 150 degrees F for 6 hours.
2. Divide everything between plates and serve.

Nutrition:
calories 325
fat 18
fiber 1
carbs 16
protein 36

Pork Roast and Olives Salsa

Preparation time: 10 minutes
Cooking time: 6 hours
Servings: 4
Ingredients:

- 4 spring onions, chopped
- 2 tablespoons balsamic vinegar
- 2 tablespoons lime juice
- 2 tablespoons olive oil
- 1 tablespoon chives, chopped
- Salt and black pepper to the taste
- 2 pounds pork roast, sliced
- 1 cup green olives, pitted and sliced
- 1 cup cherry tomatoes, halved

Directions:

1. In a sous vide bag, combine the roast with the olives, tomatoes and the other ingredients, seal the bag, introduce in your preheated water oven and cook at 170 degrees F for 6 hours.
2. Divide everything between plates and serve right away.

Nutrition:
calories 390
fat 16
fiber 2
carbs 22
protein 16

Lamb and Spinach Salad

Preparation time: 10 minutes
Cooking time: 5 hours
Servings: 4
Ingredients:

- 2 garlic cloves, minced
- ½ cup pecans, toasted
- 1 cup cherry tomatoes, halved
- 2 cups spinach
- 1 tablespoon lime juice
- 1 cup mint, chopped
- 2 tablespoons olive oil
- 2 pounds lamb stew meat, cut into strips
- Salt and black pepper to the taste
- 1 teaspoon turmeric powder

Directions:

1.	In a sous vide bag, combine the lamb with the turmeric, garlic, half of the oil, salt and pepper, toss, seal the bag, submerge in the preheated water oven, cook at 180 degrees F for 5 hours, cool down and transfer to a salad bowl.
2.	Add the rest of the ingredients, toss and serve.
Nutrition:
calories 334
fat 33
fiber 3
carbs 14
protein 7

Harrisa Lamb Mix

Preparation time: 10 minutes
Cooking time: 3 hours
Servings: 4
Ingredients:
- 2 teaspoons oregano, dried
- 2 teaspoons rosemary, dried
- ¼ cup parsley, chopped
- 2 teaspoons harissa
- Salt and black pepper to the taste
- 2 pounds lamb stew meat, roughly cubed
- 2 tablespoons olive oil
- 2 garlic cloves, minced

Directions:
1.	In a sous vide bag, mix the lamb with the oil, garlic and the other ingredients, toss, seal the bag, submerge in your preheated water oven and cook them at 160 degrees F for 3 hours.
2.	Divide between plates and serve with a side salad.
Nutrition:
calories 345
fat 32
fiber 6
carbs 14
protein 34

Lamb with Fennel and Tomatoes

Preparation time: 10 minutes
Cooking time: 3 hours
Servings: 4
Ingredients:
- 2 tablespoons balsamic vinegar
- Salt and black pepper to the taste
- 1 tablespoon mint, chopped
- 2 pounds lamb racks
- 2 fennel bulbs, sliced
- 1 cup cherry tomatoes, halved
- 2 tablespoons olive oil

Directions:
1.	In a sous vide bag, combine the lamb with the fennel and the other ingredients, seal the bag, submerge in the preheated water oven, cook at 182 degrees F for 3 hours, divide between plates and serve.

Nutrition:
calories 230
fat 3
fiber 3
carbs 14
protein 17

Beef and Yogurt Mix

Preparation time: 10 minutes
Cooking time: 4 hours
Servings: 4
Ingredients:
- 1 cup Greek yogurt
- 1 teaspoon rosemary, dried
- 1 tablespoon chives, chopped
- 1 teaspoon thyme, dried
- Salt and black pepper to the taste
- 1 bay leaf
- 2 garlic cloves, minced
- 2 tablespoons olive oil
- 1 tablespoon lime juice
- 1 tablespoon lime zest, grated
- 2 pounds beef stew meat, cut into strips

Directions:
1.	In a sous vide bag, combine the beef with the oil, lime juice and the other ingredients, toss, seal the bag, submerge in the preheated water oven and cook at 170 degrees F for 4 hours.
2.	Divide the mix between plates and serve with a side salad.
Nutrition:
calories 435
fat 16
fiber 6
carbs 18
protein 45

Paprika Pork and Chili

Preparation time: 10 minutes
Cooking time: 6 hours
Servings: 4
Ingredients:
- 2 tablespoons lemon zest, grated
- Salt and black pepper to the taste
- ½ teaspoon celery salt
- A pinch of cayenne pepper
- 1 tablespoon garlic, minced
- 2 pound pork shoulder, sliced
- 1 tablespoon chili sauce
- ½ teaspoon sweet paprika
- 2 tablespoons olive oil

Directions:
1.	In a big sous vide bag, combine the pork with the chili sauce, paprika and the other ingredients, toss, seal it, introduce in your preheated water oven and cook at 170 degrees F for 6 hours.
2.	Divide between plates and serve with a side salad.
Nutrition:

calories 480
fat 5
fiber 6
carbs 16
protein 25

Greek Rosemary Lamb Chops

Preparation time: 10 minutes
Cooking time: 6 hours
Servings: 4
Ingredients:
- 1 tablespoon mint, chopped
- Salt and black pepper to the taste
- 3 garlic cloves, minced
- 2 pounds lamb chops
- 2 tablespoons olive oil
- 2 tablespoons rosemary, chopped
- ½ cup Greek yogurt

Directions:
1. In a large sous vide bag, combine the lamb with the oil, rosemary and the other ingredients, seal the bag , submerge in the water oven and cook at 140 degrees F for 6 hours.
2. Divide the chops between plates and serve with a side salad.

Nutrition:
calories 275
fat 2
fiber 1
carbs 12
protein 26

Coconut Pork Chops and Curry

Preparation time: 10 minutes
Cooking time: 6 hours
Servings: 4
Ingredients:
- 1 tablespoon rosemary, chopped
- 2 garlic cloves, minced
- ½ teaspoon chili powder
- 1 teaspoon cumin, ground
- Salt and black pepper to the taste
- ¼ cup lime juice
- 2 pounds pork chops
- 2 tablespoons avocado oil
- 2 tablespoons coconut butter, melted
- 2 tablespoons red curry paste

Directions:
1. In a large sous vide bag, combine the pork chops with the lime juice, oil and the other ingredients, seal the bag, submerge in your preheated water oven and cook at 145 degrees F for 6 hours.
2. Divide the pork chops between plates and serve them with a side salad.

Nutrition:
calories 360
fat 8
fiber 1

carbs 16
protein 26

Tomato and Eggplant Stew

Preparation time: 5 minutes
Cooking time: 30 minutes
Servings: 4
Ingredients:
- 1 tablespoon olive oil
- 2 garlic cloves, minced
- 1 teaspoon chili powder
- ½ cup tomato passata
- 1 tablespoon basil, chopped
- A pinch of salt and black pepper
- 1 pound tomatoes, cut into wedges
- 2 eggplants, cubed
- 1 red onion, chopped

Directions:
1. In a sous vide bag, mix the tomatoes with the eggplants, onion and the other ingredients, toss, seal the bag, submerge in the water oven and cook at 160 degrees F for 30 minutes.
2. Divide the stew into bowls and serve.

Nutrition:
calories 181
fat 7.3
fiber 1.4
carbs 4.6
protein 1.1

Lentils Stew

Preparation time: 10 minutes
Cooking time: 30 minutes
Servings: 4
Ingredients:
- 2 tablespoons olive oil
- A pinch of salt and black pepper
- 1 bunch cilantro, chopped
- ½ teaspoon chili powder
- ½ teaspoon sweet paprika
- 1 tablespoon cilantro, chopped
- 1 cup canned lentils, drained
- 2 spring onions, chopped
- ½ cup mild salsa
- 2 garlic cloves, minced

Directions:
1. In a sous vide bag, mix the lentils with the salsa and the other ingredients, toss, seal the bag, submerge in the water oven and cook at 165 degrees F for 30 minutes.
2. Divide the stew into bowls and serve.

Nutrition:
calories 671
fat 15.6
fiber 27.5
carbs 87.5

protein 27.1

Rice and Turmeric Veggies

Preparation time: 10 minutes
Cooking time: 30 minutes
Servings: 4
Ingredients:

- 1 cup white rice
- 1 cup chicken stock
- ½ teaspoon turmeric powder
- Juice of ½ lemon
- 2 tablespoons parsley, chopped
- A pinch of salt and black pepper
- 1 red bell pepper, cubed
- 1 zucchini, cubed
- 1 eggplant, cubed
- ½ cup cherry tomatoes, halved
- 1 tablespoon olive oil
- 1 red onion, chopped
- 2 garlic cloves, minced

Directions:

1.   In a sous vide bag, mix the veggies with the rice, stock and the other ingredients, toss, seal the bag, submerge in the water oven and cook at 170 degrees F for 30 minutes.
2.   Divide into bowls and serve.

Nutrition:
calories 342
fat 17.4
fiber 16.5
carbs 27.7
protein 26.4

Pork Bowls

Preparation time: 10 minutes
Cooking time: 30 minutes
Servings: 4
Ingredients:

- 1 yellow onion, chopped
- ½ teaspoon chili powder
- A pinch of salt and black pepper
- 2 garlic cloves, minced
- ½ cup tomato passata
- 1/3 cup parsley, chopped
- 1 pound pork stew meat, cubed
- 2 sweet potatoes, peeled and cubed
- 1 tablespoon olive oil

Directions:

1.   In s sous vide bag, mix the pork with the sweet potatoes and the other ingredients, toss, seal the bag, submerge in the water oven and cook at 170 degrees F for 30 minutes.
2.   Divide into bowls and serve for lunch.

Nutrition:
calories 435
fat 18.5
fiber 13.6
carbs 27.8
protein 25.6

Sweet Potato Bowls and Shrimp

Preparation time: 10 minutes
Cooking time: 20 minutes
Servings: 4
Ingredients:

- 2 spring onions, chopped
- 1 tablespoon chives, chopped
- ½ teaspoon sweet paprika
- ½ teaspoon chili powder
- A pinch of salt and black pepper
- Juice of ½ lemon
- 1 cup sweet potatoes, peeled and cubed
- 1 tablespoon balsamic vinegar
- ½ pound shrimp, peeled and deveined

Directions:

1.   In a sous vide bag, mix the shrimp with the vinegar, potatoes and the other ingredients, toss, seal the bag, submerge in the water oven and cook at 140 degrees F fro 20 minutes.
2.   Divide everything into bowls and serve.

Nutrition:
calories 253
fat 11.5
fiber 3.4
carbs 16.5
protein 23.2

Chicken and Eggplants

Preparation time: 10 minutes
Cooking time: 30 minutes
Servings: 4
Ingredients:

- 2 eggplants, cubed
- ½ teaspoon chili powder
- ½ teaspoon hot paprika
- 2 tablespoons balsamic vinegar
- ¼ cup parsley, chopped
- 1 pound chicken breast, skinless, boneless and cubed
- 2 spring onions, chopped
- Juice of 1 lime
- ½ cup tomato passata

Directions:

1.   In a sous vide bag, mix the chicken with the eggplants and the other ingredients, toss, seal the bag,

submerge in the water oven and cook at 170 degrees F for 30 minutes.

2.   Divide everything between plates and serve for lunch.

Nutrition:

calories 266

fat 12.2

fiber 4.5

carbs 15.7

protein 3.7

Turkey Hash

Preparation time: 10 minutes

Cooking time: 30 minutes

Servings: 4

Ingredients:

- ¼ cup chicken stock
- ¼ teaspoon red pepper flakes, crushed
- ¼ teaspoon garlic powder
- 2 tablespoons lemon juice
- ¼ cup parsley, chopped
- 1 red onion, chopped
- 1 cup hash browns
- 1 pound turkey breast, skinless, boneless and cubed
- 1 tablespoon olive oil

Directions:

1.   In a sous vide bag, mix the turkey with the onion, hash browns and the other ingredients, seal the bag and cook in the water oven at 170 degrees F for 30 minutes.

2.   Divide between plates and serve for lunch.

Nutrition:

calories 364

fat 16.8

fiber 5.5

carbs 26.8

protein 23.4

Eggplant Stew

Preparation time: 10 minutes

Cooking time: 25 minutes

Servings: 4

Ingredients:

- ½ teaspoon cumin, ground
- Zest and juice of 1 lemon
- A pinch of salt and black pepper
- 1 cup tomato passata
- 1 tablespoon parsley, chopped
- 1 pound eggplant, cubed
- 2 tablespoons olive oil
- 1 red onion, chopped
- 2 garlic cloves, minced

Directions:

1.   In a sous vide bag, mix the eggplants with the onion and the other ingredients, seal the bag and cook in the water oven at 170 degrees F for 25 minutes.

2.   Divide the stew into bowls and serve.

Nutrition:

calories 512

fat 16.4

fiber 17.5

carbs 78

protein 17.2

Turmeric Shrimp Mix

Preparation time: 5 minutes

Cooking time: 20 minutes

Servings: 4

Ingredients:

- ½ teaspoon turmeric powder
- 1 tablespoon lime juice
- A pinch of salt and black pepper
- ¼ cup chives, chopped
- 1 pound shrimp, peeled and deveined
- 2 spring onions, chopped
- 1 tablespoon avocado oil

Directions:

1.   In a sous vide bag, mix the shrimp with the spring onions and the other ingredients, seal the bag and cook in the water oven at 160 degrees F for 20 minutes.

2.   Divide everything into bowls and serve.

Nutrition:

calories 28

fat 12.7

fiber 1.7

carbs 5.8

protein 36.5

Tomato Mix and Beef

Preparation time: 10 minutes

Cooking time: 1 hour

Servings: 4

Ingredients:

- 1 tablespoon olive oil
- 1 teaspoon cumin, ground
- ½ teaspoon garam masala
- ½ teaspoon oregano, dried
- A pinch of salt and black pepper
- ¼ cup chives, chopped
- 1 pound beef stew meat, ground
- 1 cup cherry tomatoes, halved
- ¼ tablespoon balsamic vinegar
- 1 red onion, chopped

Directions:
1.   In a sous vide bag, mix the beef with the tomatoes, vinegar and the other ingredients, toss, seal the bag, submerge in the water oven and cook at 160 degrees F for 1 hours.
2.   Divide everything into bowls and serve.
Nutrition:
calories 354
fat 19.2
fiber 4.5
carbs 24.7
protein 11.2

Lentils and Quinoa Stew

Preparation time: 10 minutes
Cooking time: 30 minutes
Servings: 4
Ingredients:
- ½ cup tomato passata
- 1 tablespoon olive oil
- ½ teaspoon sweet paprika
- ½ teaspoon red pepper flakes, crushed
- 1 tablespoon cilantro, chopped
- Salt and black pepper to the taste
- 1 cup canned lentils, drained and rinsed
- 1 cup quinoa, cooked
- 1 zucchini, cubed
- 1 yellow onion, chopped

Directions:
1.   In a sous vide bag, mix the lentils with the quinoa, zucchini and the other ingredients, toss, seal the bag and cook in the water oven at 160 degrees F for 30 minutes.
2.   Divide into bowls and serve for lunch.
Nutrition:
calories 263
fat 18.5
fiber 4.5
carbs 19.8
protein 14.5

Chickpeas Stew

Preparation time: 10 minutes
Cooking time: 30 minutes
Servings: 4
Ingredients:
- Juice of 1 lime
- ¼ cup dill, chopped
- Salt and black pepper to the taste
- ½ teaspoon sweet paprika
- ½ teaspoon rosemary, dried
- 2 cups canned chickpeas, drained
- ½ cup tomato passata

- 1 yellow onion, chopped
- 1 carrot, peeled and sliced

Directions:
1.   In a sous vide bag, mix the chickpeas with the passata, onion and the other ingredients, toss, seal the bag and cook in the water oven at 160 degrees F for 30 minutes.
2.   Divide into bowls and serve.
Nutrition:
calories 264
fat 17.5
fiber 4.8
carbs 28.7
protein 16.3

Peppers Stew

Preparation time: 10 minutes
Cooking time: 25 minutes
Servings: 2
Ingredients:
- 2 garlic cloves, minced
- A pinch of salt and black pepper
- 2 tablespoons tomato paste
- ¼ cup parsley, chopped
- ½ pound red bell peppers, cut into strips
- ½ cup cherry tomatoes, halved
- 1 red onion, chopped
- 1 tablespoon olive oil

Directions:
1.   In a sous vide bag, mix the peppers with the tomatoes and the other ingredients, seal the bag, and cook in the water oven at 165 degrees F for 25 minutes.
2.   Divide the stew into bowls and serve.
Nutrition:
calories 273
fat 11.2
fiber 3.4
carbs 15.7
protein 5.6

Potato Stew

Preparation time: 10 minutes
Cooking time: 30 minutes
Servings: 4
Ingredients:
- 1 carrot, sliced
- ½ cup cilantro, chopped
- 2 tablespoons ginger, grated
- 1 teaspoon turmeric powder
- 1 tablespoon chives, chopped
- A pinch of salt and black pepper
- 1 red onion, chopped

- 1 tablespoon olive oil
- 1 pound gold potatoes, peeled and cut into wedges
- ½ cup tomato passata

Directions:

1. In a sous vide bag, mix the potatoes with the onion, the oil and the other ingredients, seal the bag, submerge in the water oven and cook at 170 degrees F for 30 minutes.
2. Divide into bowls and serve.

Nutrition:

calories 238

fat 7.3

fiber 6.3

carbs 32

protein 14

Green Beans Salad

Preparation time: 10 minutes

Cooking time: 25 minutes

Servings: 4

Ingredients:

- 2 tablespoons balsamic vinegar
- 1 pound green beans, trimmed and halved
- ½ teaspoon turmeric powder
- ½ teaspoon chili powder
- A pinch of salt and black pepper
- 1 red onion, chopped
- 1 tablespoon olive oil
- 1 tablespoon lime juice
- 1 cup cherry tomatoes, halved
- 1 cup kalamata olives, pitted and halved

Directions:

1. In a sous vide bag, mix the green beans with the onion, oil and the other ingredients, seal the bag and cook in the water oven at 165 degrees F fro 25 minutes.
2. Divide into bowls and serve for lunch.

Nutrition:

calories 264

fat 17.5

fiber 4.5

carbs 23.7

protein 11.5

SOUS VIDE SIDE DISH RECIPES

Cauliflower Salad

Preparation time: 10 minutes
Cooking time: 30 minutes
Servings: 2
Ingredients:
- Juice of 1 lime
- 2 tablespoons balsamic vinegar
- 6 tablespoons olive oil
- Salt and black pepper to the taste
- 1 pound cauliflower florets
- ½ cup black olives, pitted and sliced

Directions:
1. In a big sous vide bag mix the cauliflower with the olives and the other ingredients, toss, seal it, submerge it in the preheated water oven and cook at 183 degrees F for 30 minutes.
2. Divide between plates and serve as a side salad.

Nutrition:
calories 172
fat 4
fiber 5
carbs 8
protein 6

Pear Salad and Spinach

Preparation time: 10 minutes
Cooking time: 20 minutes
Servings: 4
Ingredients:
- A pinch of salt and black pepper
- 2 Frisee heads, torn
- 1 cup walnuts, toasted
- 1 tablespoon lemon juice
- 1 tablespoon balsamic vinegar
- 2 pears, peeled, cored and cubed
- 1 pound baby spinach
- 2 tablespoons olive oil

Directions:
1. In a sous vide bag, mix the pears with half of the oil, salt, pepper, walnuts and lemon juice, seal the bag, submerge in the water oven and cook at 158 degrees F for 20 minutes.
2. In a bowl, mix the pears with the spinach and the rest of the ingredients, toss, and serve as a side dish.

Nutrition:
calories 183
fat 4
fiber 6
carbs 8
protein 5

Balsamic Beet Salad

Preparation time: 10 minutes
Cooking time: 1 hour
Servings: 4
Ingredients:
- Salt and black pepper to the taste
- 2 tablespoons olive oil
- ½ teaspoon sweet paprika
- 2 bunches red beets, trimmed, peeled and cut into wedges
- 2/3 cup walnuts, toasted
- 2 and ½ tablespoons balsamic vinegar

Directions:
1. In a sous vide bag, mix the beets with the walnuts and the other ingredients, seal the bag, put it your preheated water oven and cook at 180 degrees F for 1 hour.
2. Divide between plates and serve as a side salad.

Nutrition:
calories 188
fat 4
fiber 6
carbs 8
protein 5

Glazed Beets

Preparation time: 10 minutes
Cooking time: 1 hour
Servings: 4
Ingredients:
- 1 tablespoon sugar
- 1 tablespoon parsley, chopped
- 1 pound beets, peeled and cut into medium chunks
- Salt and black pepper to the taste
- 2 tablespoons butter, melted

Directions:
1. In a sous vide bag, combine the beets with the butter and the other ingredients, toss, seal the bag, submerge in the preheated water oven and cook at 183 degrees F for 1 hour.
2. Divide them between plates and serve.

Nutrition:
calories 177
fat 2
fiber 5
carbs 7
protein 5

Orange Green Beans

Preparation time: 10 minutes
Cooking time: 40 minutes
Servings: 4
Ingredients:
- 2 tablespoons butter, melted
- Zest of 2 oranges, grated
- Juice of 2 oranges
- 1 pound green beans, trimmed and halved
- A pinch of salt and black pepper

- ½ teaspoon chili powder
- ½ teaspoon coriander, ground

Directions:

1. In a sous vide bag, combine the green beans with the butter and the other ingredients, toss, seal the bag, submerge in the preheated water oven and cook at 185 degrees F for 40 minutes.
2. Divide the mix between plates and serve.

Nutrition:

calories 152

fat 2

fiber 5

carbs 5

protein 3

Lime Brussels Sprouts

Preparation time: 10 minutes

Cooking time: 30 minutes

Servings: 4

Ingredients:

- A pinch of cayenne pepper
- 1 tablespoon avocado oil
- ½ teaspoon chili powder
- ½ teaspoon rosemary, dried
- 1 pound Brussels sprouts, trimmed and halved
- 1 tablespoon lime juice
- Salt and black pepper to the taste
- 1 teaspoon sweet paprika

Directions:

1. In a sous vide bag, combine the sprouts with the lime juice, salt, pepper and the other ingredients, toss, seal the bag, introduce in your preheated water oven and cook at 183 degrees F for 30 minutes.
2. Divide between plates and serve as a side dish.

Nutrition:

calories 121

fat 3

fiber 2

carbs 5

protein 3

Buttery Squash Mix

Preparation time: 10 minutes

Cooking time: 1 hour

Servings: 4

Ingredients:

- 1 teaspoon turmeric powder
- 2 pounds summer squash, quartered and sliced
- ½ cup coconut cream
- 2 tablespoons butter, melted
- A pinch of salt and black pepper
- 3 scallions, chopped

Directions:

1. Divide the squash, butter and the other ingredients into sous vide bags, seal them, submerge

them in the preheated water oven and cook at 176 degrees F for 1 hour.

2. Divide this mix between plates and serve as a side dish.

Nutrition:

calories 152

fat 3

fiber 6

carbs 12

protein 3

Parmesan Fennel

Preparation time: 10 minutes

Cooking time: 2 hours

Servings: 4

Ingredients:

- ½ teaspoon coriander, ground
- ½ cup parmesan, grated
- Salt and black pepper to the taste
- 2 fennel bulbs, trimmed and quartered
- 2 tablespoons butter, melted
- ½ teaspoon rosemary, dried

Directions:

1. Divide the fennel quarters into sous vide bags, add the butter and the other ingredients except the parmesan, toss, seal the bags, submerge them in the preheated water oven and cook at 183 degrees F for 2 hours.
2. Divide fennel between plates, sprinkle parmesan on top and serve as a side dish.

Nutrition:

calories 181

fat 2

fiber 6

carbs 9

protein 5

Soy Mushrooms

Preparation time: 10 minutes

Cooking time: 1 hour

Servings: 4

Ingredients:

- ½ teaspoon turmeric powder
- ½ teaspoon garam masala
- Salt and black pepper to the taste
- Juice of 1 lime
- 1 bay leaf
- 2 tablespoons olive oil
- ½ teaspoon rosemary, dried
- 1 tablespoon soy sauce
- 1 pound white mushrooms, halved

Directions:

1. In a sous vide bag, combine the mushrooms with the rosemary, oil and the other ingredients, toss, seal the bag, submerge in the preheated water oven and cook at 180 degrees F for 1 hour.
2. Divide mushrooms between plates and serve as a side dish.

Nutrition:

calories 161
fat 3
fiber 6
carbs 7
protein 5

Balsamic Carrots and Parsnips

Preparation time: 10 minutes
Cooking time: 2 hours
Servings: 4
Ingredients:
- 2 pounds baby carrots, peeled
- ½ pound parsnips, peeled and cut into matchsticks
- 2 tablespoon olive oil
- 1 tablespoon balsamic vinegar
- 2 tablespoons sugar
- ½ teaspoon rosemary, dried
- 1 tablespoon chives, chopped
- Salt and black pepper to the taste

Directions:
1. In a sous vide bag, combine the carrots with the parsnips, oil, vinegar and the other ingredients, seal the bag, submerge in your preheated water oven and cook at 185 degrees F for 2 hours.
2. Divide between plates and serve as a side dish.

Nutrition:
calories 121
fat 2
fiber 5
carbs 5
protein 4

Thai Eggplant Mix

Preparation time: 10 minutes
Cooking time: 2 hours
Servings: 4
Ingredients:
- 2 tablespoons balsamic vinegar
- 1 tablespoon olive oil
- Salt and black pepper to the taste
- 2 tablespoons lime juice
- 2 tablespoons soy sauce
- 2 tablespoons chives, chopped
- 2 pounds eggplants, peeled and roughly cubed
- 3 garlic cloves, minced
- 2 Thai chilies, chopped

Directions:
1. In a sous vide bag, combine the eggplants with the garlic, chilies and the other ingredients, toss, seal the bag, submerge in the preheated water oven and cook at 185 degrees F for 2 hours.
2. Divide the mix between plates and serve as a side dish.

Nutrition:
calories 212
fat 4

fiber 5
carbs 12
protein 4

Peppers and Eggplant Mix

Preparation time: 10 minutes
Cooking time: 2 hours
Servings: 4
Ingredients:
- 1 pound eggplant, roughly cubed
- 2 red bell peppers, cut into strips
- 2 tablespoons balsamic vinegar
- 2 tablespoons olive oil
- 4 garlic cloves, minced
- Salt and black pepper to the taste
- 1 red onion, sliced
- 1 tablespoon basil, chopped

Directions:
1. In a sous vide bag, combine the eggplants with the peppers, vinegar and the other ingredients, toss, seal the bag, submerge in the preheated water oven and cook at 180 degrees F for 2 hours.
2. Divide between plates and serve as a side dish.

Nutrition:
calories 189
fat 3
fiber 4
carbs 6
protein 4

Peppers and Seeds Mix

Preparation time: 10 minutes
Cooking time: 2 hours
Servings: 4
Ingredients:
- 2 tablespoons olive oil
- Juice of 1 lime
- 2 garlic cloves, minced
- 1 tablespoon basil, chopped
- Salt and black pepper to the taste
- 1 pound red bell peppers, cut into strips
- 1 tablespoon sunflower seeds
- 1 tablespoon pine nuts, toasted

Directions:
1. In a sous vide bag, combine the peppers with the seeds, nuts and the other ingredients, toss, introduce in your preheated water oven and cook at 180 degrees F for 2 hours.
2. Divide between plates and serve.

Nutrition:
calories 126
fat 1
fiber 3
carbs 6
protein 3

Parsley Asparagus

Preparation time: 10 minutes

Cooking time: 30 minutes
Servings: 2
Ingredients:
- Juice of 1 lime
- ¼ cup olive oil
- 1 teaspoon mustard powder
- Salt and black pepper to the taste
- 1 pound asparagus, trimmed
- 1 tablespoon balsamic vinegar
- 1 tablespoon parsley, chopped

Directions:
1. In a sous vide bag, combine the asparagus with the vinegar, parsley and the other ingredients, toss, seal the bag, submerge it in your preheated water oven and cook at 185 degrees F for 30 minutes.
2. Divide this between plates and serve.

Nutrition:
calories 144
fat 3
fiber 6
carbs 15
protein 4

Olives and Cauliflower

Preparation time: 10 minutes
Cooking time: 2 hours
Servings: 2
Ingredients:
- Salt and black pepper to the taste
- 2 tablespoons olive oil
- 2 tablespoons balsamic vinegar
- 2 tablespoons cilantro, chopped
- 1 pound asparagus, trimmed
- 1 tablespoon balsamic vinegar
- 1 tablespoon parsley, chopped

Directions:
1. In a sous vide bag, combine the cauliflower with the olives, cream and the other ingredients, toss, seal the bag, submerge into preheated water oven and cook at 180 degrees F for 2 hours.
2. Divide between plates and serve as a side dish.

Nutrition:
calories 151
fat 4
fiber 2
carbs 12
protein 4

Tarragon Mushrooms

Preparation time: 10 minutes
Cooking time: 1 hour
Servings: 4
Ingredients:
- Salt and black pepper to the taste
- 2 tablespoons olive oil
- ½ teaspoon tarragon, dried
- 2 tablespoons balsamic vinegar
- 1 pound brown mushrooms, halved

- Juice of 1 lime
- ½ teaspoon chili powder

Directions:
1. In a sous vide bag, combine the mushrooms with the lime juice, chili powder and the other ingredients, seal the bag, introduce in the preheated water oven and cook at 182 degrees F for 1 hour.
2. Divide between plates and serve as a side dish.

Nutrition:
calories 100
fat 4
fiber 4
carbs 7
protein 4

Creamy Spinach

Preparation time: 10 minutes
Cooking time: 50 minutes
Servings: 2
Ingredients:
- 1 teaspoon turmeric powder
- ½ teaspoon curry powder
- Salt and black pepper to the taste
- 1 tablespoon butter, melted
- 2 garlic cloves, minced
- 1 pound baby spinach
- ½ cup heavy cream

Directions:
1. In a sous vide bag, mix the spinach with the garlic and the other ingredients, seal the bag, submerge in the preheated water oven and cook at 175 degrees F for 50 minutes.
2. Divide between plates and serve as a side dish.

Nutrition:
calories 133
fat 10
fiber 4
carbs 4
protein 2

Parsley Cauliflower

Preparation time: 10 minutes
Cooking time: 2 hours
Servings: 4
Ingredients:
- 2 pounds cauliflower florets
- 1 tablespoon lemon juice
- 1 tablespoon lemon zest, grated
- Salt and black pepper to the taste
- 1 tablespoon parsley, chopped
- 3 tablespoons olive oil
- 2 tablespoons soy sauce

Directions:
1. In a sous vide bag, combine the cauliflower with the lemon juice and the other ingredients, toss, seal, introduce in the preheated water oven and cook at 180 degrees F for 2 hours.

2.	Divide between plates and serve.
Nutrition:
calories 128
fat 2
fiber 3
carbs 7
protein 6

Mushroom and Broccoli Mix

Preparation time: 10 minutes
Cooking time: 1 hour
Servings: 4
Ingredients:
- 2 tablespoons olive oil
- Salt and black pepper to the taste
- 2 garlic cloves, minced
- A handful parsley, chopped
- 1 pound broccoli florets
- ½ pound white mushrooms, halved
- 2 tablespoons balsamic vinegar

Directions:
1.	In a sous vide bag, combine the broccoli with the mushrooms, vinegar and the other ingredients, toss, seal the bag, introduce in your preheated water bag and cook at 175 degrees F for 1 hour.
2.	Divide between plates and serve.
Nutrition:
calories 160
fat 4
fiber 6
carbs 2
protein 12

Cumin Okra

Preparation time: 10 minutes
Cooking time: 40 minutes
Servings: 4
Ingredients:
- 1 tablespoon balsamic vinegar
- Salt and black pepper to the taste
- 1 tablespoon chives, chopped
- 1 pound okra, sliced
- 2 tablespoons olive oil
- 1 red onion, sliced

Directions:
1.	In a sous vide bag, combine the okra with the oil and the other ingredients, toss, seal the bag, submerge in the preheated water oven and cook at 180 degrees F for 40 minutes.
2.	Divide between plates and serve as a side dish.
Nutrition:
calories 170
fat 2
fiber 3
carbs 12
protein 6

Okra Mix and Eggplant

Preparation time: 10 minutes
Cooking time: 1 hour
Servings: 4
Ingredients:
- 1 tablespoon red wine vinegar
- ½ teaspoon coriander, ground
- ½ teaspoon cumin, ground
- Salt and black pepper to the taste
- ¼ cup chives, chopped
- 1 pound eggplant, sliced into thin rounds
- ½ pound okra, sliced
- 1 tablespoon olive oil
- 1 tablespoon lemon zest, grated

Directions:
1.	In a sous vide bag, combine the eggplant with the okra, oil and the other ingredients, toss, seal the bag, submerge in the preheated water oven and cook at 183 degrees F for 1 hour.
2.	Divide between plates and serve.
Nutrition:
calories 105
fat 1
fiber 1
carbs 6
protein 7

Lemony Okra

Preparation time: 10 minutes
Cooking time: 30 minutes
Servings: 4
Ingredients:
- Salt and black pepper to the taste
- ¼ cup almonds, blanched
- 2 tablespoons chives, chopped
- ½ teaspoon turmeric powder
- 1 pound okra, sliced
- Juice of 1 lemon
- Zest of 1 lemon, grated

Directions:
1.	In a sous vide bag, combine the okra with the lemon juice, zest and the other ingredients, seal the bag, introduce it in the preheated water oven and cook at 180 degrees F for 30 minutes.
2.	Divide the mix between plates and serve as a side dish.
Nutrition:
calories 170
fat 15
fiber 4
carbs 7
protein 4

Cheesy Broccoli

Preparation time: 10 minutes
Cooking time: 1 hour
Servings: 4
Ingredients:
- 1 teaspoon chili powder

- 1 teaspoon cumin, ground
- 1 tablespoon goat cheese, crumbled
- Salt and black pepper to the taste
- 3 tablespoons olive oil
- 1 pound broccoli florets
- 1 garlic clove, minced

Directions:

1. In a sous vide bag, combine the broccoli with the garlic, chili and the other ingredients except the cheese, seal the bag, submerge in the preheated water oven and cook at 180 degrees F for 1 hour.
2. Divide broccoli between plates, sprinkle cheese all over and serve as a side dish.

Nutrition:

calories 173
fat 14
fiber 3
carbs 6
protein 5

Okra Mix and Tomato

Preparation time: 10 minutes
Cooking time: 1 hour
Servings: 4
Ingredients:

- 1 tablespoon soy sauce
- 1 tablespoon balsamic vinegar
- 1 teaspoon chili powder
- 1 tablespoon cilantro, chopped
- Salt and black pepper to the taste
- 1 pound cherry tomatoes, halved
- ½ pound okra, sliced
- 2 tablespoons olive oil

Direction:

1. In a sous vide bag, combine the tomatoes with the okra, oil and the other ingredients, seal, submerge in the preheated water oven and cook at 185 degrees F for 1 hour.
2. Divide between plates and serve as a side dish.

Nutrition:

calories 165
fat 11
fiber 4
carbs 6
protein 3

Italian Tomatoes

Preparation time: 10 minutes
Cooking time: 1 hour
Servings: 4
Ingredients:

- Salt and black pepper to the taste
- 1 garlic clove, minced
- 1 teaspoon Italian seasoning
- 1 tablespoon dill, chopped
- 1 red onion, sliced
- 1 pound tomatoes, cut into wedges
- 1 tablespoon olive oil

- ½ teaspoon sweet paprika

Directions:

1. In a sous vide bag, combine the tomatoes with the onion, oil and the other ingredients, seal the bag, submerge into the preheated water oven and cook at 180 degrees F for 1 hour.
2. Divide the mix between plates and serve as a side dish.

Nutrition:

calories 120
fat 3
fiber 2
carbs 6
protein 4

Mushroom Salad

Preparation time: 10 minutes
Cooking time: 1 hour
Servings: 4
Ingredients:

- 1 cup cherry tomatoes, halved
- 1 cup kalamata olives, pitted and halved
- 1 cup baby spinach
- 1 tablespoon chives, chopped
- 2 tablespoons avocado oil
- 1 pound cremini mushrooms, cut into quarters
- 1 tablespoon balsamic vinegar
- 2 tablespoons red wine
- ½ teaspoon chili powder
- Salt and black pepper to the taste

Directions:

1. In a sous vide bag, combine the mushrooms with the oil, vinegar and the other ingredients, toss, seal the bag, submerge in the preheated water oven and cook at 180 degrees F for 1 hour.
2. Divide between plates and serve as a side dish.

Nutrition:

calories 160
fat 4
fiber 2
carbs 6
protein 6

Coriander Tomato and Spinach Mix

Preparation time: 10 minutes
Cooking time: 1 hour
Servings: 6
Ingredients:

- ½ pounds tomatoes, halved
- ½ pound baby spinach
- Juice of 1 lime
- 1 teaspoon coriander, ground
- ½ teaspoon chili powder
- 1 tablespoon extra virgin olive oil
- 3 garlic cloves, minced
- 1 tablespoon basil, chopped

Directions:

1.   In a sous vide bag, combine the tomatoes with the spinach and the other ingredients, seal the bag, submerge in the preheated water oven and cook at 180 degrees F for 1 hour.
2.   Divide between plates and serve as a side dish.

Nutrition:
calories 200
fat 2
fiber 2
carbs 7
protein 10

Tomato and Mango Salsa

Preparation time: 10 minutes
Cooking time: 1 hour
Servings: 4
Ingredients:
- 1 pound cherry tomatoes, halved
- 1 cup mango, peeled and cubed
- ½ cup black olives, pitted and halved
- 1 tablespoon olive oil
- 1 tablespoon balsamic vinegar
- Salt and black pepper to the taste
- 1/3 cup red onion, cut into wedges
- ¼ cup cilantro, finely chopped
- 3 tablespoons lemon juice

Directions:
1.   In a sous vide bag, mix the tomatoes with the mango, olives and the other ingredients, seal the bag, submerge in the preheated water oven and cook at 140 degrees F for 1 hour.
2.   Divide the mix between plates and serve as a side dish.

Nutrition:
calories 100
fat 1
fiber 2
carbs 7
protein 4

Pineapple Mix and Balsamic Tomato

Preparation time: 5 minutes
Cooking time: 1 hour
Servings: 4
Ingredients:
- 2 tablespoons balsamic vinegar
- 1 tablespoon chives, chopped
- Salt and black pepper to the taste
- 1 pound tomatoes, cut into wedges
- 1 cup pineapple, peeled and cubed
- 2 tablespoons extra virgin olive oil

Directions:
1.   In a sous vide bag, combine the tomatoes with the pineapple and the other ingredients, seal the bag, submerge in the preheated water oven and cook at 140 degrees F for 1 hour.
2.   Divide between plates and serve as a side dish.

Nutrition:
calories 100
fat 2
fiber 2
carbs 8
protein 9

Eggplant and Pearl Onion Mix

Preparation time: 10 minutes
Cooking time: 1 hour
Servings: 4
Ingredients:
- 1 pound eggplant, roughly cubed
- 1 cup pearl onions, peeled
- 2 tablespoons olive oil
- 1 tablespoon lemon juice
- 1 teaspoon mustard powder
- ½ teaspoon onion powder
- 1 tablespoon balsamic vinegar
- 1 tablespoon fresh oregano, chopped
- Salt and black pepper to the taste

Directions:
1.   In a sous vide bag, combine the eggplants with the onions and the other ingredients, seal, submerge in the preheated water oven and cook at 180 degrees F for 1 hour.
2.   Divide the mix between plates serve as a side dish.

Nutrition:
calories 160
fat 3
fiber 2
carbs 7
protein 8

Spicy Beets and Okra

Preparation time: 10 minutes
Cooking time: 1 hour
Servings: 4
Ingredients:
- 2 red chilies, chopped
- 1 teaspoon chili powder
- 2 tablespoons balsamic vinegar
- 1 teaspoon oregano, dried
- ¼ teaspoon basil, dried
- 1 tablespoon balsamic vinegar
- Salt and black pepper to the taste
- 1 pound beets, peeled and cubed
- 1 cup okra, sliced
- 2 tablespoons olive oil

Directions:
1.   In a sous vide bag, combine the beets with the okra, oil and the other ingredients, toss, seal the bag, submerge in the water bath and cook at 180 degrees F for 1 hour.
2.   Divide the mix between plates and serve

Nutrition:
calories 150
fat 1

fiber 2
carbs 7
protein 8

Coconut Endives and Radish

Preparation time: 10 minutes
Cooking time: 30 minutes
Servings: 4
Ingredients:
- 1 tablespoon lemon juice
- 1 shallot, chopped
- 1 tablespoon balsamic vinegar
- 6 tablespoons coconut cream
- Salt and black pepper to the taste
- 1 tablespoon parsley, chopped
- 2 endives, roots and ends cut and thinly sliced crosswise
- 1 cup radishes, halved
- 2 tablespoons avocado oil

Directions:
1. In a sous vide bag, combine the endives with the radishes and the other ingredients, seal it, submerge in the preheated water oven and cook at 180 degrees F for 30 minutes.
2. Divide between plates and serve as a side dish.

Nutrition:
calories 170
fat 3
fiber 5
carbs 7
protein 10

Cabbage and Carrots Mix

Preparation time: 10 minutes
Cooking time: 50 minutes
Servings: 4
Ingredients:
- 1 yellow onion, chopped
- 2 tablespoons capers, drained
- Juice of 1 lemon
- Salt and black pepper to the taste
- 2 tablespoons olive oil
- 1 red cabbage, shredded
- 2 carrots, peeled and shredded
- 2 tablespoons balsamic vinegar

Directions:
1. In a sous vide bag, combine the cabbage with the carrots and the other ingredients, seal the bag, submerge in the preheated water oven and cook at 185 degrees F for 50 minutes.
2. Divide everything between plates and serve as a side dish.

Nutrition:
calories 119
fat 7
fiber 3
carbs 7
protein 2

Kale and Spring Onions Mix

Preparation time: 10 minutes
Cooking time: 20 minutes
Servings: 4
Ingredients:
- 3 garlic cloves, minced
- 2 tablespoons lime juice
- ½ teaspoon chili powder
- ½ teaspoon rosemary, chopped
- 2 tablespoons chives, chopped
- 1 tablespoon olive oil
- 1 pound baby kale
- 1 cup spring onions, chopped
- 1/3 cup almonds, toasted

Directions:
1. In a sous vide bag, combine the kale with the spring onions, oil and the other ingredients, seal the bag, introduce in your preheated water oven and cook at 180 degrees F for 20 minutes.
2. Divide the mix between plates and serve as a side dish.

Nutrition:
calories 170
fat 11
fiber 3
carbs 7
protein 4

Simple Cabbage and Avocado Mix

Preparation time: 10 minutes
Cooking time: 1 hour
Servings: 4
Ingredients:
- 2 tablespoons olive oil
- Juice of 1 lime
- ½ teaspoon sweet paprika
- Salt and black pepper to the taste
- 1 pound green cabbage, roughly shredded
- 1 cup avocado, peeled, pitted and cubed
- ½ cup kalamata olives, pitted and halved
- 1 cup cherry tomatoes, halved

Directions:
1. In a sous vide bag, combine the cabbage with the avocado, olives and the other ingredients, seal the bag, submerge in the preheated water oven and cook at 180 degrees F for 1 hour
2. Divide the mix between plates and serve as a side dish.

Nutrition:
calories 160
fat 4
fiber 2
carbs 7
protein 7

Green Beans and Walnuts Mix

Preparation time: 10 minutes
Cooking time: 1 hour
Servings: 4

Ingredients:
- 1 tablespoon balsamic vinegar
- 2 tablespoons olive oil
- Salt and black pepper to the taste
- 5 scallions, chopped
- A handful cilantro, chopped
- 1 pound green beans, trimmed
- 1 cup walnuts, chopped
- 1 tablespoon soy sauce

Directions:
1. In a sous vide bag, combine the green beans with the walnuts, soy sauce and the other ingredients, seal the bag, submerge in your preheated water oven and cook at 185 degrees F for 1 hour.
2. Divide the mix between plates and serve as a side dish.

Nutrition:
calories 170
fat 5
fiber 3
carbs 4
protein 6

Lemon Olives and Radish Mix

Preparation time: 10 minutes
Cooking time: 30 minutes
Servings: 4
Ingredients:
- 2 tablespoons olive oil
- 2 garlic cloves, minced
- 1 tablespoon lemon juice
- 1 teaspoon sweet paprika
- 1 teaspoon lemon zest, grated
- Salt and black pepper to the taste
- 1 cup black olives, pitted
- 1 cup kalamata olives, pitted
- 1 cup radishes, halved

Directions:
1. In a sous vide bag, combine the olives with the radishes, oil and the other ingredients, seal the bag, submerge into your preheated water oven and cook at 134 degrees F for 30 minutes.
2. Divide between plates and serve.

Nutrition:
calories 130
fat 20
fiber 4
carbs 7
protein 1

Cauliflower and Chard Mix

Preparation time: 10 minutes
Cooking time: 1 hour
Servings: 6
Ingredients:
- 1 pound cauliflower florets
- 1 cup red chard, torn
- 1 tablespoon olive oil
- 1 tablespoon lemon juice

Ingredients (continued):
- 1 tablespoon balsamic vinegar
- 1 tablespoon lemon zest, grated
- ½ teaspoon garlic powder
- ½ teaspoon rosemary, dried
- Salt and black pepper to the taste
- 1 cup red onion, chopped
- 1 tablespoon chives, chopped

Directions:
1. In a sous vide bag, combine the cauliflower with the chard, oil and the other ingredients, toss, seal the bag, submerge in the preheated water oven and cook at 185 degrees F for 1 hour.
2. Divide the mix between plates and serve as a side salad.

Nutrition:
calories 171
fat 20
fiber 2
carbs 3
protein 4

Ginger Broccoli and Radish Mix

Preparation time: 10 minutes
Cooking time: 40 minutes
Servings: 4
Ingredients:
- 1 pound broccoli florets
- ½ pound radish, halved
- 2 tablespoons olive oil
- 1 tablespoon soy sauce
- 2 teaspoons coriander seeds, crushed
- 1 yellow onion, chopped
- Salt and black pepper to the taste
- A pinch of red pepper, crushed
- 1 tablespoon ginger, grated
- 1 garlic clove, minced
- 1 tablespoon chives, chopped

Directions:
1. In a sous vide bag, combine the broccoli with the radishes, oil and the other ingredients, seal the bag, submerge in the preheated water oven and cook at 183 degrees F for 40 minutes.
2. Divide the mix between plates and serve as a side dish.

Nutrition:
calories 150
fat 4
fiber 2
carbs 7
protein 12

Apple and Zucchini Mix

Preparation time: 10 minutes
Cooking time: 1 hour
Servings: 4
Ingredients:
- 1 bunch green onion, chopped
- ½ teaspoon sweet paprika
- ½ teaspoon rosemary, dried

- Salt and black pepper to the taste
- 1 tablespoon parsley, chopped
- 2 apples, cored and cut into wedges
- 1 pound zucchinis, roughly cubed
- 1 tablespoon olive oil
- Juice of 1 lime

Directions:

1. In a sous vide bag, mix the zucchinis with the apples, oil and the other ingredients, toss, seal the bag, submerge in the preheated water oven and cook at 180 degrees F for 1 hour.
2. Divide between plates and serve as a side dish.

Nutrition:

calories 170

fat 7

fiber 4

carbs 6

protein 10

Creamy Garlic Spinach and Corn

Preparation time: 10 minutes
Cooking time: 40 minutes
Servings: 4
Ingredients:

- 1 cup heavy cream
- 1 tablespoon chives, chopped
- 1 teaspoon garlic, minced
- Salt and black pepper to the taste
- ½ teaspoon nutmeg, ground
- 2 tablespoons butter, melted
- 1 pound baby spinach
- 1 cup corn
- 1 teaspoon turmeric powder
- ½ teaspoon coriander, ground

Directions:

1. In a sous vide bag, combine the spinach with the corn, turmeric and the other ingredients, toss, seal the bag, submerge in the preheated water bag and cook at 170 degrees F for 40 minutes.
2. Divide everything between plates and serve as a side dish.

Nutrition:

calories 245

fat 24

fiber 3

carbs 4

protein 6

Lemon Greens Mix

Preparation time: 10 minutes
Cooking time: 20 minutes
Servings: 4
Ingredients:

- 2 garlic cloves, minced
- 1 tablespoon olive oil
- 1 cup collard greens, chopped
- 1 cup red chard, torn
- 1 cup baby kale

- 1 cup baby spinach
- ½ teaspoon chili powder
- 1 teaspoon lemon juice
- 1 tablespoon butter, melted
- Salt and black pepper to the taste

Directions:

1. In a sous vide bag, combine the greens with the garlic, oil and the other ingredients, seal the bag, submerge in the preheated water oven and cook at 185 degrees F for 20 minutes.
2. Divide the mix between plates and serve.

Nutrition:

calories 151

fat 6

fiber 3

carbs 7

protein 8

Spicy Collards Greens

Preparation time: 10 minutes
Cooking time: 20 minutes
Servings: 4
Ingredients:

- 1 tablespoon olive oil
- 2 pounds collard greens, torn
- 2 red chilies, chopped
- 1 teaspoon hot paprika
- ½ teaspoon garam masala
- 1 tablespoon lemon juice
- 1 teaspoon red pepper flakes, crushed
- Salt and black pepper to the taste
- 1 yellow onion, chopped

Directions:

1. In a sous vide bag, mix the greens with the oil, chilies and the other ingredients, seal the bag, submerge in the preheated water oven and cook at 180 degrees F for 20 minutes.
2. Divide between plates and serve as a side dish.

Nutrition:

calories 150

fat 12

fiber 2

carbs 4

protein 8

Spinach, Mango and Tomatoes

Preparation time: 10 minutes
Cooking time: 20 minutes
Servings: 4
Ingredients:

- Juice and zest of 1 lime
- ½ teaspoon rosemary, dried
- 1 tablespoon apple cider vinegar
- Salt and black pepper to the taste
- 1 pound baby spinach
- ½ pound cherry tomatoes, halved
- 1 cup mango, peeled and cubed
- 2 tablespoons olive oil

Directions:
1.	In a sous vide bag, combine the spinach with the tomatoes, mango and the other ingredients, seal the bag, submerge in the preheated water oven and cook at 180 degrees F for 20 minutes.
2.	Divide the whole mix between plates and serve.
Nutrition:
calories 150
fat 8
fiber 1
carbs 3
protein 7

Mustard Greens, Olives and Kale Salad

Preparation time: 5 minutes
Cooking time: 20 minutes
Servings: 4
Ingredients:
- 2 garlic cloves, minced
- 1 pound baby kale
- 2 tomatoes, cubed
- 1 cup kalamata olives, pitted and halved
- 1 cup black olives, pitted and halved
- 1 pound mustard greens, torn
- 1 tablespoon olive oil
- ½ cup scallions, chopped
- Juice of 1 lime
- Salt and black pepper to the taste
- 3 tablespoons veggie stock
- 1 tablespoon chives, chopped

Directions:
1.	In a sous vide bag, combine the kale with the olives, greens and the other ingredients, toss seal the bag, submerge in the preheated water oven and cook at 180 degrees F for 20 minutes.
2.	Divide between plates, and serve as a side dish.
Nutrition:
calories 120
fat 3
fiber 1
carbs 7
protein 6

Greens and Shallots Mix

Preparation time: 10 minutes
Cooking time: 20 minutes
Servings: 4
Ingredients:
- 1 cup cherry tomatoes halved
- 1 tablespoon olive oil
- Salt and black pepper to the taste
- 2 tablespoons soy sauce
- 2 teaspoons ginger, grated
- 2 cups mustard greens, torn
- 1 cup shallots, chopped
- ½ cup black olives, pitted and halved

Directions:

1.	In a sous vide bag, combine the greens with the shallots and the other ingredients, toss, seal the bag, submerge into preheated water oven and cook at 180 degrees F for 20 minutes.
2.	Divide between plates and serve as a side dish.
Nutrition:
calories 140
fat 2
fiber 1
carbs 6
protein 7

Jalapeno Greens Mix

Preparation time: 10 minutes
Cooking time: 20 minutes
Servings: 4
Ingredients:
- 1 tablespoon avocado oil
- 1 teaspoon coriander seeds
- 1 cup shallots, chopped
- 1 tablespoon garlic, minced
- 1 tablespoon ginger, grated
- Salt and black pepper to the taste
- ½ teaspoon paprika
- 1 pound mustard greens, torn
- 1 cup red chard, torn
- 1 cup baby kale
- 2 jalapeno peppers, chopped
- 1 tablespoon balsamic vinegar

Directions:
1.	In a sous vide bag, combine the greens with the jalapenos and the other ingredients, seal the bag, submerge in the preheated water oven and cook at 185 degrees F for 20 minutes.
2.	Divide the mix between plates and serve as a side dish.
Nutrition:
calories 143
fat 6
fiber 3
carbs 7
protein 7

Sprouts Salad

Preparation time: 10 minutes
Cooking time: 40 minutes
Servings: 4
Ingredients:
- 1 green apple, cored and cubed
- 1 cup cherry tomatoes, halved
- 1 cup shallots, chopped
- 1 pound Brussels sprouts, trimmed and halved
- 2 tablespoons olive oil
- Juice of ½ lemon
- ½ teaspoon chili powder
- 1 tablespoon balsamic vinegar
- Salt and black pepper to the taste

Directions:
1.   In a sous vide bag, mix the sprouts with the shallots, tomatoes and the other ingredients, seal the bag, submerge in the preheated water oven and cook at 183 degrees F for 40 minutes.
2.   Divide between plates and serve as a side dish.
Nutrition:
calories 160
fat 3
fiber 1
carbs 6
protein 6

Mango and Radishes Mix

Preparation time: 10 minutes
Cooking time: 40 minutes
Servings: 4
Ingredients:
* 1 tablespoon balsamic vinegar
* ½ teaspoon chili powder
* 2 scallions, chopped
* Salt and black pepper to the taste
* 1 tablespoon chives, chopped
* 1 pound radishes, halved
* 1 cup mango, peeled and cubed
* 1 tablespoon olive oil

Directions:
1.   In a sous vide bag, mix the radishes with the mango and the other ingredients, seal the bag, submerge in the preheated water oven and cook at 185 degrees F for 40 minutes.
2.   Divide between plates and serve.
Nutrition:
calories 30
fat 1
fiber 0.4
carbs 1
protein 1

Creamy Radish and Corn Mix

Preparation time: 10 minutes
Cooking time: 30 minutes
Servings: 4
Ingredients:
* ½ cup heavy cream
* 1 tablespoon butter, melted
* 1 tablespoon green onion, chopped
* 1 tablespoon chives, chopped
* Salt and black pepper to the taste
* ½ pound radishes, halved
* 1 cup corn

Directions:
1.   In a sous vide bag, combine the radishes with the corn and the other ingredients, toss, seal the bag, submerge in the preheated water oven and cook at 185 degrees F for 30 minutes.
2.   Divide everything between plates and serve as a side dish.

Nutrition:
calories 140
fat 23
fiber 3
carbs 6
protein 5

Balsamic Carrots

Preparation time: 10 minutes
Cooking time: 30 minutes
Servings: 4
Ingredients:
* 1 pound baby carrots, peeled
* 2 tablespoons olive oil
* 2 tablespoons balsamic vinegar
* 1 teaspoon rosemary, dried
* A pinch of salt and black pepper
* 1 teaspoon chili powder

Directions:
1.   In a sous vide bag, mix the carrots with the vinegar and the other ingredients, seal and cook in the water oven at 170 degrees F for 30 minutes.
2.   Divide between plates and serve.
Nutrition:
calories 149
fat 5
fiber 3
carbs 33
protein 4

Creamy Corn

Preparation time: 10 minutes
Cooking time: 20 minutes
Servings: 2
Ingredients:
* ½ teaspoon turmeric powder
* A pinch of salt and black pepper
* 1 tablespoon cilantro, chopped
* 2 cups fresh corn
* 2 spring onions, chopped
* ½ cup heavy cream

Directions:
1.   In a sous vide bag, mix the corn with the cream and the other ingredients, seal the bag, submerge in the water oven and cook at 165 degrees F for 20 minutes.
2.   Divide the mix between plates and serve as a side dish.
Nutrition:
calories 293
fat 19
fiber 2
carbs 28
protein 6

Rosemary Broccoli Mix

Preparation time: 10 minutes
Cooking time: 30 minutes
Servings: 4

Ingredients:
- 1 pound broccoli florets
- 1 tablespoon avocado oil
- 2 scallions, chopped
- Juice of 1 lime
- 1 tablespoon rosemary, chopped
- 1 tablespoon coriander powder
- 1 tablespoon chives, chopped
- A pinch of salt and black pepper

Directions:
1. In a sous vide bag, mix the broccoli with the oil, scallions and the other ingredients, seal the bag and cook in the water oven and cook at 160 degrees F for 30 minutes.
2. Divide the mix between plates and serve as a side dish.

Nutrition:
calories 168
fat 12
fiber 6
carbs 14
protein 5

Creamy Tomatoes

Preparation time: 10 minutes
Cooking time: 20 minutes
Servings: 2
Ingredients:
- ½ teaspoon chili powder
- ¼ cup heavy cream
- A pinch of salt and black pepper
- 1 tablespoon dill, chopped
- 4 scallions, chopped
- 1 tablespoon avocado oil
- 1 pound cherry tomatoes, halved

Directions:
1. In a sous vide bag, mix the tomatoes with the scallions and the other ingredients, seal the bag and cook in the water oven at 165 degrees F for 20 minutes.
2. Divide the mix between plates and serve.

Nutrition:
calories 122
fat 7
fiber 3
carbs 10
protein 4

Hot Cauliflower

Preparation time: 10 minutes
Cooking time: 20 minutes
Servings: 4
Ingredients:
- 1 tablespoon avocado oil
- 1 teaspoon chili powder
- Juice of 1 lime
- 1 red chili pepper, chopped
- 1 pound cauliflower florets
- 2 garlic cloves, minced
- A pinch of salt and black pepper
- ½ teaspoon turmeric powder
- ½ teaspoon red pepper flakes, crushed

Directions:
1. In a sous vide bag, mix the cauliflower with the oil, chili and the other ingredients, toss, seal the bag and cook in the water oven at 170 degrees F for 20 minutes.
2. Divide between plates and serve as a side dish.

Nutrition:
calories 166
fat 13
fiber 3
carbs 9.6
protein 5

Ginger Green Beans

Preparation time: 10 minutes
Cooking time: 25 minutes
Servings: 4
Ingredients:
- 1 tablespoon avocado oil
- 1 red chili pepper, minced
- 1 tablespoon ginger, grated
- 2 garlic cloves, minced
- Salt and black pepper to the taste
- 1 tablespoon cilantro, chopped
- 2 cups green beans, trimmed and halved
- 1 tablespoon lemon zest, grated
- 1 tablespoon balsamic vinegar

Directions:
1. In a sous vide bag, mix the green beans with the vinegar, lemon zest and the other ingredients, seal the bag, submerge in the water oven and cook at 160 degrees F for 25 minutes.
2. Divide the mix between plates and serve as a side dish.

Nutrition:
calories 256
fat 14
fiber 5
carbs 15
protein 5

Dill Eggplant

Preparation time: 5 minutes
Cooking time: 30 minutes
Servings: 4
Ingredients:
- 1 red onion, chopped
- Juice of 1 lime
- ½ teaspoon coriander, ground
- ½ teaspoon rosemary, dried
- A pinch of salt and black pepper
- 1 pound eggplant, roughly cubed
- 1 tablespoon dill, chopped
- 1 tablespoon olive oil

Directions:

1.   In a sous vide bag, mix the eggplant with the dill, oil and the other ingredients, seal the bag and cook in the water oven at 170 degrees F for 30 minutes.
2.   Divide the mix between plates and serve.
Nutrition:
calories 230
fat 12
fiber 4
carbs 8
protein 5

Chives Potatoes

Preparation time: 10 minutes
Cooking time: 30 minutes
Servings: 2
Ingredients:
- 2 tablespoons butter, melted
- 1 pound gold potatoes, peeled and cut into wedges
- 2 tablespoons balsamic vinegar
- A pinch of salt and black pepper
- 1 tablespoon chives, chopped

Directions:
1.   In a sous vide bag, mix the potatoes with the melted butter and the other ingredients, seal the bag and cook in the water oven and cook at 180 degrees F for 30 minutes.
2.   Divide between plates and serve as a side dish.
Nutrition:
calories 152
fat 4
fiber 4
carbs 12
protein 5.3

Black Beans Mix

Preparation time: 5 minutes
Cooking time: 20 minutes
Servings: 4
Ingredients:
- 2 cups canned black beans, drained and rinsed
- 1 tablespoon coriander, chopped
- 2 tablespoons butter, soft
- 1 tablespoon balsamic vinegar
- 1 tablespoon chives, chopped
- A pinch of salt and white pepper

Directions:
1.   In a sous vide bag, mix the beans with the coriander and the other ingredients, toss, seal the bag and cook in the water oven at 170 degrees F for 20 minutes.
2.   Divide between plates and serve as a side dish.
Nutrition:
calories 170
fat 6
fiber 3
carbs 22
protein 5

Dill Peas

Preparation time: 10 minutes
Cooking time: 25 minutes
Servings: 2
Ingredients:
- ½ teaspoon rosemary, dried
- 1 teaspoon turmeric powder
- A pinch of salt and black pepper
- 1 tablespoon dill, chopped
- 1 tablespoon olive oil
- 2 cups green peas
- Juice of 1 lime

Directions:
1.   In a sous vide bag, mix the peas with the oil, lime juice and the other ingredients, toss, seal the bag and cook in the water oven at 150 degrees F for 25 minutes.
2.   Divide the mix between plates and serve as a side dish,
Nutrition:
calories 220
fat 15
fiber 4
carbs 18
protein 4

SOUS VIDE SNACK AND APPETIZER RECIPES

Turkey Meatballs

Preparation time: 10 minutes
Cooking time: 3 hours
Servings: 8
Ingredients:
- 1 red onion, chopped
- 1 tablespoon chives, chopped
- 2 tablespoons parsley, chopped
- 3 tablespoons parmesan, grated
- 1 pound turkey breast, skinless, boneless and ground
- Salt and black pepper to the taste
- 1 egg, whisked
- 1 tablespoon coconut flour

Directions:
1. In a bowl, mix the meat with the egg, flour and the other ingredients, stir well and shape medium meatballs out of this mix.
2. Put the meatballs in a sous vide bag, seal, put it in the water oven and cook them at 135 degrees F for 3 hours.
3. Arrange the meatballs on a platter and serve them as an appetizer.

Nutrition:
calories 200
fat 6
fiber 6
carbs 8
protein 5

Pearl Onions Bowls

Preparation time: 10 minutes
Cooking time: 1 hour
Servings: 8
Ingredients:
- 2 cups pearl onions, peeled
- 2 tablespoons olive oil
- 1 tablespoon balsamic vinegar
- 1 tablespoon goat cheese, crumbled

Directions:
1. In a sous vide bag, mix the pearl onions with the oil and the other ingredients, toss, seal the bag, submerge them in the preheated water oven and cook at 185 degrees F for 1 hour.
2. Divide into bowls and serve as a snack.

Nutrition:
calories 162
fat 5
fiber 6
carbs 9
protein 5

Thyme Shrimp Platter

Preparation time: 10 minutes
Cooking time: 20 minutes
Servings: 4
Ingredients:
- Salt and black pepper to the taste
- 2 tablespoons thyme, chopped
- 1 pound shrimp, peeled and deveined
- Juice of 1 lime
- 2 spring onions, chopped

Directions:
1. In a sous vide bag, mix the shrimp with the lime juice and the other ingredients, toss, seal, put the bag in the water oven and cook at 150 degrees F for 20 minutes.
2. Arrange the shrimp on a platter, and serve.

Nutrition:
calories 181
fat 3
fiber 5
carbs 7
protein 6

Cauliflower Spread

Preparation time: 10 minutes
Cooking time: 1 hour
Servings: 12
Ingredients:
- 1 yellow onion, cut into wedges
- ¾ cup heavy cream
- ½ teaspoon chili powder
- Salt and black pepper to the taste
- ¼ cup chicken stock
- 1 pound cauliflower florets
- ¼ cup mayonnaise

Directions:
1. In a sous vide bag, mix the cauliflower with the chicken stock, onion, salt and pepper, seal the bag, submerge in the water oven and cook at 183 degrees F for 1 hour.
2. Transfer this to a blender, add the rest of the ingredients, pulse well, divide into bowls and serve as a party spread.

Nutrition:
calories 100
fat 4
fiber 1
carbs 7
protein 1

Coconut Cheese Dip

Preparation time: 10 minutes
Cooking time: 30 minutes
Servings: 4
Ingredients:
- 2 cups mozzarella cheese, shredded
- ¼ cup coconut cream
- 2 tablespoons garlic, chopped
- 1 red chili, chopped
- 1 tablespoon chives, chopped
- 2 teaspoons cumin, ground

- A pinch of salt and white pepper

Directions:

1. In a sous vide bag, mix the cheese with the cream, garlic and the other ingredients, seal the bag, submerge in the preheated water oven and cook at 175 degrees F for 30 minutes.
2. Transfer the cheese dip to a bowl and serve.

Nutrition:

calories 150

fat 14

fiber 2

carbs 4

protein 2

Shrimp and Pineapple Bowls

Preparation time: 10 minutes

Cooking time: 30 minutes

Servings: 2

Ingredients:

- 1 cup pineapple, peeled and cubed
- 1 tablespoon lime juice
- 1 tablespoons mint, chopped
- 2 tablespoons olive oil
- 2 pounds shrimp, peeled and deveined
- 1 cup black olives, pitted and halved

Directions:

1. In a sous vide bag, mix the shrimp with the pineapple and the other ingredients, seal, submerge in the preheated water oven and cook at 140 degrees F for 30 minutes.
2. Divide into bowls and serve.

Nutrition:

calories 205

fat 12

fiber 2

carbs 6

protein 14

Peppers Salsa

Preparation time: 10 minutes

Cooking time: 1 hour

Servings: 6

Ingredients:

- 1 tablespoon olive oil
- Juice of 1 lime
- ½ teaspoon chili powder
- Salt and black pepper to the taste
- 1 teaspoon garlic powder
- 1 teaspoon sweet paprika
- ½ teaspoon oregano, dried
- ¼ teaspoon red pepper flakes
- 1 tablespoon chives, chopped
- 1 pound red bell peppers, roughly cubed
- 1 cup cherry tomatoes, halved
- 1 cup spring onions, chopped
- 1 cup kalamata olives, pitted and halved

Directions:

1. In a sous vide bag, combine the bell peppers with the tomatoes, spring onions and the other ingredients, toss, seal, submerge in the preheated water oven and cook at 185 degrees F for 1 hour.
2. Divide into small bowls and serve.

Nutrition:

calories 250

fat 22

fiber 3

carbs 6

protein 15

Radish Chips

Preparation time: 10 minutes

Cooking time: 30 minutes

Servings: 4

Ingredients:

- Salt and black pepper to the taste
- ½ teaspoon rosemary, dried
- Cooking spray
- Juice of 1 lime
- ½ pound radishes, thinly sliced
- ½ teaspoon chili powder

Directions:

1. Spray the radish chips with cooking spray, add the chili powder and the other ingredients, transfer the mix to a sous vide bag, seal, submerge in the preheated water oven and cook at 183 degrees F for 30 minutes.
2. Divide into bowls and serve as a snack.

Nutrition:

calories 150

fat 4

fiber 2

carbs 6

protein 4

Zucchini Salsa

Preparation time: 10 minutes

Cooking time: 30 minutes

Servings: 4

Ingredients:

- 4 spring onions, chopped
- ½ teaspoon rosemary, dried
- Salt and black pepper to the taste
- 2 tablespoons olive oil
- 2 tablespoons balsamic vinegar
- 1 pound zucchinis, cubed
- 1 cup cherry tomatoes, halved
- 1 cup avocado, peeled, pitted and cubed

Directions:

1. In a sous vide bag, combine the zucchinis with the cherry tomatoes and the other ingredients, seal, submerge in the preheated water oven and cook at 183 degrees F for 30 minutes.
2. Divide into bowls and serve.

Nutrition:

calories 100

fat 3

fiber 7

carbs 3

protein 7

Crab Dip

Preparation time: 10 minutes
Cooking time: 30 minutes
Servings: 8
Ingredients:

- ½ teaspoon turmeric powder
- 2 spring onions, chopped
- 2 tablespoons lemon juice
- Salt and black pepper to the taste
- 4 garlic cloves, minced
- 1 tablespoon chives, chopped
- Salt and black pepper to the taste
- 2 cups crab meat
- ½ cup mayonnaise
- ½ cup heavy cream
- 8 ounces cream cheese

Directions:
1. In a sous vide bag, mix the crab with the mayo, cream and the other ingredients, seal the bag, submerge in the preheated water oven and cook at 154 degrees F for 30 minutes.
2. Divide into bowls and serve as a snack.

Nutrition:
calories 180
fat 7
fiber 2
carbs 4
protein 6

Olives Balls

Preparation time: 10 minutes
Cooking time: 10 minutes
Servings: 12
Ingredients:

- 4 tablespoons butter, melted
- 2 cups black olives, pitted and chopped
- 1 cup kalamata olives, pitted and chopped
- 2 eggs
- 1 cup almond flour
- ¼ teaspoon sweet paprika
- 1/3 cup parmesan, grated
- Salt and black pepper to the taste
- 1 tablespoon garlic, minced
- 3 tablespoons whipping cream

Directions:
1. In a bowl, combine the olives with the eggs, butter and the other ingredients, stir well and shape medium balls out of this mix
2. Divide the balls in sous vide bags, seal them, submerge them in the water oven and cook at 180 degrees F for 10 minutes.
3. Serve as a party appetizer.

Nutrition:
calories 60
fat 5
fiber 1
carbs 0.7

protein 2

Spinach Dip

Preparation time: 10 minutes
Cooking time: 10 minutes
Servings: 6
Ingredients:

- 8 ounces cream cheese, soft
- 1 tablespoon parsley, chopped
- 1 tablespoon lemon juice
- Salt and black pepper to the taste
- 1 tablespoon chives, chopped
- ½ pound baby spinach
- ½ cup coconut cream

Directions:
1. In a sous vide bag, combine the spinach with the cream and the other ingredients, seal the bag, submerge it in the preheated water oven and cook at 180 degrees F for 10 minutes.
2. Transfer to a blender, pulse well, divide into small bowls and serve as a party dip.

Nutrition:
calories 245
fat 12
fiber 3
carbs 6
protein 8

Stuffed Mushrooms

Preparation time: 10 minutes
Cooking time: 1 hour
Servings: 4
Ingredients:

- 1 cup black olives, pitted and chopped
- 1 pound white mushroom caps
- Salt and black pepper to the taste
- 1 teaspoon curry powder
- 4 ounces cream cheese, soft
- Salt and black pepper to the taste
- 1 teaspoon garlic powder
- 1 red onion, chopped
- 2 spring onions, chopped

Directions:
1. In a bowl, combine the spring onions with the garlic powder and the other ingredients except the mushroom caps, stir well and stuff the mushrooms with this mix.
2. Divide them into sous vide bags, seal them, submerge them in your preheated water oven and cook at 180 degrees F for 1 hour.
3. Arrange on a platter and serve.

Nutrition:
calories 204
fat 12
fiber 3
carbs 7
protein 14

Spicy Meatballs

Preparation time: 10 minutes
Cooking time: 1 hour
Servings: 12
Ingredients:
- 4 spring onions, chopped
- Salt and black pepper to the taste
- ¼ cup almond flour
- ½ teaspoon garlic powder
- 2 tablespoon basil, chopped
- 2 eggs, whisked
- 1 pound beef stew meat, ground
- 1 tablespoon garlic, minced
- ½ teaspoon chili powder
- ½ teaspoon hot paprika

Directions:
1. In a bowl, combine the meat with the eggs and the other ingredients, stir well and shape medium meatballs out of this mix.
2. Divide them into sous vide bags and keep them in the freezer for 10 minutes.
3. Submerge sous vide bags in the preheated water oven and cook at 145 degrees F for 1 hour.
4. Arrange the meatballs on a platter and serve.

Nutrition:
calories 130
fat 6
fiber 3
carbs 5
protein 7

Parmesan Chicken Wings

Preparation time: 10 minutes
Cooking time: 4 hours
Servings: 6
Ingredients:
- 1 tablespoon sugar
- Salt and black pepper to the taste
- ½ teaspoon Italian seasoning
- ½ cup parmesan cheese, grated
- 2 pounds chicken wings, halved
- 2 tablespoons olive oil
- 1 tablespoon soy sauce

Directions:
1. In a sous vide bag, combine the chicken wings with the oil and the other ingredients except the parmesan, toss, seal the bag, submerge them in the preheated water oven and cook at 170 degrees F for 4 hours.
2. Arrange the chicken wings on a platter, sprinkle the parmesan on top and serve as an appetizer.

Nutrition:
calories 154
fat 8
fiber 1
carbs 6
protein 14

Cauliflower Bowls

Preparation time: 10 minutes
Cooking time: 50 minutes
Servings: 8
Ingredients:
- 2 eggs, whisked
- 2 cups cauliflower florets
- 1/3 cup parmesan, grated
- 1/3 cup breadcrumbs
- 2 tablespoons chives, chopped
- Cooking spray
- Salt and black pepper to the taste

Directions:
1. In a sous vide bag, combine the cauliflower with salt and pepper, grease with cooking spray, toss, seal the bag, submerge it in your preheated water oven and cook at 183 degrees F for 40 minutes.
2. In a bowl, mix the cauliflower with the rest of the ingredients, toss well, transfer the bites to another sous vide bag, seal, submerge them in the water oven and cook them at 180 degrees F for 10 minutes.
3. Divide into bowls and serve as a snack.

Nutrition:
calories 140
fat 4
fiber 2
carbs 7
protein 7

Artichoke Dip

Preparation time: 10 minutes
Cooking time: 1 hour
Servings: 8
Ingredients:
- ½ cup cream cheese
- 1 cup mozzarella cheese, shredded
- 1 teaspoon turmeric powder
- Salt and black pepper to the taste
- 1 tablespoon chives, chopped
- 1 cup heavy cream
- 4 spring onions, chopped
- 2 cups canned artichoke hearts, drained and chopped
- 1 tablespoon olive oil
- 2 garlic cloves, minced

Directions:
1. In a sous vide bag, combine the artichokes with the cream and the other ingredients, whisk, seal the bag, submerge them in the preheated water oven and cook at 183 degrees F for 1 hour.
2. Divide into bowls and serve as a dip.

Nutrition:
calories 144
fat 12
fiber 2
carbs 5
protein 5

Shrimp Bites

Preparation time: 10 minutes
Cooking time: 30 minutes
Servings: 6
Ingredients:

- 2 pounds shrimp, peeled and deveined
- Salt and black pepper to the taste
- A drizzle of olive oil
- 1 tablespoon chives, chopped
- 3 tablespoons lemon juice
- 4 garlic cloves, minced
- ½ teaspoon chili powder

Directions:
1. In a sous vide bag, combine the shrimp with the oil, chives and the other ingredients, toss, seal the bag, submerge in the preheated water oven and cook them at 160 degrees F for 30 minutes.
2. Divide into bowls and serve.

Nutrition:
calories 182
fat 12
fiber 1
carbs 6
protein 14

Lemon Oysters

Preparation time: 10 minutes
Cooking time: 30 minutes
Servings: 4
Ingredients:

- 1 tablespoon parsley, chopped
- A pinch of sweet paprika
- 2 tablespoons chives, chopped
- 8 oysters, shucked
- Juice of 1 lemon
- Zest of 1 lemon, grated
- ½ teaspoon chili powder

Directions:
1. Top each oyster with lemon juice, zest and the other ingredients, put them in separate sous vide bags, seal them, submerge them in the preheated water oven and cook them at 140 degrees F for 30 minutes.
2. Arrange on a platter and serve them as an appetizer.

Nutrition:
calories 100
fat 1
fiber 1
carbs 4
protein 1

Parsley Calamari Bites

Preparation time: 10 minutes
Cooking time: 40 minutes
Servings: 4
Ingredients:

- 2 garlic cloves, minced
- 2 cups calamari rings
- 1 tablespoon lime juice
- ½ teaspoon sweet paprika
- 1 tablespoon olive oil
- Salt and black pepper to the taste
- ¼ cup parsley, chopped

Directions:
1. In a sous vide bag, combine the calamari with the garlic and the other ingredients, seal the bag, submerge it in the preheated water oven and cook them at 130 degrees F for 40 minutes.
2. Divide into bowls and serve as an appetizer.

Nutrition:
calories 240
fat 12
fiber 1
carbs 5
protein 25

Salmon Salsa

Preparation time: 10 minutes
Cooking time: 40 minutes
Servings: 4
Ingredients:

- 1 teaspoon sweet paprika
- 2 red onions, chopped
- 1 cup cherry tomatoes, halved
- 2 tablespoons cilantro, chopped
- Juice of 2 limes
- Salt and black pepper to the taste
- 1 pound salmon fillets, skinless, boneless and cubed
- 1 tablespoon olive oil
- Salt and black pepper to the taste
- 1 teaspoon turmeric powder
- 2 red chilies, minced

Directions:
1. In a sous vide bag, combine the salmon with the oil, turmeric and the other ingredients, toss, seal the bag, submerge in the preheated water oven and cook them at 140 degrees F for 40 minutes.
2. Divide into bowls and serve as an appetizer.

Nutrition:
calories 250
fat 14
fiber 4
carbs 5
protein 15

Tuna Bites

Preparation time: 15 minutes
Cooking time: 30 minutes
Servings: 6
Ingredients:

- 1 pound tuna fillets, boneless and roughly cubed
- 1 tablespoon olive oil
- 1 tablespoon soy sauce
- 1 teaspoon chili powder
- ½ teaspoon dill, dried

- 1 tablespoon parsley, chopped
- Salt and black pepper to the taste

Directions:
1. In a sous vide bag, combine the tuna with the oil, soy sauce and the other ingredients, toss, seal, submerge in the preheated water oven and cook at 130 degrees F for 30 minutes.
2. Arrange the tuna bites on a platter and serve them as an appetizer.

Nutrition:
calories 170
fat 2
fiber 1
carbs 6
protein 6

Cucumber Salad and Shrimp

Preparation time: 10 minutes
Cooking time: 30 minutes
Servings: 4
Ingredients:
- 1 tablespoon olive oil
- Salt and black pepper to the taste
- 2 tablespoons lime juice
- 2 teaspoons chili garlic sauce
- 1 tablespoon chives, chopped
- 3 cucumbers, cut with a spiralizer
- ½ cup mint, chopped
- 2 pounds shrimp, peeled and deveined
- 1 cup black olives, pitted and halved

Directions:
1. In a sous vide bag, combine the shrimp with the cucumbers, mint and the other ingredients, toss, seal the bag, submerge it in your preheated water oven and cook at 140 degrees F for 30 minutes.
2. Divide into bowls and serve.

Nutrition:
calories 150
fat 2
fiber 3
carbs 6
protein 6

Lemon Mussels

Preparation time: 5 minutes
Cooking time: 20 minutes
Servings: 4
Ingredients:
- 2 pounds mussels, debearded and scrubbed
- ½ teaspoon rosemary, dried
- ½ teaspoon sweet paprika
- 1 tablespoon butter, melted
- 1 tablespoon lemon juice

Directions:
1. Put the mussels in a sous vide bag, add the rosemary and the other ingredients, seal the bag, submerge in the preheated water oven and cook at 194 degrees F for 20 minutes.
2. Arrange mussels on a platter, and serve.

Nutrition:
calories 100
fat 1
fiber 1
carbs 6
protein 2

Squid Salad

Preparation time: 10 minutes
Cooking time: 2 hours
Servings: 2
Ingredients:
- 1 tablespoon balsamic vinegar
- A pinch of cayenne pepper
- Salt and black pepper to the taste
- 1 tablespoons lemon juice
- 1 tablespoon chives, chopped
- 1 teaspoon sriracha sauce
- 1 pound squid, cut into medium rings
- 1 cup cherry tomatoes, halved
- 1 cup kalamata olives, pitted and halved
- 1 cup zucchinis, cubed
- 2 tablespoons olive oil

Directions:
1. In a sous vide bag, combine the squid rings with the tomatoes, olives and the other ingredients, toss, seal, submerge in the preheated water oven and cook at 136 degrees F for 2 hours.
2. Divide the salad into bowls and serve.

Nutrition:
calories 245
fat 32
fiber 3
carbs 12
protein 17

Radish Salad and Calamari

Preparation time: 10 minutes
Cooking time: 2 hours
Servings: 4
Ingredients:
- Juice of 1 lime
- A splash of Worcestershire sauce
- Salt and black pepper to the taste
- ½ teaspoon turmeric powder
- 1 tablespoon chives, chopped
- 2 cups calamari rings
- 1 cup radishes, sliced
- 1 cup kalamata olives, pitted and halved
- 1 tablespoon olive oil

Directions:
1. In a sous vide bag, combine the calamari with the radishes and the other ingredients, seal the bag, submerge in the preheated water oven and cook at 145 degrees F for 2 hours.
2. Divide into bowls and serve as an appetizer.

Nutrition:
calories 368
fat 23

fiber 3
carbs 10
protein 34

Mango Salad and Octopus

Preparation time: 10 minutes
Cooking time: 5 hours
Servings: 2
Ingredients:
- 1 tablespoon balsamic vinegar
- 4 tablespoons olive oil
- 1 tablespoon chives, chopped
- Juice of 1 lemon
- Salt and black pepper to the taste
- 2 tablespoons parsley, chopped
- 2 pounds octopus, rinsed
- 1 cup mango, peeled and cubed
- 1 cup cherry tomatoes, halved
- 1 cup black olives, pitted and halved
- 1 cup cucumber, cubed

Directions:
1. Put the octopus in a sous vide bag, drizzle half of the oil over it, season with salt and pepper, seal the bag, submerge it in the preheated water oven and cook at 170 degrees F for 5 hours.
2. Chop octopus, transfer to a bowl, add the rest of the ingredients, toss, divide into bowls and serve.

Nutrition:
calories 200
fat 10
fiber 3
carbs 6
protein 23

Clam Bowls

Preparation time: 10 minutes
Cooking time: 20 minutes
Servings: 4
Ingredients:
- 1 cup chicken stock
- 14 ounces baby clams
- 1 cup heavy cream
- 1 cup onion, chopped
- 1 tablespoon chives, chopped
- 1 cup shallots, chopped
- 1 cup corn
- 1 cup kalamata olives, pitted and halved
- Juice of 1 lime
- ½ teaspoon chili powder
- Salt and black pepper to the taste

Directions:
1. Put the clams in a sous vide bag, add salt, pepper and the stock, seal the bag, submerge it in the preheated water oven and cook at 190 degrees F for 20 minutes.
2. Open the clams, transfer the meat to a bowl, add the rest of the ingredients, toss, divide between plates and serve.

Nutrition:
calories 220
fat 12
fiber 7
carbs 8
protein 13

Italian Shrimp Salad

Preparation time: 10 minutes
Cooking time: 30 minutes
Servings: 4
Ingredients:
- 1 pound shrimp, peeled and deveined
- Salt and black pepper to the taste
- 2 tablespoons lime juice
- 2 teaspoons mint, chopped
- 1 tablespoon tarragon, chopped
- 1 tablespoon lemon juice
- 1 teaspoon lime zest, grated
- ½ cup heavy cream
- 2 tablespoons avocado oil
- 1 cup pineapple, peeled and cubed
- 1 cup avocado, peeled, pitted and cubed
- 1 cup radishes, cubed

Directions:
1. In a sous vide bag, combine the shrimp with the oil, pineapple and the other ingredients, seal the bag, submerge it in the preheated water oven and cook at 140 degrees F for 30 minutes.
2. Divide small bowls and serve as an appetizer.

Nutrition:
calories 180
fat 11
fiber 2
carbs 8
protein 13

Cod Salsa

Preparation time: 10 minutes
Cooking time: 40 minutes
Servings: 4
Ingredients:
- ½ cup spring onions, chopped
- 2 pounds cod fillets, boneless and cubed
- 1 cup radishes, cubed
- 1 cup mango, peeled and cubed
- 1 cup green olives, pitted and halved
- Juice of 1 lime
- 1 tablespoon avocado oil
- 1 teaspoon red pepper flakes, crushed
- 1 tablespoon parsley, chopped
- 5 garlic cloves, minced

Directions:
1. In a sous vide bag, combine the cod with the spring onions and the other ingredients, seal the bag, submerge in the preheated water oven and cook them at 180 degrees F for 40 minutes.

2.	Divide the mix into bowls and serve as an appetizer.
Nutrition:
calories 204
fat 15
fiber 2
carbs 3
protein 4

Shrimp Salsa and Apple

Preparation time: 10 minutes
Cooking time: 30 minutes
Servings: 4
Ingredients:
- Juice of ½ lemon
- 2 garlic cloves, minced
- Salt and black pepper to the taste
- Juice of ½ lemon
- 1 tablespoon chives, chopped
- 2 thyme springs, chopped
- 2 pounds shrimp, peeled and deveined
- 1 cup green apple, cored and cubed
- 1 cup cherry tomatoes, halved
- 2 tablespoons balsamic vinegar
- 1 tablespoon olive oil

Directions:
1.	In a sous vide bag, combine the shrimp with the apple, tomatoes and the other ingredients, seal, submerge in the preheated water oven and cook them at 180 degrees F for 30 minutes.
2.	Divide the mix appetizer bowls and serve.
Nutrition:
calories 140
fat 2
fiber 1
carbs 8
protein 10

Shrimp and Pico De Gallo

Preparation time: 10 minutes
Cooking time: 30 minutes
Servings: 4
Ingredients:
- ¼ cup red onion, chopped
- Salt and black pepper to the taste
- Zest of 1 lime, grated
- 1 tablespoon chives, chopped
- Juice of 1 lime
- 1 pound shrimp, peeled and deveined
- 1 tablespoon olive oil
- ½ teaspoon sweet paprika
- A handful cilantro, chopped
- 2 tomatoes, cubed
- 1 jalapeno pepper, chopped

Directions:
1.	In a sous vide bag, combine the shrimp with the oil, paprika and the other ingredients, toss, seal the bag, submerge in the preheated water oven and cook them at 185 degrees F for 30 minutes.

2.	Divide into bowls and serve.
Nutrition:
calories 100
fat 2
fiber 6
carbs 8
protein 1

Radish Salad and Scallops

Preparation time: 10 minutes
Cooking time: 1 hour
Servings: 2
Ingredients:
- 1 tablespoon chives, chopped
- 1 tablespoon parsley, chopped
- Juice of 1 lime
- Zest of 1 lime, grated
- 2 tablespoons olive oil
- Salt and black pepper to the taste
- 6 scallops
- 1 cup radishes, halved
- 1 cup cherry tomatoes, halved
- 1 cup kalamata olives, pitted and halved

Directions:
1.	Season scallops with salt and pepper, put them in a sous vide bag, seal, submerge in the preheated water oven and cook them at 140 degrees F for 1 hour.
2.	In a bowl, combine the scallops with the radishes, tomatoes and the other ingredients, toss and serve as an appetizer.
Nutrition:
calories 240
fat 14
fiber 4
carbs 12
protein 15

Tuna Salad

Preparation time: 10 minutes
Cooking time: 40 minutes
Servings: 4
Ingredients:
- 1 cup broccoli florets
- 2 tablespoons green onions, chopped
- A pinch of salt and black pepper
- Some cloves sprouts
- 2 tablespoons soy sauce
- 1 tablespoon apple cider vinegar
- A pinch of salt and black pepper
- 1 tablespoon cilantro, chopped
- 1 pound tuna fillets, boneless and cubed
- 2 beets, peeled and cubed
- 1 cup kalamata olives, pitted and halved
- 1 tablespoon olive oil

Directions:
1.	In a sous vide bag, combine the tuna with the beets, olives and the other ingredients, toss gently, seal it, submerge it in the preheated water

oven, cook at 130 degrees F for 40 minutes, transfer small bowls and serve as an appetizer.
Nutrition:
calories 281
fat 12
fiber 6
carbs 6
protein 15

Tuna Bites and Mint Sauce

Preparation time: 10 minutes
Cooking time: 40 minutes
Servings: 4
Ingredients:
- Salt and black pepper to the taste
- 2 tablespoons olive oil
- Juice of ½ lemon
- 1 cup mint leaves
- 2 tablespoons chives, chopped
- 1 tablespoon pine nuts, toasted and chopped
- 1 tablespoon water
- Salt and black pepper to the taste
- 2 pounds tuna fillets, boneless and cubed
- 1 tablespoon turmeric powder
- 1 tablespoon ginger, grated
- ½ teaspoon sweet paprika

Directions:
1. In a blender, combine the mint with the oil, lemon juice, pine nuts, water, salt and pepper and pulse well.
2. In a sous vide bag, combine the tuna with the turmeric, the other ingredients and the mint sauce, toss, seal the bag, submerge in the water oven and cook at 175 degrees F for 40 minutes.
3. Arrange the tuna and sauce on a platter and serve as an appetizer.
Nutrition:
calories 140
fat 5
fiber 1
carbs 7
protein 9

Bbq Chicken Meatballs

Preparation time: 10 minutes
Cooking time: 2 hours
Servings: 4
Ingredients:
- Salt and black pepper to the taste
- 2 tablespoons lime juice
- Cooking spray
- ½ cup almond flour
- ¼ cup cheddar cheese, grated
- 1 tablespoon cilantro, chopped
- 1 pound chicken meat, ground
- 1 cup bbq sauce
- 2 eggs, whisked
- 4 scallions, chopped

Directions:
1. In a bowl, mix the chicken with the eggs, scallions and the other ingredients except the cooking spray and the bbq sauce, stir and shape medium meatballs out of this mix.
2. Divide the meatballs into sous vide bags, grease them with cooking spray, cover with the bbq sauce, seal the bags, submerge in the preheated water oven and cook them at 150 degrees F for 2 hours.
3. Arrange the meatballs on a platter and serve them as an appetizer.
Nutrition:
calories 156
fat 11
fiber 1
carbs 2
protein 12

Creamy Corn Dip

Preparation time: 10 minutes
Cooking time: 30 minutes
Servings: 4
Ingredients:
- 2 cups corn
- 1 cup heavy cream
- 1 cup cream cheese
- 4 spring onions, chopped
- ½ teaspoon turmeric powder
- Juice of 1 lime
- 1 handful cilantro, chopped
- 2 garlic cloves, minced
- 1 jalapeno pepper, chopped
- Salt and black pepper to the taste

Directions:
1. In a vide bag, combine the corn with the cream, cream cheese and the other ingredients, toss, seal, submerge in the preheated water oven and cook at 160 degrees F for 30 minutes.
2. Divide the mix into bowls and serve as a party dip.
Nutrition:
calories 172
fat 5
fiber 1
carbs 5
protein 12

Chicken Salad

Preparation time: 10 minutes
Cooking time: 1 hour
Servings: 4
Ingredients:
- 1 cup kalamata olives, pitted and cubed
- 1 cup mango, peeled and cubed
- 2 tablespoons lime juice
- Salt and black pepper to the taste
- 1 teaspoon sweet paprika
- 1 green bell pepper, cubed

- 1 red onion, chopped
- 1 tablespoon cilantro, chopped
- 1 tablespoon chives, chopped
- 2 pounds chicken breasts, skinless, boneless and cut into strips
- 1 cup baby kale
- 1 teaspoon chili powder
- 2 tablespoons olive oil
- 1 tablespoon balsamic vinegar

Directions:

1. In a sous vide bag, mix the chicken with the kale, chili powder and the other ingredients, toss, seal the bag, submerge in the preheated water oven and cook them at 170 degrees F for 1 hour.
2. Divide the mix into bowls and serve.

Nutrition:

calories 240
fat 10
fiber 2
carbs 5
protein 20

Duck and Spinach Salad

Preparation time: 10 minutes
Cooking time: 1 hour and 30 minutes
Servings: 4
Ingredients:

- 2 tablespoons olive oil
- ¾ cup raspberries
- 1 tablespoon lime juice
- Salt and black pepper to the taste
- 2 cups baby spinach
- Salt and black pepper to the taste
- ½ cup walnuts, chopped
- 1 tablespoon chives, chopped
- 2 pounds duck breast, boneless and skin scored
- 1 red onion, chopped
- 2 tablespoons red vinegar

Directions:

1. Season the duck with salt and pepper, drizzle half of the oil, divide into 2 sous vide bags, seal the bags, submerge them in the preheated water oven and cook at 140 degrees F for 1 hour and 30 minutes.
2. In a bowl, combine the spinach with the other ingredients and toss.
3. Slice duck breasts, add them to the salad, toss and serve as an appetizer.

Nutrition:

calories 355
fat 40
fiber 4
carbs 6
protein 18

Stuffed Peppers

Preparation time: 10 minutes
Cooking time: 1 hour
Servings: 4
Ingredients:

- Salt and black pepper to the taste
- 1 small yellow onion, chopped
- 2 tablespoons spring onions, chopped
- 1 pound beef stew meat, ground
- 2 tomatoes, chopped
- 1 tablespoon olive oil
- 8 bell peppers, tops cut off and seeds removed
- 2/3 cup tomato sauce

Directions:

1. In a bowl mix the beef with the onion, spring onions, tomatoes, salt and pepper, stir and stuff the peppers with this mix.
2. Divide the stuffed peppers into individual sous vide bags, also divide the tomato sauce, seal them, submerge in the water oven and cook at 185 degrees F for 1 hour.
3. Arrange the peppers on a platter and serve.

Nutrition:

calories 200
fat 6,
fiber 3
carbs 6
protein 14

Chicken Dip

Preparation time: 10 minutes
Cooking time: 1 hour and 10 minutes
Servings: 4
Ingredients:

- 1 tablespoon chives, chopped
- 1 pound chicken breast, skinless, boneless and ground
- 1 tablespoon olive oil
- 1 yellow onion, chopped
- 1 cup baby spinach
- 1 cup heavy cream
- Juice of 1 lime
- 1 teaspoon turmeric powder
- 1 cup cream cheese
- Salt and black pepper to the taste

Directions:

1. Heat up a pan with the oil over medium heat, add the onion and the meat and brown for 10 minutes.
2. In a bowl, mix browned meat with the other ingredients, stir well and divide into 4 ramekins.
3. Put the ramekins in the water oven, fill it with water halfway and cook the dip at 160 degrees F for 1 hour.
4. Serve as a party dip.

Nutrition:

calories 260
fat 45
fiber 4
carbs 5
protein 16

Chinese Beef Bites

Preparation time: 10 minutes
Cooking time: 3 hours
Servings: 4
Ingredients:

- 3 tablespoons balsamic vinegar
- 1 teaspoon five spice
- ½ teaspoon allspice, ground
- 3 tablespoons balsamic vinegar
- ¼ cup scallions, chopped
- 2 pounds beef stew meat, cubed
- 2 tablespoons olive oil
- Salt and black pepper to the taste

Directions:
1. In a bowl, mix beef bites with the oil, vinegar and the other ingredients, toss, transfer to a sous vide bag, submerge in the preheated water oven and cook at 160 degrees F for 3 hours.
2. Arrange on a platter and serve.

Nutrition:
calories 415
fat 23
fiber 3
carbs 8
protein 27

Mushroom Dip

Preparation time: 10 minutes
Cooking time: 1 hour
Servings: 6
Ingredients:

- 1 teaspoon Italian seasoning
- 4 tablespoons hot sauce
- ½ cup mozzarella, shredded
- 1 cup heavy cream
- 4 spring onions, chopped
- Salt and black pepper to the taste
- 1 pound mushrooms, sliced
- 1 tablespoon olive oil
- 4 ounces cream cheese
- ½ teaspoon rosemary, dried

Directions:
1. Heat up a pan with the oil over medium heat, add the mushrooms, cook for 10 minutes and transfer to a bowl.
2. Add the rest of the ingredients, toss well and divide into 6 ramekins.
3. Arrange the ramekins in the water oven, cover them with tin foil, fill the water oven with water halfway and cook at 170 degrees F for 1 hour.
4. Serve the mix as a party dip.

Nutrition:
calories 200
fat 4
fiber 1
carbs 7
protein 7

Shrimp Meatballs

Preparation time: 10 minutes
Cooking time: 1 hour
Servings: 6
Ingredients:

- ½ cup coconut flour
- 2 pounds shrimp, peeled, deveined and chopped
- 2 eggs, whisked
- 4 scallions, chopped
- Salt and black pepper to the taste
- 3 teaspoons soy sauce
- 1 tablespoon chives, chopped
- Cooking spray
- ½ teaspoon mustard powder
- ¼ teaspoon sweet paprika

Directions:
1. In a bowl, mix the shrimp with the scallions, flour and the other ingredients except the cooking spray, stir well and shape medium meatballs out of this mix.
2. Divide the shrimp meatballs into sous vide bags, grease them with the cooking spray, seal the bags, submerge in the water oven and cook at 140 degrees F for 1 hour.
3. Arrange them on a platter and serve as an appetizer

Nutrition:
calories 332
fat 18
fiber 1
carbs 7
protein 15

Sausage Bites

Preparation time: 10 minutes
Cooking time: 1 hour and 30 minutes
Servings: 4
Ingredients:

- Salt and black pepper to taste
- 1 teaspoon sweet paprika
- 3 tablespoons tomato sauce
- ¼ teaspoon red pepper flakes
- ¼ teaspoon onion powder
- ½ teaspoon garlic powder
- 1 pound beef sausages, sliced
- 1 tablespoon olive oil
- 1 tablespoon balsamic vinegar

Directions:
1. In large sous vide bag, mix the sausage bites with the oil, vinegar and the other ingredients, toss, seal, submerge in the preheated water oven and cook them at 140 degrees F for 1 hour and 30 minutes
2. Divide the sausage bites into bowls and serve as a snack.

Nutrition:
calories 316
fat 35
fiber 3
carbs 4

protein 16

Radish Dip

Preparation time: 10 minutes
Cooking time: 1 hour
Servings: 6
Ingredients:

- 1 pound radishes, chopped
- 1 cup scallions, chopped
- 1 cup heavy cream
- 1 cup cream cheese
- 1 tablespoon chives, chopped
- Juice of 1 lime
- Salt and black pepper to the taste
- ½ teaspoon garlic powder
- 1 tablespoon parsley, chopped

Directions:
1.   In a bowl, mix the radishes with the scallions, cream and the other ingredients, stir well and divide into 6 ramekins.
2.   Cover the ramekins with tin foil, put them in the water oven, add water halfway into the oven, and cook at 140 degrees F for 1 hour.
3.   Serve as a party dip.
Nutrition:
calories 325
fat 23
fiber 4
carbs 6
protein 22

Sriracha Turkey Bites

Preparation time: 10 minutes
Cooking time: 2 hours
Servings: 4
Ingredients:

- 2 pounds turkey breast, skinless, boneless and cubed
- 1 tablespoon olive oil
- 1 tablespoon soy sauce
- 2 tablespoons tomato sauce
- 2 teaspoons sriracha sauce
- ¼ cup chives, chopped
- ½ teaspoon chili powder
- Salt and black pepper to the taste

Directions:
1.   In a sous vide bag, combine the turkey with the oil, sriracha sauce and the other ingredients, toss, seal the bag, submerge in the preheated water oven, cook at 146 degrees F for 2 hours, arrange on a platter and serve as an appetizer.
Nutrition:
calories 320
fat 23
fiber 0
carbs 12
protein 37

Beet Salsa

Preparation time: 10 minutes
Cooking time: 1 hour
Servings: 4
Ingredients:

- Juice of 1 lime
- 2 tablespoons olive oil
- Salt and black pepper to the taste
- ½ teaspoon herbs de Provence
- 2 red onions, chopped
- 1 tablespoon chives, chopped
- 1 pound red beets, peeled and cubed
- 1 cup green olives, pitted and halved
- 1 cup cherry tomatoes, halved

Directions:
1.   In a large sous vide bag, combine the beets with the olives and the other ingredients, toss, seal the bag, introduce in the preheated water oven and cook at 185 degrees F for 1 hour.
2.   Serve as a snack.
Nutrition:
calories 320
fat 8
fiber 4
carbs 12
protein 10

Shrimp Salad and Fennel

Preparation time: 10 minutes
Cooking time: 50 minutes
Servings: 4
Ingredients:

- 1 tablespoon lime juice
- 2 tablespoons olive oil
- ¼ cup walnuts, toasted and chopped
- 2 tablespoons cilantro, chopped
- 1 tablespoon chives, chopped
- Salt and black pepper to the taste
- A pinch of cayenne pepper
- 1 pound shrimp, peeled and deveined
- 2 fennel bulbs, sliced
- 1 cup mango, peeled and cubed
- 1 cup kalamata olives, pitted and cubed

Directions:
1. In a large sous vide bag, combine the shrimp with the mango, fennel and the other ingredients, toss, seal, submerge in the preheated water oven, cook them at 146 degrees F for 50 minutes, divide between appetizer plates and serve.
Nutrition:
calories 200
fat 10
fiber 1
carbs 6
protein 7

Pesto Radish and Corn Dip

Preparation time: 10 minutes
Cooking time: 1 hour
Servings: 4

Ingredients:
- 1 pound radishes, cubed
- 2 cups corn
- 3 tablespoons basil pesto
- 1 cup heavy cream
- 1 cup cream cheese
- 1 tablespoon chives, chopped
- Salt and black pepper to the taste

Directions:
1. In a bowl, mix the radishes with the corn, pesto and the other ingredients, whisk and divide into 4 ramekins.
2. Cover the ramekins with tin foil, put them in the water oven, fill it halfway with water and cook the dip at 180 degrees F for 1 hour.
3. Serve the mix as a party dip warm.

Nutrition:
calories 357
fat 23
fiber 5
carbs 8
protein 26

Balsamic Salmon Bites

Preparation time: 10 minutes
Cooking time: 20 minutes
Servings: 6
Ingredients:
- 1 pound salmon fillets, boneless and cubed
- 2 tablespoons olive oil
- ½ tablespoon honey
- 2 tablespoons balsamic vinegar
- 1 tablespoon parsley, chopped

Directions:
1. In a sous vide bag, mix the salmon with the oil and the other ingredients, toss, seal the bag and cook in the water oven at 170 degrees F for 20 minutes.
2. Arrange the bites on a platter and serve as an appetizer.

Nutrition:
calories 222
fat 11.2
fiber 4.5
carbs 3.4
protein 12.6

Spicy Lentils Bowls

Preparation time: 10 minutes
Cooking time: 20 minutes
Servings: 4
Ingredients:
- 2 cups canned lentils, drained and rinsed
- 1 tablespoon olive oil
- 1 teaspoon hot paprika
- Juice of 1 lime
- 1 red chili pepper, chopped
- ½ tablespoon red pepper, crushed
- A pinch of salt and black pepper

- 1 tablespoon chives, chopped

Directions:
1. In a sous vide bag, mix the lentils with the paprika and the other ingredients, toss, seal the bag, submerge in the water oven and cook at 160 degrees F for 20 minutes.
2. Divide the mix into bowls and serve as a snack.

Nutrition:
calories 200
fat 11.2
fiber 2.4
carbs 5.3
protein 2.3

Eggplant Dip

Preparation time: 10 minutes
Cooking time: 25 minutes
Servings: 4
Ingredients:
- A pinch of salt and black pepper
- 2 scallions, chopped
- 1 tablespoon parsley, chopped
- 1 red onion, chopped
- 1 cup heavy cream
- 1 cup eggplant, chopped
- ½ teaspoon rosemary, dried

Directions:
1. In a sous vide bag, mix the eggplants with the cream and the other ingredients, seal the bag and cook in the water oven at 170 degrees F for 25 minutes.
2. Transfer to a blender, pulse well divide into bowls, and serve the dip right away.

Nutrition:
calories 232
fat 9.8
fiber 2.3
carbs 5.7
protein 4.3

Chickpeas Spread

Preparation time: 10 minutes
Cooking time: 25 minutes
Servings: 6
Ingredients:
- 1 cup canned chickpeas, drained and rinsed
- 2 tablespoons chives, chopped
- A pinch of salt and black pepper
- 2 tablespoons olive oil
- 2 tablespoons tahini paste
- 2 tablespoons lime juice
- 2 scallions, chopped

Directions:
1. In a sous vide bag, mix the chickpeas with the oil, lime juice and the other ingredients, seal the bag and cook in the water oven at 170 degrees F for 25 minutes.

2.	Transfer the mix to a blender, pulse well, divide into bowls and serve.
Nutrition:
calories 300
fat 12
fiber 4
carbs 12
protein 5

Garlic Chicken Bites

Preparation time: 10 minutes
Cooking time: 40 minutes
Servings: 6
Ingredients:
- 2 pounds chicken breast, skinless, boneless and cubed
- 4 garlic cloves, minced
- 2 tablespoons olive oil
- 1 tablespoon balsamic vinegar
- ½ cup honey
- A pinch of salt and black pepper
- ½ teaspoon hot paprika

Directions:
1.	In a sous vide bag, mix the chicken with the garlic and the other ingredients, toss, seal, and cook in the water oven at 180 degrees F for 40 minutes.
2.	Arrange on a platter and serve as an appetizer.
Nutrition:
calories 234
fat 11
fiber 3
carbs 20
protein 12

Coconut Dip

Preparation time: 5 minutes
Cooking time: 20 minutes
Servings: 4
Ingredients:
- 1 cup coconut cream
- ½ cup coconut flakes
- ½ teaspoon turmeric powder
- 1 tablespoon olive oil
- 1 cup almonds, chopped
- A pinch of salt and black pepper

Directions:
1.	In a blender, mix the cream with the almonds and the other ingredients, pulse well and divide into 4 ramekins.
2.	Put the ramekins in the water bath, fill it with water halfway, and cook at 180 degrees F for 20 minutes.
3.	Serve right away as a party dip.
Nutrition:
calories 132
fat 1
fiber 2
carbs 6

protein 5

Pesto Dip

Preparation time: 5 minutes
Cooking time: 20 minutes
Servings: 4
Ingredients:
- 2 tablespoons basil pesto
- 1 cup Greek yogurt
- 4 scallions, chopped
- 1 tablespoon lime zest, grated
- 1 tablespoon lime juice
- 1 tablespoon olive oil
- ½ teaspoon garam masala
- A pinch of salt and black pepper

Directions:
1.	In a blender, mix the yogurt with the pesto and the other ingredients, pulse well and transfer to 4 ramekins.
2.	Put the ramekins in the water oven and cook at 180 degrees F for 20 minutes.
3.	Serve as a dip.
Nutrition:
calories 140
fat 4
fiber 3
carbs 6
protein 6

Olives Bowls and Shrimp

Preparation time: 5 minutes
Cooking time: 20 minutes
Servings: 4
Ingredients:
- 2 pounds shrimp, peeled and deveined
- 1 tablespoon avocado oil
- 1 cup kalamata olives, pitted and halved
- 1 tablespoon chives, chopped
- Juice of 1 lime
- 1 tablespoon balsamic vinegar
- 1 tablespoon capers, drained
- 2 spring onions, chopped

Directions:
1.	In a sous vide bag, mix the shrimp with the oil, olives and the other ingredients, seal the bag and cook in the water oven at 180 degrees F for 20 minutes.
2.	Divide the mix into bowls and serve as an appetizer.
Nutrition:
calories 170
fat 9
fiber 4
carbs 7
protein 6

Mussels Bowls

Preparation time: 5 minutes
Cooking time: 20 minutes

Servings: 4
Ingredients:
- ½ cup white wine
- ½ teaspoon Italian seasoning
- 1 tablespoon olive oil
- 1 tablespoon chives, chopped
- 1 pound mussels, scrubbed
- 2 scallions, chopped
- 1 cup kalamata olives, pitted and halved
- ½ cup cherry tomatoes, halved
- Juice of 1 lime

Directions:
1. In a sous vide bag, mix the mussels with the scallions and the other ingredients, seal the bag, submerge in the water oven and cook at 170 degrees F for 20 minutes.
2. Divide into bowls and serve as an appetizer.

Nutrition:
calories 180
fat 3
fiber 3
carbs 7
protein 9

Walnuts Bowls

Preparation time: 5 minutes
Cooking time: 20 minutes
Servings: 4
Ingredients:
- 2 cups walnuts
- ½ teaspoon hot paprika
- 1 tablespoon olive oil
- 1 teaspoon red pepper flakes, crushed
- 1 tablespoon lime juice
- 1 tablespoon capers, drained
- 1 tablespoon chives, chopped

Directions:
1. In a sous vide bag, mix the walnuts with the paprika and the other ingredients, toss, seal, submerge in the water oven and cook at 180 degrees F for 20 minutes.
2. Divide the mix into bowls and serve as a snack.

Nutrition:
calories 150
fat 9
fiber 2
carbs 6
protein 6

SOUS VIDE FISH AND SEAFOOD RECIPES

Lemon Salmon

Preparation time: 10 minutes
Cooking time: 30 minutes
Servings: 4
Ingredients:

- 1 pound salmon fillets, boneless and cubed
- ½ teaspoon turmeric powder
- 1 tablespoon lemon juice
- 1 tablespoon rosemary, chopped
- A pinch of salt and black pepper
- 1 tablespoon chives, chopped

Directions:

1. In a sous vide bag, mix the salmon with the turmeric and the other ingredients, seal the bag, and cook at 180 degrees F for 30 minutes.
2. Divide between plates and serve.

Nutrition:
calories 198
fat 7
fiber 2
carbs 6
protein 7

Chili Tuna

Preparation time: 10 minutes
Cooking time: 30 minutes
Servings: 4
Ingredients:

- 2 tablespoons avocado oil
- 1 pound tuna fillets, boneless and cubed
- 2 red chilies, chopped
- ½ teaspoon chili powder
- 1 tablespoon chives, chopped
- A pinch of salt and black pepper

Directions:

1. In a sous vide bag, mix the tuna with the oil and the other ingredients, seal, and cook in the water oven at 200 degrees F for 30 minutes.
2. Divide the mix into bowls and serve.

Nutrition:
calories 221
fat 8
fiber 3
carbs 6
protein 7

Shrimp and Tomatoes Mix

Preparation time: 5 minutes
Cooking time: 20 minutes
Servings: 4
Ingredients:

- 1 pound shrimp, peeled and deveined
- 1 tablespoon olive oil
- 1 cup cherry tomatoes, halved
- 1 tablespoon lemon juice
- 3 garlic cloves, crushed
- A pinch of salt and black pepper

Directions:

1. In a sous vide bag, mix the shrimp with the tomatoes and the other ingredients, seal and cook in the water oven at 180 degrees F for 20 minutes.
2. Divide the mix into bowls and serve.

Nutrition:
calories 235
fat 8
fiber 4
carbs 7
protein 9

Paprika Cod

Preparation time: 10 minutes
Cooking time: 25 minutes
Servings: 4
Ingredients:

- ½ cup white wine
- 1 teaspoon sweet paprika
- A pinch of salt and black pepper
- 1 tablespoon avocado oil
- 2 pounds cod fillets, boneless

Directions:

1. In a sous vide bag, mix the cod with the wine and the other ingredients, seal and cook in the water oven at 170 degrees F for 25 minutes.
2. Divide everything into bowls and serve.

Nutrition:
calories 211
fat 8
fiber 4
carbs 8
protein 8

Shrimp and Spinach

Preparation time: 10 minutes
Cooking time: 20 minutes
Servings: 4
Ingredients:

- 1 cup baby spinach
- ½ teaspoon chili powder
- ½ teaspoon red pepper flakes, crushed
- 2 tablespoons avocado oil
- A pinch of salt and black pepper
- 1 tablespoon chives, chopped
- 1 pound shrimp, peeled and deveined
- Juice of 1 lemon

Directions:

1. In a sous vide bag, mix the shrimp with the lemon juice and the other ingredients, seal and cook n the water oven at 170 degrees F for 20 minutes.
2. Transfer the mix to bowls and serve.

Nutrition:
calories 193
fat 7
fiber 3

carbs 6
protein 6

Cod and Green Beans

Preparation time: 5 minutes
Cooking time: 25 minutes
Servings: 4
Ingredients:
- ½ teaspoon ginger, ground
- Juice of 1 lime
- 1 tablespoon chives, chopped
- A pinch of salt and black pepper
- 1 pound cod fillets, boneless and roughly cubed
- 1 cup green beans, trimmed and halved
- 1 tablespoon olive oil

Directions:
1. In a sous vide bag, mix the cod with the green beans and the other ingredients, seal the bag, submerge in the water oven and cook at 180 degrees F for 25 minutes.
2. Divide the mix into bowls and serve.

Nutrition:
calories 200
fat 11
fiber 4
carbs 5
protein 12

Turmeric Tuna

Preparation time: 10 minutes
Cooking time: 25 minutes
Servings: 4
Ingredients:
- ½ teaspoon sweet paprika
- 2 spring onions, chopped
- Juice of ½ lemon
- 1 tablespoon chives, chopped
- 1 pound tuna fillets, boneless and roughly cubed
- 1 teaspoon turmeric powder
- 1 tablespoon avocado oil

Directions:
1. In a sous vide bag, mix the tuna with the turmeric, oil and the other ingredients, seal the bag and cook in the water oven at 180 degrees F for 25 minutes.
2. Divide the mix between plates and serve.

Nutrition:
calories 200
fat 12
fiber 3
carbs 7
protein 9

Salmon and Avocado Mix

Preparation time: 5 minutes
Cooking time: 25 minutes
Servings: 4

Ingredients:
- 1 pound salmon fillets, boneless and roughly cubed
- 1 cup avocado, peeled, pitted and cubed
- 2 scallions, chopped
- Juice of 1 lime
- 1 tablespoon olive oil
- A pinch of salt and black pepper
- 1 teaspoon ginger powder
- ½ teaspoon basil, dried
- 1 tablespoon cilantro, chopped

Directions:
1. In a sous vide bag, mix the salmon with the avocado, scallions and the other ingredients, seal and cook in the water oven at 176 degrees F for 25 minutes.
2. Divide the mix into bowls and serve.

Nutrition:
calories 232
fat 10
fiber 4
carbs 6
protein 9

Shrimp and Corn

Preparation time: 10 minutes
Cooking time: 20 minutes
Servings: 4
Ingredients:
- 1 pound shrimp, peeled and deveined
- 1 cup corn
- 3 scallions, minced
- ½ teaspoon garam masala
- 1 tablespoon olive oil
- 1 tablespoon lemon juice
- 1 tablespoon chives, chopped
- Salt and black pepper to the taste

Directions:
1. In a sous vide bag, mix the shrimp with the corn and the other ingredients, seal and cook in the water oven at 165 degrees F for 20 minutes.
2. Divide the mix into between plates and serve.

Nutrition:
calories 182
fat 7
fiber 3
carbs 6
protein 9

Lemon Cod and Peas

Preparation time: 5 minutes
Cooking time: 30 minutes
Servings: 4
Ingredients:
- 2 spring onions, chopped
- ½ teaspoon red pepper flakes, crushed
- ½ tablespoon lemon juice
- 1 tablespoon lemon zest, grated

- 1 tablespoon chives, chopped
- A pinch of salt and black pepper
- 1 pound cod fillets, boneless
- 1 cup peas
- 1 tablespoon avocado oil

Directions:

1. In a sous vide bag, mix the cod with the peas and the other ingredients, seal the bag and cook in the water oven at 180 degrees F for 30 minutes.
2. Divide between plates and serve.

Nutrition:

calories 210
fat 8
fiber 3
carbs 6
protein 14

Ginger Cod

Preparation time: 5 minutes
Cooking time: 30 minutes
Servings: 4
Ingredients:

- 1 red onion, chopped
- ½ teaspoon turmeric powder
- 2 tablespoons avocado oil
- Salt and black pepper to the taste
- 1 tablespoon chives, chopped
- 1 pound cod fillets, boneless
- Juice of 1 lime
- 1 tablespoon ginger, grated

Directions:

1. In a sous vide bag, mix the cod with the lime juice and the other ingredients, seal the bag and cook in the water oven at 180 degrees F for 30 minutes.
2. Divide between plates and serve.

Nutrition:

calories 200
fat 12
fiber 3
carbs 6
protein 11

Salmon and Olives

Preparation time: 5 minutes
Cooking time: 30 minutes
Servings: 4
Ingredients:

- 2 garlic cloves, minced
- 1 tablespoon olive oil
- Salt and black pepper to the taste
- 1 pound salmon fillets, boneless
- 1 cup kalamata olives, pitted and halved
- ½ teaspoon rosemary, dried
- ¼ cup tomato passata

Directions:

1. In a sous vide bag, mix the salmon with the olives, rosemary and the other ingredients, seal the bag and cook in the water oven at 170 degrees F for 30 minutes.

2. Divide everything between plates and serve.

Nutrition:

calories 132
fat 9
fiber 2
carbs 5
protein 11

Curry Shrimp

Preparation time: 10 minutes
Cooking time: 25 minutes
Servings: 4
Ingredients:

- ½ cup coconut cream
- 1 tablespoon yellow curry paste
- A pinch of salt and black pepper
- 2 tablespoons cilantro, chopped
- 1 pound shrimp, peeled and deveined
- 2 scallions, chopped
- 2 tablespoons avocado oil

Directions:

1. In a sous vide bag, mix the shrimp with the scallions and the other ingredients, seal and cook in the water oven at 165 degrees F for 25 minutes.
2. Divide the mix into bowls and serve.

Nutrition:

calories 200
fat 12
fiber 2
carbs 6
protein 11

Chives Shrimp Mix

Preparation time: 5 minutes
Cooking time: 20 minutes
Servings: 4
Ingredients:

- 2 pounds shrimp, peeled and deveined
- 2 tablespoons chives, chopped
- 1 cup white wine
- 2 tablespoons olive oil
- Juice of 1 lime
- 1 teaspoon sweet paprika
- Salt and black pepper to the taste

Directions:

1. In a sous vide bag, mix the shrimp with the wine and the other ingredients, seal the bag and cook in the water oven at 170 degrees F for 20 minutes.
2. Divide the mix into bowls and serve.

Nutrition:

calories 200
fat 12
fiber 2
carbs 6
protein 9

Pesto Sea Bass

Preparation time: 10 minutes
Cooking time: 35 minutes

Servings: 4
Ingredients:

- ½ teaspoon turmeric powder
- ½ teaspoon chili powder
- 1 tablespoon chives, chopped
- A pinch of salt and black pepper
- 1 pound sea bass fillets, boneless and roughly cubed
- 2 tablespoons basil pesto
- 1 tablespoon olive oil
- Juice of 1 lime

Directions:
1.   In a sous vide bag, mix the fish with the pesto and the other ingredients, seal the bag and cook in the water oven at 180 degrees F for 35 minutes.
2.   Divide the mix between plates and serve.
Nutrition:
calories 211
fat 13
fiber 2
carbs 7
protein 11

Shrimp and Pineapple Bowls

Preparation time: 5 minutes
Cooking time: 20 minutes
Servings: 4
Ingredients:

- 1 red chili pepper, chopped
- 2 scallions, chopped
- 2 tablespoons chives, chopped
- A pinch of salt and black pepper
- 1 pound shrimp, peeled and deveined
- 1 tablespoon olive oil
- Juice of ½ lemon
- 1 cup pineapple, peeled and cubed

Directions:
1.   In a sous vide bag, mix the shrimp with the oil, lemon juice and the other ingredients, seal the bag, submerge in the water oven and cook at 170 degrees F for 20 minutes.
2.   Divide the mix into bowls and serve.
Nutrition:
calories 200
fat 12
fiber 4
carbs 6
protein 8

Garlic Sea Bass

Preparation time: 5 minutes
Cooking time: 35 minutes
Servings: 4
Ingredients:

- 2 tablespoons olive oil
- ½ teaspoon sweet paprika
- ½ teaspoon rosemary, dried
- A pinch of salt and black pepper

- 1 tablespoon cilantro, chopped
- 1 pound sea bass fillets, boneless
- 4 garlic cloves, minced
- 1 tablespoon lime zest, grated
- 1 tablespoon lime juice

Directions:
1.   In 4 sous vide bags, mix the sea bass fillets with the garlic, lime juice and the other ingredients, seal them, submerge in the water oven and cook at 180 degrees F for 30 minutes.
2.   Divide the mix between plates and serve with a side salad.
Nutrition:
calories 232
fat 7
fiber 3
carbs 7
protein 9

Shrimp and Broccoli

Preparation time: 5 minutes
Cooking time: 25 minutes
Servings: 4
Ingredients:

- 2 pounds shrimp, peeled and deveined
- 1 cup broccoli florets
- Juice of ½ lemon
- 2 tablespoons balsamic vinegar
- 1 red onion, chopped
- 2 tablespoons avocado oil
- A pinch of salt and black pepper
- 1 tablespoon cilantro, chopped

Directions:
1.   In a large sous vide bag, mix the shrimp with the broccoli, lemon juice and the other ingredients, toss, seal the bag and cook in the water oven at 170 degrees F for 25 minutes.
2.   Divide the mix between plates and serve.
Nutrition:
calories 232
fat 9
fiber 2
carbs 6
protein 8

Brussels Sprouts and Tuna

Preparation time: 10 minutes
Cooking time: 30 minutes
Servings: 4
Ingredients:

- 1 tablespoon soy sauce
- 1 tablespoon balsamic vinegar
- 3 scallions, chopped
- 1 tablespoon olive oil
- ½ teaspoon sweet paprika
- ½ teaspoon chili powder
- A pinch of salt and black pepper
- 1 tablespoon chives, chopped

- 1 pound tuna fillets, boneless and roughly cubed
- 1 cup Brussels sprouts, trimmed and halved
- 1 tablespoon lime juice

Directions:

1. In a large sous vide bag, mix the tuna with the sprouts, lime juice and the other ingredients, seal the bag and cook in the water oven at 180 degrees F for 30 minutes.
2. Divide the mix between plates and serve.

Nutrition:

calories 200

fat 13

fiber 3

carbs 6

protein 11

Avocado Mix and Mackerel

Preparation time: 5 minutes

Cooking time: 30 minutes

Servings: 4

Ingredients:

- Juice of 1 lime
- 1 tablespoon avocado oil
- 1 tablespoon balsamic vinegar
- ½ teaspoon turmeric powder
- A pinch of salt and black pepper
- 1 tablespoon chives, chopped
- 1 pound mackerel fillets, boneless
- 1 cup avocado, peeled, pitted and cubed
- 3 scallions, minced

Directions:

1. In a sous vide bag, mix the mackerel with the avocado, scallions and the other ingredients, seal the bag and cook in the water oven at 180 degrees F for 30 minutes.
2. Divide the mix between plates and serve.

Nutrition:

calories 200

fat 12

fiber 2

carbs 6

protein 9

Tuna and Asparagus

Preparation time: 10 minutes

Cooking time: 25 minutes

Servings: 4

Ingredients:

- 1 pound tuna fillets, boneless
- ¼ pound asparagus spears, trimmed
- ½ cup white wine
- 1 tablespoon avocado oil
- 1 tablespoon lime juice
- A pinch of salt and black pepper
- 2 tablespoons chives, chopped

Directions:

1. Divide the tuna, asparagus and the other ingredients in 4 sous vide bags, seal and submerge them in the water oven.
2. Cook at 180 degrees F for 25 minutes, divide the whole mix between plates and serve.

Nutrition:

calories 200

fat 12

fiber 2

carbs 5

protein 6

Cod and Carrots

Preparation time: 10 minutes

Cooking time: 35 minutes

Servings: 4

Ingredients:

- 1 teaspoon lemon juice
- 1 tablespoon cilantro, chopped
- ½ teaspoon sweet paprika
- ½ teaspoon chili powder
- A pinch of salt and black pepper
- 1 tablespoon olive oil
- 1 pound cod fillets, boneless and cubed
- 2 cups baby carrots, peeled

Directions:

1. In a large sous vide bag, mix the cod with the oil, carrots and the other ingredients, seal and submerge it in the water oven.
2. Cook at 180 degrees F for 35 minutes, divide the mix between plates and serve.

Nutrition:

calories 192

fat 9

fiber 2

carbs 8

protein 7

Chili Cod

Preparation time: 10 minutes

Cooking time: 35 minutes

Servings: 4

Ingredients:

- 1 tablespoon lime juice
- ½ teaspoon rosemary, dried
- 1 tablespoon olive oil
- ½ cup chicken stock
- A pinch of salt and black pepper
- 1 tablespoon chives, chopped
- 1 pound cod fillets, skinless, boneless and cubed
- 1 red chili pepper, chopped
- 1 teaspoon chili powder
- 1 red onion, chopped

Directions:

1. In a large sous vide bag, mix the cod with the chili pepper, chili powder and the other ingredients, seal the bag and cook in the water oven at 180 degrees F for 35 minutes.

2.   Divide the mix between plates and serve.
Nutrition:
calories 210
fat 9
fiber 2
carbs 6
protein 7

Beans and Balsamic Salmon

Preparation time: 5 minutes
Cooking time: 35 minutes
Servings: 4
Ingredients:
- 1 tablespoon avocado oil
- Juice of 1 lime
- 2 tablespoons balsamic vinegar
- 2 tablespoons parsley, chopped
- A pinch of salt and black pepper
- 4 salmon fillets, boneless and cubed
- 1 cup canned black beans, drained and rinsed
- 3 garlic cloves, minced

Directions:
1.   In a sous vide bag, mix the salmon with the black beans, garlic and the other ingredients, seal the bag, submerge in the water oven and cook at 180 degrees F for 35 minutes.
2.   Divide the mix between plates and serve.
Nutrition:
calories 200
fat 10
fiber 2
carbs 5
protein 9

Lemon Trout and Cabbage

Preparation time: 10 minutes
Cooking time: 35 minutes
Servings: 4
Ingredients:
- 1 pound trout fillets, boneless
- 1 cup red cabbage, shredded
- 1 tablespoon soy sauce
- 3 scallions, minced
- 2 tablespoons avocado oil
- 2 tablespoons lemon juice
- 1 teaspoon lemon zest, grated
- 1 tablespoon chives, chopped
- A pinch of salt and black pepper

Directions:
1.   In a large sous vide bag, mix the trout with the cabbage, soy sauce and the other ingredients, seal, submerge the bag and cook in the water oven at 180 degrees F for 35 minutes.
2.   Divide everything between plates and serve.
Nutrition:
calories 200
fat 13
fiber 3

carbs 6
protein 11

Chili Mussels and Lime

Preparation time: 10 minutes
Cooking time: 40 minutes
Servings: 4
Ingredients:
- 1 pound mussels, scrubbed
- 1 tablespoon olive oil
- Juice of 1 lime
- 2 red chilies, minced
- 1 teaspoon turmeric powder
- ½ cup white wine
- A pinch of salt and black pepper

Directions:
1.   In a sous vide bag, combine the mussels with the oil, lime juice and the other ingredients, seal the bag, submerge in preheated water bath and cook at 170 degrees F for 40 minutes.
2.   Divide the mussels into bowls and serve.
Nutrition:
calories 198
fat 7
fiber 2
carbs 6
protein 7

Chives Cod

Preparation time: 10 minutes
Cooking time: 40 minutes
Servings: 4
Ingredients:
- 1 tablespoon avocado oil
- 1 pound cod fillets, boneless
- 2 tablespoons chives, chopped
- 2 garlic cloves, minced
- ¼ cup white wine
- A pinch of salt and black pepper

Directions:
1.   In a sous vide bag, mix the cod with the oil and the other ingredients, seal the bag, submerge in the water bath and cook at 180 degrees F for 40 minutes.
2.   Divide between plates and serve with a side salad.
Nutrition:
calories 221
fat 8
fiber 3
carbs 6
protein 7

Pineapple with Tuna Bites

Preparation time: 5 minutes
Cooking time: 40 minutes
Servings: 4
Ingredients:

- 1 pounds tuna fillets, boneless, skinless and cubed
- 1 cup pineapple, peeled and cubed
- 1 tablespoon avocado oil
- Juice of 1 lime
- 3 garlic cloves, crushed
- 1 tablespoon chives, chopped
- A pinch of salt and black pepper

Directions:

1. In a sous vide bag, mix the tuna bites with the pineapple, oil and the other ingredients, seal the bag, submerge in the water bath and cook at 180 degrees F for 40 minutes.
2. Divide between plates and serve.

Nutrition:
calories 235
fat 8
fiber 4
carbs 7
protein 9

Sea Bass and Avocado

Preparation time: 10 minutes
Cooking time: 40 minutes
Servings: 4
Ingredients:

- Juice of 1 lime
- ½ teaspoon rosemary, dried
- ½ teaspoon turmeric powder
- 1 teaspoon sweet paprika
- A pinch of salt and black pepper
- 1 tablespoon olive oil
- 1 pound sea bass fillets, boneless
- 1 cup avocado, peeled, pitted and cubed

Directions:

1. In a sous vide bag, mix the sea bass with the oil, avocado and the other ingredients, seal the bag and cook in the water bath for 40 minutes at 180 degrees F.
2. Divide everything between plates and serve.

Nutrition:
calories 211
fat 8
fiber 4
carbs 8
protein 8

Smoked Salmon and Chives

Preparation time: 10 minutes
Cooking time: 20 minutes
Servings: 4
Ingredients:

- 1 tablespoon chives, chopped
- ¼ cup lime juice
- 2 scallions, chopped
- 1 tablespoon smoked paprika
- A pinch of salt and black pepper
- 1 pound smoked salmon fillets, boneless
- 1 tablespoon olive oil

- 1 cup baby spinach

Directions:

1. In a sous vide bag, mix the smoked salmon with the oil, spinach and the other ingredients, seal the bag, submerge in the water bath and cook at 180 degrees F for 20 minutes.
2. Transfer the mix to bowls and serve.

Nutrition:
calories 193
fat 7
fiber 3
carbs 6
protein 6

Shrimp and Eggplant

Preparation time: 5 minutes
Cooking time: 20 minutes
Servings: 4
Ingredients:

- 1 pound shrimp, peeled and deveined
- 1 tablespoon avocado oil
- 2 eggplants, cubed
- 1 red onion, chopped
- 4 garlic cloves, minced
- 1 tablespoon chives, chopped
- A pinch of salt and black pepper

Directions:

1. In a sous vide bag, mix the shrimp with the eggplant, oil and the other ingredients, seal the bag, submerge in preheated water bath and cook at 170 degrees F for 20 minutes.
2. Divide the mix into bowls and serve.

Nutrition:
calories 200
fat 11
fiber 4
carbs 5
protein 12

Garlic Mackerel

Preparation time: 10 minutes
Cooking time: 30 minutes
Servings: 4
Ingredients:

- ½ teaspoon turmeric powder
- ½ teaspoon garam masala
- Juice of ½ lemon
- 1 tablespoon chives, chopped
- 1 pound mackerel fillets, boneless
- 4 garlic cloves, minced
- 1 tablespoon avocado oil

Directions:

1. In a sous vide bag, mix the mackerel with the garlic, oil and the other ingredients, seal the bag, submerge in the water bath and cook at 180 degrees F for 30 minutes.
2. Divide between plates and serve with a side salad.

Nutrition:

calories 200
fat 12
fiber 3
carbs 7
protein 9

Coconut Cod

Preparation time: 5 minutes
Cooking time: 40 minutes
Servings: 4
Ingredients:
- 1 pound cod fillets, boneless, skinless and cubed
- 1 tablespoon olive oil
- 1 cup coconut cream
- ½ teaspoon turmeric powder
- ½ teaspoon cumin, ground
- A pinch of salt and black pepper
- 1 tablespoon chives, chopped

Directions:
1. Divide the cod, oil, cream and the other ingredients in 2 sous vide bags, seal, submerge them in the water bath and cook at 180 degrees F for 40 minutes.
2. Divide into bowls and serve.

Nutrition:
calories 232
fat 10
fiber 4
carbs 6
protein 9

Shrimp and Peas

Preparation time: 10 minutes
Cooking time: 20 minutes
Servings: 4
Ingredients:
- 1 tablespoon lemon zest, grated
- ½ teaspoon oregano, dried
- 1 teaspoon chili powder
- Salt and black pepper to the taste
- 1 pound shrimp, peeled and deveined
- 1 tablespoon olive oil
- 1 cup fresh peas
- ¼ cup lemon juice

Directions:
1. In a sous vide bag, mix the shrimp with the oil, peas and the other ingredients, seal and cook at 180 degrees F for 20 minutes.
2. Divide the mix into bowls and serve.

Nutrition:
calories 182
fat 7
fiber 3
carbs 6
protein 9

Italian Mackerel

Preparation time: 10 minutes

Cooking time: 35 minutes
Servings: 4
Ingredients:
- 1 pound mackerel fillets, boneless
- 4 spring onions, chopped
- 1 tablespoon Italian seasoning
- Juice of 1 lime
- 2 green chilies, chopped
- A pinch of salt and black pepper
- 1 tablespoon rosemary, chopped

Directions:
1. In a sous vide bag, mix the mackerel with the spring onions, seasoning and the other ingredients, seal the bag and cook in the water bath at 180 degrees F for 35 minutes.
2. Divide the mix between plates and serve.

Nutrition:
calories 210
fat 8
fiber 3
carbs 6
protein 14

Honey Cod

Preparation time: 5 minutes
Cooking time: 30 minutes
Servings: 4
Ingredients:
- 1 tablespoon balsamic vinegar
- 2 tablespoons honey
- Salt and black pepper to the taste
- Juice of 1 lime
- 1 tablespoon chives, chopped
- 1 pound cod fillets, boneless
- 2 tablespoons olive oil
- ½ teaspoon coriander, ground

Directions:
1. In a sous vide bag, mix the cod with the oil, honey, coriander and the other ingredients, seal the bag, submerge in the water bath and cook at 175 degrees F for 30 minutes.
2. Divide the mix into bowls and serve.

Nutrition:
calories 200
fat 12
fiber 3
carbs 6
protein 11

Basil Shrimp

Preparation time: 5 minutes
Cooking time: 20 minutes
Servings: 4
Ingredients:
- 1 tablespoon olive oil
- ½ teaspoon rosemary, dried
- ½ teaspoon cumin, ground
- 2 garlic cloves, minced
- Salt and black pepper to the taste

* 1 pound shrimp, peeled and deveined
* Juice of 1 lemon
* 1 tablespoon basil, chopped

Directions:

1. In a sous vide bag, mix the shrimp with the lemon juice and the other ingredients, seal the bag, submerge in the water bath and cook at 180 degrees F for 20 minutes.
2. Divide everything between plates and serve.

Nutrition:

calories 132
fat 9
fiber 2
carbs 5
protein 11

Curry Sea Bass

Preparation time: 10 minutes
Cooking time: 40 minutes
Servings: 4
Ingredients:

* 1 pound sea bass fillets, boneless
* 1 tablespoon olive oil
* ½ teaspoon rosemary, dried
* Juice of 1 lime
* ½ teaspoon curry powder
* 1 red onion, chopped
* A pinch of salt and black pepper
* 2 tablespoons cilantro, chopped

Directions:

1. In a sous vide bag, mix the sea bass with the oil and the other ingredients, seal the bag, submerge in the water bath and cook at 180 degrees F for 40 minutes.
2. Divide the mix between plates and serve with a side salad.

Nutrition:

calories 200
fat 12
fiber 2
carbs 6
protein 11

Calamari and Mushrooms

Preparation time: 10 minutes
Cooking time: 35 minutes
Servings: 4
Ingredients:

* ½ cup white wine
* 2 tablespoons avocado oil
* Juice of 1 lime
* 1 tablespoon rosemary, dried
* Salt and black pepper to the taste
* 1 tablespoon parsley, chopped
* 1 pound calamari rings
* 1 cup brown mushrooms, halved
* 4 scallions, minced

Directions:

1. In a sous vide bag, mix the calamari with the mushrooms, scallions and the other ingredients, seal the bag, submerge in the water bath and cook at 180 degrees F for 35 minutes.
2. Divide the mix between plates and serve.

Nutrition:

calories 200
fat 12
fiber 2
carbs 6
protein 9

Curry Trout and Green Beans

Preparation time: 10 minutes
Cooking time: 35 minutes
Servings: 4
Ingredients:

* 4 trout fillets, boneless
* ½ pound green beans, trimmed and halved
* 1 tablespoon green curry paste
* 1 cup coconut cream
* 1 tablespoon avocado oil
* ½ teaspoon basil, dried
* ½ teaspoon curry powder
* A pinch of salt and black pepper

Directions:

1. In a sous vide bag, mix the trout with the green beans, curry paste and the other ingredients, seal the bag, submerge in the water bath and cook at 180 degrees F for 35 minutes.
2. Divide the whole mix between plates and serve.

Nutrition:

calories 211
fat 13
fiber 2
carbs 7
protein 11

Coriander Shrimp Mix

Preparation time: 5 minutes
Cooking time: 20 minutes
Servings: 4
Ingredients:

* 1 pound shrimp, peeled and deveined
* Juice of 1 lime
* 1 tablespoon olive oil
* ½ cup white wine
* ½ teaspoon turmeric powder
* 2 tablespoons coriander, chopped
* A pinch of salt and black pepper

Directions:

1. In a sous vide bag, mix the shrimp with the oil, lime juice and the other ingredients, seal the bag, submerge in the water bath and cook at 180 degrees F for 20 minutes.
2. Divide the mix into bowls and serve.

Nutrition:

calories 200

fat 12
fiber 4
carbs 6
protein 8

Shrimp and Mustard Sauce

Preparation time: 5 minutes
Cooking time: 20 minutes
Servings: 4
Ingredients:
- 1 tablespoon lime zest, grated
- ½ teaspoon rosemary, dried
- A pinch of salt and black pepper
- 1 tablespoon cilantro, chopped
- 1 pound shrimp, peeled and deveined
- 1 tablespoon mustard
- 1 cup heavy cream
- ½ teaspoon garam masala

Directions:
1. In a sous vide bag, mix the shrimp with the mustard, heavy cream and the other ingredients, seal the bag and cook in the water bath and cook at 175 degrees F for 25 minutes.
2. Divide the mix into bowls and serve.

Nutrition:
calories 232
fat 7
fiber 3
carbs 7
protein 9

Shrimp and Quinoa

Preparation time: 5 minutes
Cooking time: 20 minutes
Servings: 4
Ingredients:
- 1 pound shrimp, peeled and deveined
- 1 cup quinoa, cooked
- ½ cup lemon juice
- ½ teaspoon turmeric powder
- 1 tablespoon capers, drained
- ½ cup tomatoes, cubed
- 1 tablespoon olive oil
- 1 red onion, chopped
- ½ teaspoon sweet paprika
- A pinch of salt and black pepper
- 1 tablespoon cilantro, chopped

Directions:
1. In a sous vide bag, mix the shrimp with the quinoa, lemon juice and the other ingredients, seal the bag, submerge in the water bath and cook at 180 degrees F for 20 minutes.
2. Divide into bowls and serve.

Nutrition:
calories 232
fat 9
fiber 2
carbs 6
protein 8

Shrimp and Rice

Preparation time: 5 minutes
Cooking time: 30 minutes
Servings: 4
Ingredients:
- 1 cup baby spinach
- 1 red onion, sliced
- 1 tablespoon olive oil
- ½ teaspoon sweet paprika
- A pinch of salt and black pepper
- 1 tablespoon chives, chopped
- 1 pound shrimp, peeled and deveined
- 1 cup wild rice
- 1 cup chicken stock
- 1 tablespoon lime zest, grated

Directions:
1. In a sous vide bag, mix the shrimp with the rice, stock and the other ingredients, seal the bag, submerge in the water bath and cook at 180 degrees F for 30 minutes.
2. Divide the mix into bowls and serve.

Nutrition:
calories 200
fat 13
fiber 3
carbs 6
protein 11

Parsley Cod

Preparation time: 5 minutes
Cooking time: 30 minutes
Servings: 4
Ingredients:
- 1 pound cod fillets, boneless
- 1 tablespoon capers, drained
- 1 tablespoon parsley, chopped
- 1 cup heavy cream
- ½ teaspoon turmeric powder
- Juice of 1 lime
- 1 tablespoon olive oil
- ½ teaspoon garam masala
- A pinch of salt and black pepper

Directions:
1. In a sous vide bag, mix the cod with the capers, parsley and the other ingredients, toss gently, seal the bag, and cook in the water bath at 180 degrees F for 30 minutes.
2. Divide between plates and serve.

Nutrition:
calories 200
fat 12
fiber 2
carbs 6
protein 9

Cod, Olives and Zucchinis

Preparation time: 10 minutes
Cooking time: 30 minutes
Servings: 4

Ingredients:
- ¼ cup chicken stock
- 1 tablespoon lime juice
- ½ teaspoon sweet paprika
- A pinch of salt and black pepper
- 2 tablespoons chives, chopped
- 1 pound cod fillets, boneless and roughly cubed
- 1 cup black olives, pitted and halved
- 2 zucchinis, cubed
- 2 tablespoons olive oil
- 3 spring onions, chopped

Directions:
1. Divide the cod, olives, zucchinis and the other ingredients between 2 sous vide bags, seal them and cook in the water bath at 180 degrees F for 30 minutes.
2. Divide between plates and serve.

Nutrition:
calories 200
fat 12
fiber 2
carbs 5
protein 6

Creamy Salmon Mix

Preparation time: 5 minutes
Cooking time: 30 minutes
Servings: 4
Ingredients:
- 1 tablespoon lime zest, grated
- 1 yellow onion, chopped
- ½ teaspoon turmeric powder
- ½ teaspoon chili powder
- A pinch of salt and black pepper
- 1 tablespoon chives, chopped
- 1 pound salmon fillets, boneless and roughly cubed
- 1 cup heavy cream
- 1 tablespoon lime juice

Directions:
1. In a big sous vide bag, mix the salmon with the cream, lime juice and the other ingredients, seal the bag and cook in the water bath at 175 degrees F for 30 minutes
2. Divide the mix into bowls and serve.

Nutrition:
calories 210
fat 9
fiber 2
carbs 6
protein 7

Trout and Capers Mix

Preparation time: 10 minutes
Cooking time: 30 minutes
Servings: 4
Ingredients:
- Juice of 1 lime
- 2 tablespoons chives, chopped
- ½ teaspoon chili powder
- A pinch of salt and black pepper
- 1 pound trout fillets, boneless
- 2 tablespoons capers, drained
- 1 red onion, sliced
- 1 tablespoon olive oil
- ½ cup white wine

Directions:
1. In a large sous vide bag, mix the trout fillets with the capers, onion and the other ingredients, seal the bag and cook in the water bath at 175 degrees F for 30 minutes.
2. Divide the mix between plates and serve.

Nutrition:
calories 200
fat 10
fiber 2
carbs 5
protein 9

Balsamic Sea Bass

Preparation time: 5 minutes
Cooking time: 30 minutes
Servings: 4
Ingredients:
- 1 pound sea bass fillets, boneless
- 2 tablespoons balsamic vinegar
- 1 cup kalamata olives, pitted and halved
- 2 tablespoons olive oil
- 2 tablespoons garlic, minced
- A pinch of salt and black pepper

Directions:
1. In a sous vide bag, mix the sea bass with the vinegar, olives and the other ingredients, seal the bag, submerge in the water bath and cook at 180 degrees F for 30 minutes.
2. Divide everything between plates and serve.

Nutrition:
calories 200
fat 13
fiber 3
carbs 6
protein 11

Creole Calamari

Preparation time: 5 minutes
Cooking time: 35 minutes
Servings: 4
Ingredients:
- 1 pound calamari rings
- ½ cup white wine
- 2 tablespoons avocado oil
- 1 tablespoon lime juice
- 1 tablespoon Creole seasoning
- ½ teaspoon chili powder
- 1 tablespoon chives, chopped

Directions:

1.	In a sous vide bag, mix the calamari rings with the wine, oil and the other ingredients, seal the bag, submerge in the water bath and cook at 190 degrees F for 35 minutes.
2.	Divide the mix into bowls and serve.
Nutrition:
calories 211
fat 12
fiber 3
carbs 6
protein 7

Clams and Wine Sauce

Preparation time: 10 minutes
Cooking time: 25 minutes
Servings: 4
Ingredients:
- 1 pound clams, scrubbed
- ½ cup white wine
- Juice of ½ lemon
- Zest of 1 lemon, grated
- A pinch of salt and black pepper
- 1 tablespoon chives, chopped

Directions:
1.	In a sous vide bag, mix the clams with the wine, lemon juice and the other ingredients, seal the bag and cook in the water bath at 175 degrees F for 25 minutes.
2.	Divide the mix into bowls and serve.
Nutrition:
calories 198
fat 7
fiber 2
carbs 6
protein 7

Tarragon Trout

Preparation time: 10 minutes
Cooking time: 30 minutes
Servings: 4
Ingredients:
- 1 tablespoon avocado oil
- 1 pound trout fillets, boneless
- ½ teaspoon chili powder
- 1 tablespoon tarragon, chopped
- ½ cup chicken stock
- A pinch of salt and black pepper
- Juice of ½ lemon

Directions:
1.	In a large sous vide bag, mix the trout with the oil, chili powder and the other ingredients, seal the bag and cook in the water bath at 180 degrees F for 30 minutes.
2.	Divide the mix between plates and serve.
Nutrition:
calories 221
fat 8
fiber 3
carbs 6

protein 7

Shrimp, Corn and Tomato Bowls

Preparation time: 5 minutes
Cooking time: 20 minutes
Servings: 4
Ingredients:
- 1 tablespoon olive oil
- ½ teaspoon rosemary, dried
- 3 garlic cloves, crushed
- 2 tablespoons chives, chopped
- ½ cup chicken stock
- A pinch of salt and black pepper
- 1 pounds shrimp, peeled and deveined
- 1 cup corn
- 1 cup cherry tomatoes, halved
- Juice of 1 lime

Directions:
1.	In a large sous vide bag, mix the shrimp with the corn, tomatoes and the other ingredients, seal the bag and cook in the water bath at 175 degrees F for 20 minutes.
2.	Divide into bowls and serve.
Nutrition:
calories 235
fat 8
fiber 4
carbs 7
protein 9

Shrimp, Crab and Avocado Bowls

Preparation time: 10 minutes
Cooking time: 20 minutes
Servings: 4
Ingredients:
- Juice of 1 lime
- 1 tablespoon lime zest, grated
- ½ teaspoon chili powder
- 1 cup chicken stock
- 1 teaspoon sweet paprika
- A pinch of salt and black pepper
- 1 tablespoon olive oil
- 1 cup crab meat
- 1 pound shrimp, peeled and deveined
- 1 cup avocado, peeled, pitted and cubed

Directions:
1.	In a sous vide bag, mix the crab with the shrimp and the other ingredients, seal the bag and cook in the water bath at 180 degrees F for 20 minutes.
2.	Divide everything into bowls and serve.
Nutrition:
calories 211
fat 8
fiber 4
carbs 8
protein 8

Salmon and Kale

Preparation time: 10 minutes
Cooking time: 30 minutes
Servings: 4
Ingredients:

- 1 pound salmon fillets, boneless and cubed
- 1 cup baby kale
- Juice of 1 lime
- 2 tablespoons avocado oil
- 1 tablespoon smoked paprika
- A pinch of salt and black pepper
- 2 garlic cloves, minced
- 1 tablespoon cilantro, chopped

Directions:

1. In a sous vide bag, mix the salmon with the kale and the other ingredients, seal the bag and cook in the water bath at 180 degrees F for 30 minutes.
2. Transfer the mix to bowls and serve.

Nutrition:
calories 193
fat 7
fiber 3
carbs 6
protein 6

Rosemary Calamari

Preparation time: 5 minutes
Cooking time: 30 minutes
Servings: 4
Ingredients:

- 1 pound calamari rings
- Juice of 1 lime
- ½ teaspoon chili powder
- 1 tablespoon rosemary, chopped
- ½ cup red wine
- 1 red onion, chopped
- 4 garlic cloves, minced
- A pinch of salt and black pepper

Directions:

1. In a sous vide bag, mix the calamari with the lime juice and the other ingredients, seal the bag and cook in the water bath at 180 degrees F for 30 minutes.
2. Divide into bowls and serve.

Nutrition:
calories 200
fat 11
fiber 4
carbs 5
protein 12

Salmon and Sweet Potatoes

Preparation time: 10 minutes
Cooking time: 30 minutes
Servings: 4
Ingredients:

- 2 sweet potatoes, peeled and cubed
- 2 spring onions, chopped
- 2 tablespoons olive oil
- 1 tablespoon chives, chopped

- 1 pound salmon fillets, boneless
- 1 cup chicken stock
- ½ teaspoon garam masala
- ½ teaspoon sweet paprika

Directions:

1. In a large sous vide bag, mix the salmon with the stock, garam masala and the other ingredients, seal the bag and cook in the water bath at 180 degrees F for 30 minutes.
2. Divide the mix into bowls and serve.

Nutrition:
calories 200
fat 12
fiber 3
carbs 7
protein 9

Creamy Cod and Zucchinis

Preparation time: 5 minutes
Cooking time: 30 minutes
Servings: 4
Ingredients:

- 1 pound cod fillets, boneless, skinless and cubed
- 2 zucchinis, cubed
- 1 tablespoon olive oil
- 1 cup heavy cream
- A pinch of salt and black pepper
- ½ teaspoon turmeric powder
- 1 tablespoon cilantro, chopped

Directions:

1. In a sous vide bag, mix the cod with the zucchinis and the other ingredients, seal the bag and cook in the water bath at 180 degrees F for 30 minutes.
2. Divide the mix into bowls and serve.

Nutrition:
calories 232
fat 10
fiber 4
carbs 6
protein 9

Salmon with Quinoa and Rice

Preparation time: 6 minutes
Cooking time: 30 minutes
Servings: 4
Ingredients:

- 2 spring onions, chopped
- 1 tablespoon olive oil
- ½ teaspoon rosemary, dried
- 1 teaspoon sweet paprika
- Salt and black pepper to the taste
- 1 pound smoked salmon, skinless and flaked
- 1 cup quinoa, cooked
- 1 cup corn
- 1 cup chicken stock
- 1 tablespoon olive oil

Directions:
1.   In a large sous vide bag, mix the salmon with the corn, quinoa and the other ingredients, seal the bag and cook in the water bath at 176 degrees F for 30 minutes.
2.   Divide the mix into bowls and serve right away.
Nutrition:
calories 182
fat 7
fiber 3
carbs 6
protein 9

Lemon Sea Bass and Olives

Preparation time: 10 minutes
Cooking time: 30 minutes
Servings: 4
Ingredients:
- ¼ cup white wine
- 2 green chilies, chopped
- ½ tablespoon lemon juice
- 1 tablespoon coriander, chopped
- A pinch of salt and black pepper
- 1 pound sea bass fillets, skinless, boneless and cubed
- 2 spring onions, chopped
- 1 cup kalamata olives, pitted and halved
- 1 cup green olives, pitted and halved
- 2 tablespoons olive oil

Directions:
1.   In a large sous vide bag, mix the sea bass with the spring onions, olives and the other ingredients, seal the bag, submerge in the water bath and cook at 180 degrees F for 30 minutes.
2.   Divide everything between plates and serve.
Nutrition:
calories 210
fat 8
fiber 3
carbs 6
protein 14

SOUS VIDE POULTRY RECIPES

Lime Duck and Eggplant Mix

Preparation time: 10 minutes
Cooking time: 1 hour
Servings: 4
Ingredients:
- Zest of 1 lime, grated
- 1 red onion, chopped
- 4 garlic cloves, minced
- 1 tablespoon chives, chopped
- A pinch of salt and black pepper
- 2 pounds duck breast, skinless, boneless and cubed
- 2 tablespoons olive oil
- 2 eggplants, cubed
- Juice of 1 lime

Directions:
1. In a large sous vide bag, mix the duck with the oil, eggplants and the other ingredients, seal the bag and cook in the water bath at 180 degrees F for 1 hour.
2. Divide everything between plates and serve.

Nutrition:
calories 263
fat 12
fiber 3
carbs 6
protein 14

Pesto Turkey

Preparation time: 10 minutes
Cooking time: 50 minutes
Servings: 4
Ingredients:
- 1 pound turkey breasts, skinless, boneless and cubed
- ½ cup chicken stock
- 1 tablespoon basil pesto
- 1 tablespoon lime juice
- 2 tablespoons olive oil
- 1 teaspoon chili powder
- A pinch of salt and black pepper
- 1 tablespoon chives, chopped

Directions:
1. In a large sous vide bag, mix the turkey with the stock, pesto and the other ingredients, seal the bag and cook in the water bath at 180 degrees F for 50 minutes.
2. Divide everything between plates and serve.

Nutrition:
calories 16
fat 8
fiber 2
carbs 5
protein 9

Mustard Chicken and Capers

Preparation time: 10 minutes
Cooking time: 50 minutes
Servings: 4
Ingredients:
- 2 tablespoons avocado oil
- 2 pounds chicken breasts, skinless, boneless and cut into strips
- 1 tablespoon capers, drained
- 3 scallions minced
- 1 tablespoon mustard
- 1 tablespoon lime zest, grated
- Juice 1 lime
- ¾ cup chicken stock
- A pinch of salt and black pepper
- 1 tablespoon parsley, chopped

Directions:
1. In a large sous vide bag, mix the chicken with the oil, capers and the other ingredients, seal the bag and cook in the water bath at 180 degrees F for 50 minutes.
2. Divide the mix between plates and serve.

Nutrition:
calories 200
fat 9
fiber 2
carbs 5
protein 10

Orange Chicken Mix

Preparation time: 10 minutes
Cooking time: 2 hours
Servings: 4
Ingredients:
- 1 pound chicken breast, skinless, boneless and roughly cubed
- 1 cup orange, peeled and cut into segments
- 1 tablespoon avocado oil
- 1 cup orange juice
- 1 tablespoon chives, chopped
- A pinch of salt and black pepper

Directions:
1. In a large sous vide bag, mix the chicken with the orange, oil and the other ingredients, toss, seal the bag, submerge in the water bath and cook at 175 degrees F for 2 hours.
2. Divide the mix into bowls and serve.

Nutrition:
calories 200
fat 7
fiber 2
carbs 6
protein 11

Turkey with Sauce

Preparation time: 10 minutes
Cooking time: 1 hour
Servings: 4

Ingredients:
- 1 cup heavy cream
- 1 tablespoon olive oil
- 1 red onion, sliced
- ½ teaspoon garam masala
- 1 red chili, minced
- 1 teaspoon sweet paprika
- ½ cup chives, chopped
- 1 pound turkey breasts, skinless, boneless and cubed
- 1 tablespoon mustard
- 1 tablespoon lime zest, grated

Directions:
1. In a large sous vide bag, combine the turkey with the mustard, cream and the other ingredients, toss, seal the bag, submerge in the water bath, cook at 170 degrees F for 1 hour, divide the mix between plates and serve.

Nutrition:
calories 210
fat 8
fiber 2
carbs 6
protein 11

Italian Turkey and Carrots

Preparation time: 10 minutes
Cooking time: 1 hour
Servings: 4
Ingredients:
- 1 pound turkey breast, skinless, boneless and roughly cubed
- ½ pound baby carrots, peeled
- 1 cup chicken stock
- 1 tablespoon avocado oil
- 1 teaspoon Italian seasoning
- ½ teaspoon rosemary, dried
- ½ teaspoon turmeric powder
- A pinch of salt and black pepper
- 1 tablespoon cilantro, chopped

Directions:
1. Divide the turkey, carrots, stock and the other ingredients into 4 sous vide bags and seal them.
2. Submerge in the water bath, cook at 170 degrees F for 1 hour, divide between plates and serve.

Nutrition:
calories 220
fat 8
fiber 2
carbs 5
protein 11

Chicken and Green Beans

Preparation time: 10 minutes
Cooking time: 1 hour
Servings: 4
Ingredients:
- 1 red onion, chopped
- 1 cup tomato passata

- 2 tablespoons olive oil
- Salt and black pepper to the taste
- 1 tablespoon cilantro, chopped
- 1 pound chicken breasts, skinless, boneless and cut into strips
- 2 cups green beans, trimmed and halved
- 1 teaspoon curry powder
- ½ teaspoon chili powder
- ½ teaspoon rosemary, dried

Directions:
1. Divide the chicken, green beans, curry powder and the other ingredients into 2 sous vide bags, seal them, submerge in the water bath, cook at 170 degrees F for 1 hour, divide the mix between plates and serve.

Nutrition:
calories 192
fat 12
fiber 3
carbs 5
protein 12

Duck and Tomatoes

Preparation time: 10 minutes
Cooking time: 1 hour and 10 minutes
Servings: 4
Ingredients:
- 1 pound duck breasts, skinless, boneless and cubed
- 1 cup cherry tomatoes, halved
- ½ cup chicken stock
- Juice of 1 lime
- ½ teaspoon chili powder
- ½ teaspoon cumin, ground
- 2 tablespoons olive oil
- ½ teaspoon coriander, ground
- ½ teaspoon turmeric powder
- 1 tablespoon chives, chopped

Directions:
1. In a sous vide bag, mix the duck with the tomatoes, stock and the other ingredients, seal the bag and cook in the water bath at 170 degrees F for 1 hour and 10 minutes.
2. Divide the mix between plates and serve.

Nutrition:
calories 200
fat 7
fiber 1
carbs 5
protein 12

Garlic Chicken Mix

Preparation time: 10 minutes
Cooking time: 1 hour
Servings: 4
Ingredients:
- 1 pound chicken breast, skinless, boneless and cubed
- 1 tablespoon olive oil

- 4 garlic cloves, minced
- Juice of 1 lime
- ½ teaspoon coriander, ground
- 3 scallions, chopped
- A pinch of salt and black pepper
- 1 tablespoon parsley, chopped

Directions:
1. In a sous vide bag, mix the chicken with the oil, garlic and the other ingredients, seal the bag and cook in the water bath at 170 degrees F for 1 hour.
2. Divide the mix between plates and serve.

Nutrition:
calories 231
fat 7
fiber 2
carbs 6
protein 12

Chicken and Avocado

Preparation time: 10 minutes
Cooking time: 45 minutes
Servings: 4
Ingredients:
- 1 pound chicken breast, skinless, boneless and cubed
- 1 cup avocado, peeled, pitted and cubed
- 1 tablespoon olive oil
- Juice of 1 lime
- 2 scallions, chopped
- ½ teaspoon sweet paprika
- ½ teaspoon chili powder
- A pinch of salt and black pepper
- 1 tablespoon chives, chopped

Directions:
1. In a sous vide bag, mix the chicken with the avocado, oil and the other ingredients, seal the bag, submerge in the water bath and cook at 180 degrees F for 45 minutes.
2. Divide everything between plates and serve.

Nutrition:
calories 252
fat 12
fiber 4
carbs 7
protein 13

Turkey and Tomato Sauce

Preparation time: 10 minutes
Cooking time: 1 hour
Servings: 4
Ingredients:
- 1 red onion, chopped
- 2 tablespoons olive oil
- A pinch of salt and black pepper
- 1 cup tomato passata
- 1 tablespoon chives, chopped
- 1 pound turkey breasts, skinless, boneless and cubed
- 1 carrot, sliced

- 1 parsnip, sliced
- Juice of 1 lime

Directions:
1. In a sous vide bag, combine the turkey with the carrot, parsnip and the other ingredients, seal the bag, submerge into preheated water bath and cook at 175 degrees F for 1 hour.
2. Divide everything between plates and serve.

Nutrition:
calories 221
fat 14
fiber 3
carbs 7
protein 14

Turkey Medley

Preparation time: 10 minutes
Cooking time: 1 hour
Servings: 4
Ingredients:
- 1 eggplant, cubed
- 1 cup green beans, trimmed and halved
- 2 tablespoons balsamic vinegar
- A handful cilantro, chopped
- A pinch of salt and black pepper
- 1 pound turkey breast, skinless, boneless and cut into strips
- 1 tablespoon olive oil
- ½ cup white wine
- 2 scallions, chopped
- 1 cup black olives, pitted and halved

Directions:
1. In a large sous vide bag, combine the turkey with the oil, wine, scallions and the other ingredients, seal, submerge in the water oven and cook at 176 degrees F for 1 hour.
2. Divide the mix between plates and serve.

Nutrition:
calories 263
fat 14
fiber 1
carbs 8
protein 12

Chili Chicken

Preparation time: 10 minutes
Cooking time: 1 hour
Servings: 4
Ingredients:
- 1 pound chicken breast, skinless, boneless and cubed
- 2 green chilies, chopped
- Juice of 1 lime
- ½ teaspoon sweet paprika
- 2 tablespoons olive oil
- ½ cup chicken stock
- A pinch of salt and black pepper
- 1 tablespoon cilantro, chopped

Directions:

1.   In a large sous vide bag, mix the chicken with the chilies, lime juice and the other ingredients, seal the bag and cook in the water oven at 175 degrees F for 1 hour.
2.   Divide everything between plates and serve.
Nutrition:
calories 263
fat 12
fiber 3
carbs 6
protein 14

Chicken and Mango Mix

Preparation time: 10 minutes
Cooking time: 1 hour
Servings: 4
Ingredients:
- 1 teaspoon garam masala
- ½ teaspoon turmeric powder
- 1 tablespoon chives, chopped
- A pinch of salt and black pepper
- 1 pound chicken breast, skinless, boneless and sliced
- 1 cup mango, peeled and cubed
- 1 tablespoon olive oil
- Juice of 1 lime

Directions:
1.   In a sous vide bag, mix the chicken with the mango, oil and the other ingredients, seal the bag, submerge in the water oven and cook at 190 degrees F for 1 hour.
2.   Divide the mix between plates and serve.
Nutrition:
calories 253
fat 13
fiber 2
carbs 7
protein 16

Ginger Turkey

Preparation time: 10 minutes
Cooking time: 50 minutes
Servings: 4
Ingredients:
- 1 pound turkey breast, skinless, boneless and cubed
- 1 tablespoon ginger, grated
- 1 tablespoon balsamic vinegar
- Juice of ½ lime
- 3 scallions, chopped
- ¼ cup chives, chopped
- A pinch of salt and black pepper
- 1 tablespoon chives, chopped

Directions:
1.   In a sous vide bag, mix the turkey with the ginger, vinegar and the other ingredients, seal the bag and cook in the water oven at 185 degrees F for 50 minutes.
2.   Divide everything between plates and serve.

Nutrition:
calories 234
fat 14
fiber 4
carbs 7
protein 15

Turkey and Potatoes

Preparation time: 10 minutes
Cooking time: 1 hour
Servings: 4
Ingredients:
- ½ teaspoon chili powder
- 3 garlic cloves, minced
- A pinch of salt and black pepper
- 1 tablespoon cilantro, chopped
- 1 pound turkey breast, skinless, boneless and sliced
- ½ pound gold potatoes, peeled and cut into wedges
- 1 red onion, sliced
- 2 tablespoons avocado oil
- Juice of ½ lemon

Directions:
1.   In a sous vide bag, mix the turkey with the potatoes, onion and the other ingredients, seal the bag and cook in the water oven at 185 degrees F for 1 hour.
2.   Divide the mix between plates and serve.
Nutrition:
calories 263
fat 13
fiber 2
carbs 7
protein 15

Chicken and Asparagus

Preparation time: 5 minutes
Cooking time: 1 hour
Servings: 4
Ingredients:
- 1 pound chicken breasts, skinless, boneless and cubed
- 2 tablespoons avocado oil
- ½ pound asparagus, trimmed and halved
- 2 garlic cloves, minced
- ½ teaspoon sweet paprika
- 1 cup chicken stock
- 1 tablespoon cilantro, chopped
- A pinch of salt and black pepper

Directions:
1.   In a large sous vide bag, mix the chicken with the oil, and the other ingredients except the asparagus and cook in the water bath at 180 degrees F for 50 minutes.
2.   Open the bag, add the asparagus, seal the bag again, cook for another 10 minutes, divide everything between plates and serve.
Nutrition:

calories 200
fat 13
fiber 2
carbs 5
protein 16

Sage Turkey and Olives

Preparation time: 5 minutes
Cooking time: 1 hour
Servings: 4
Ingredients:
- 1 tablespoon lemon zest, grated
- 2 tablespoons olive oil
- ½ teaspoon mustard seeds, crushed
- A pinch of salt and black pepper
- 1 tablespoon chives, chopped
- 1 pound turkey breast, skinless, boneless and cubed
- 2 tablespoons sage, chopped
- Juice of ½ lemon
- 1 tablespoon garlic, minced

Directions:
1. In a large sous vide bag, mix the turkey with the sage, lemon juice and the other ingredients, seal the bag, submerge in the water oven and cook at 175 degrees F for 1 hour.
2. Divide the mix between plates and serve.

Nutrition:
calories 200
fat 12
fiber 2
carbs 6
protein 15

Chicken with Brussels Sprouts Mix

Preparation time: 10 minutes
Cooking time: 50 minutes
Servings: 4
Ingredients:
- 1 pound chicken breast, skinless, boneless and cubed
- 2 tablespoons olive oil
- 2 cups Brussels sprouts, trimmed and halved
- 2 tablespoons lime juice
- 2 tablespoons lime zest, grated
- ½ teaspoon chili powder
- 3 garlic cloves, minced
- A pinch of salt and black pepper
- 1 tablespoon parsley, chopped

Directions:
1. In a large sous vide bag, mix the chicken with the oil, sprouts and the other ingredients, toss, seal the bag, submerge in the water oven, cook at 175 degrees F for 50 minutes, divide the mix between plates and serve.

Nutrition:
calories 253
fat 14

fiber 2
carbs 7
protein 16

Turkey and Fennel

Preparation time: 10 minutes
Cooking time: 1 hour
Servings: 4
Ingredients:
- 2 pounds turkey breast, skinless, boneless and roughly cubed
- 1 tablespoon olive oil
- 2 fennel bulbs, sliced
- Juice of 1 lime
- 1 teaspoon sweet paprika
- 1 tablespoon rosemary, chopped
- A pinch of salt and black pepper
- 1 tablespoon dill, chopped

Directions:
1. In a sous vide bag, mix the turkey with the oil, fennel and the other ingredients, seal the bag, cook in the water oven at 175 degrees F for 1 hour, divide the mix between plates and serve.

Nutrition:
calories 273
fat 13
fiber 3
carbs 7
protein 17

Chicken with Endives

Preparation time: 10 minutes
Cooking time: 1 hour
Servings: 4
Ingredients:
- Zest of 1 lime, grated
- ½ teaspoon coriander, ground
- ½ teaspoon cumin, ground
- ½ teaspoon basil, dried
- ½ tablespoon olive oil
- 1 tablespoon chives, chopped
- 1 pound chicken breast, skinless, boneless and sliced
- 2 endives, shredded
- 1 red onion, sliced
- ½ cup white wine

Directions:
1. In a large sous vide bag, mix the chicken with the endives, onion and the other ingredients, toss, seal the bag, submerge in the water oven and cook at 180 degrees F for 1 hour.
2. Divide the mix between plates and serve.

Nutrition:
calories 276
fat 15
fiber 3
carbs 7
protein 16

Balsamic Turkey

Preparation time: 10 minutes
Cooking time: 1 hour
Servings: 4
Ingredients:
- 1 pound turkey breast, skinless, boneless and sliced
- 2 tablespoons olive oil
- 2 tablespoons balsamic vinegar
- 2 garlic cloves, minced
- A pinch of salt and black pepper
- 1 tablespoon chives, chopped

Directions:
1. In a sous vide bag, mix the turkey with the oil, vinegar and the other ingredients, seal the bag and cook in the water bath at 174 degrees F for 1 hour.
2. Divide the mix between plates and serve with a side salad.

Nutrition:
calories 252
fat 15
fiber 2
carbs 6
protein 15

Chicken and Squash Mix

Preparation time: 10 minutes
Cooking time: 1 hour
Servings: 4
Ingredients:
- 1 tablespoon oregano, chopped
- ½ teaspoon chili powder
- A pinch of salt and black pepper
- 1 tablespoon chives, chopped
- 1 pound chicken breast, skinless, boneless and cubed
- 1 cup butternut squash, peeled and roughly cubed
- 2 tablespoons lime juice
- 2 tablespoons olive oil
- 2 spring onions, chopped

Directions:
1. In a large sous vide bag, mix the chicken with the squash, lime juice and the other ingredients, seal the bag, submerge in the water bath and cook at 180 degrees F for 1 hour.
2. Divide everything between plates and serve.

Nutrition:
calories 234
fat 12
fiber 3
carbs 5
protein 7

Paprika Turkey Mix

Preparation time: 10 minutes
Cooking time: 50 minutes
Servings: 4

Ingredients:
- 2 pounds turkey breast, skinless, boneless and sliced
- Juice of 1 lime
- 1 tablespoon sweet paprika
- 1 tablespoon avocado oil
- 4 scallions, minced
- A pinch of salt and black pepper
- 1 tablespoon chives, chopped

Directions:
1. In a large sous vide bag, mix the turkey with the lime juice, paprika and the other ingredients, seal the bag, submerge in the water bath and cook at 175 degrees F for 50 minutes.
2. Divide everything between plates and serve.

Nutrition:
calories 263
fat 14
fiber 3
carbs 7
protein 16

BBQ Chicken Wings

Preparation time: 10 minutes
Cooking time: 1 hour
Servings: 4
Ingredients:
- ½ teaspoon chili powder
- ½ teaspoon cumin, ground
- A pinch of salt and black pepper
- 2 pounds chicken wings
- ½ cup bbq sauce
- 2 tablespoons avocado oil
- 2 tablespoons chives, chopped

Directions:
1. In a large sous vide bag, mix the chicken wings with the bbq sauce and the other ingredients, toss, seal the bag and cook in the water bath at 175 degrees F for 1 hour.
2. Divide the chicken wings between plates and serve.

Nutrition:
calories 263
fat 12
fiber 2
carbs 7
protein 18

Chicken and Salsa

Preparation time: 10 minutes
Cooking time: 1 hour
Servings: 4
Ingredients:
- 1 pound chicken breasts, skinless, boneless and cubed
- A pinch of salt and black pepper
- 1 cup cherry tomatoes, cubed
- 1 cup avocado, peeled, pitted and cubed
- 1 tablespoon basil, chopped

- Juice of 1 lime
- 2 tablespoons avocado oil
- ½ cup black olives, pitted and halved
- 3 spring onions, chopped
- 1 tablespoon balsamic vinegar

Directions:
1. In a large sous vide bag, mix the chicken with the tomatoes, avocado and the other ingredients, seal the bag and cook in the water bath at 180 degrees F for 1 hour.
2. Divide the mix between plates and serve.

Nutrition:
calories 201
fat 7
fiber 3
carbs 6
protein 8

Coconut Turkey

Preparation time: 10 minutes
Cooking time: 50 minutes
Servings: 4
Ingredients:
- 2 tablespoons avocado oil
- 3 scallions, chopped
- 1 tablespoon garam masala
- A pinch of salt and black pepper
- 1 tablespoon chives, chopped
- 2 pounds turkey breast, skinless, boneless and cubed
- 1 cup coconut cream
- 1 tablespoon lime zest, grated
- 1 tablespoon lime juice

Directions:
1. In a large sous vide bag, mix the turkey with the cream, lime juice and the other ingredients, seal the bag and cook in the water bath at 180 degrees F for 50 minutes.
2. Divide the mix between plates and serve.

Nutrition:
calories 263
fat 12
fiber 3
carbs 7
protein 15

Cumin Turkey

Preparation time: 10 minutes
Cooking time: 50 minutes
Servings: 4
Ingredients:
- 1 red onion, sliced
- 2 pounds turkey breast, skinless, boneless and sliced
- Juice of ½ lemon
- 2 tablespoons olive oil
- 2 garlic cloves, minced
- 1 tablespoon cumin, ground
- A pinch of salt and black pepper

- 2 tablespoons chives, chopped

Directions:
1. In a large sous vide bag, mix the turkey with the onion, lemon juice and the other ingredients, seal the bag and cook in the water bath at 180 degrees F for 50 minutes.
2. Divide everything between plates and serve with a side salad.

Nutrition:
calories 214
fat 14
fiber 2
carbs 6
protein 15

Chicken and Red Beans

Preparation time: 10 minutes
Cooking time: 1 hour
Servings: 4
Ingredients:
- 1 pound chicken breasts, skinless, boneless and cubed
- 1 tablespoon olive oil
- 1 cup canned red kidney beans, drained and rinsed
- ½ cup tomato sauce
- 1 red onion, sliced
- 1 tablespoon chives, chopped
- ½ teaspoon chili powder

Directions:
1. In a large sous vide bag, mix the chicken with the oil, beans and the other ingredients, seal the bag and cook in the water bath at 175 degrees F for 1 hour.
2. Divide the mix between plates and serve.

Nutrition:
calories 231
fat 12
fiber 4
carbs 7
protein 15

Rosemary Chicken

Preparation time: 10 minutes
Cooking time: 1 hour
Servings: 4
Ingredients:
- 2 pounds chicken breast, skinless, boneless and cubed
- 2 tablespoons olive oil
- Juice of 1 lime
- 1 tablespoon rosemary, chopped
- 2 garlic cloves, minced
- 1 teaspoon chili powder

Directions:
1. In a large sous vide bag, mix the chicken with the oil and the other ingredients, seal the bag and cook in the water bath at 175 degrees F for 1 hour.

2.	Divide everything between plates and serve.
Nutrition:
calories 263
fat 12
fiber 5
carbs 7
protein 16

Chicken and Peppers

Preparation time: 10 minutes
Cooking time: 1 hour
Servings: 4
Ingredients:
- ½ cup scallions, chopped
- ½ cup chicken stock
- ½ teaspoon oregano, dried
- A pinch of salt and black pepper
- 1 tablespoon cilantro, chopped
- 2 tablespoons olive oil
- 1 red bell pepper, cut into strips
- 1 green bell pepper, cut into strips
- 1 orange bell pepper, cut into strips
- 2 pound chicken breasts, skinless, boneless and roughly cubed

Directions:
1.	In a large sous vide bag, mix the chicken with the oil, peppers and the other ingredients, seal the bag and cook in the water bath at 180 degrees F for 1 hour.
2.	Divide the mix into bowls and serve.
Nutrition:
calories 242
fat 14
fiber 3
carbs 7
protein 14

Turkey and Quinoa

Preparation time: 10 minutes
Cooking time: 1 hour
Servings: 4
Ingredients:
- ½ teaspoon garam masala
- ½ teaspoon sweet paprika
- ½ teaspoon chili powder
- ½ teaspoon turmeric powder
- A pinch of salt and black pepper
- 2 pounds turkey breasts, skinless, boneless and cubed
- 2 tablespoons avocado oil
- 1 cup quinoa, cooked
- 1 cup chicken stock
- 2 spring onions, chopped

Directions:
1.	In a sous vide bag, mix the turkey with the oil, quinoa and the other ingredients, seal the bag and cook in the water bath at 170 degrees F for 1 hour.
2.	Divide everything between plates and serve.
Nutrition:

calories 232
fat 12
fiber 2
carbs 6
protein 15

Spiced Chicken Wings

Preparation time: 10 minutes
Cooking time: 1 hour
Servings: 4
Ingredients:
- ½ teaspoon cumin, ground
- ½ teaspoon cinnamon powder
- 1 red chili pepper, chopped
- 2 tablespoons olive oil
- A pinch of salt and black pepper
- 1 pound chicken wings, halved
- 1 tablespoon lime zest, grated
- ½ tablespoon lime juice
- 1 teaspoon nutmeg, ground

Directions:
1.	In a large sous vide bag, mix the chicken wings with the nutmeg and the other ingredients, toss, seal the bag and cook in the water bath at 180 degrees F for 1 hour.
2.	Divide the mix between plates and serve.
Nutrition:
calories 263
fat 14
fiber 4
carbs 6
protein 18

Turkey with Mushrooms

Preparation time: 10 minutes
Cooking time: 1 hour
Servings: 4
Ingredients:
- 1 pound turkey breast, skinless, boneless and sliced
- 1 cup mushrooms, halved
- 1 tablespoon balsamic vinegar
- 2 tablespoons lemon juice
- 1 tablespoon olive oil
- 1 teaspoon chili powder
- ¼ cup cilantro, chopped

Directions:
1.	In a large sous vide bag, mix the turkey with the mushrooms and the other ingredients, seal the bag, cook in the water bath at 175 degrees F for 1 hour, divide everything between plates and serve.
Nutrition:
calories 262
fat 16
fiber 2
carbs 8
protein 16

Turkey with Lime Sauce

Preparation time: 10 minutes
Cooking time: 1 hour
Servings: 4
Ingredients:
- 1 tablespoon avocado oil
- Juice of 1 lime
- 1 tablespoon chives, chopped
- 1 tablespoon lime zest, grated
- 1 pound turkey breast, skinless, boneless and roughly cubed
- 2 spring onions, chopped
- A pinch of salt and black pepper

Directions:
1. In a sous vide bag, mix the turkey with the lime juice and the other ingredients, seal the bag and cook in the water bath at 180 degrees F for 1 hour.
2. Divide everything between plates and serve.

Nutrition:
calories 283
fat 16
fiber 2
carbs 6
protein 17

Turkey with Lentils

Preparation time: 10 minutes
Cooking time: 50 minutes
Servings: 4
Ingredients:
- ½ teaspoon chili powder
- ½ teaspoon cumin, ground
- A pinch of salt and black pepper
- 1 tablespoon parsley, chopped
- 2 tablespoons olive oil
- 1 cup canned lentils, drained and rinsed
- 2 pounds turkey breast, boneless, skinless and roughly cubed
- ½ cup chicken stock
- ½ teaspoon sweet paprika

Directions:
1. In a large sous vide bag, mix the turkey with the lentils, oil and the other ingredients, seal the bag and cook in the water bath at 175 degrees F for 50 minutes.
2. Divide the mix between plates and serve.

Nutrition:
calories 291
fat 17
fiber 3
carbs 7
protein 16

Chicken and Leeks

Preparation time: 10 minutes
Cooking time: 1 hour
Servings: 4
Ingredients:
- ½ teaspoon hot paprika
- ½ cup chicken stock
- ½ teaspoon cumin, ground
- A pinch of salt and black pepper
- 1 tablespoon chives, chopped
- 2 pounds chicken breast, skinless, boneless and cubed
- 2 tablespoons avocado oil
- 1 cup leeks, sliced
- 2 spring onions, chopped
- Juice of ½ lemon

Directions:
1. Divide the chicken, leeks and the other ingredients into 2 sous vide bags, seal them, submerge in the water bath, cook at 180 degrees F for 1 hour, divide everything between plates and serve.

Nutrition:
calories 226
fat 9
fiber 1
carbs 6
protein 12

Turmeric Duck

Preparation time: 10 minutes
Cooking time: 1 hour and 10 minutes
Servings: 4
Ingredients:
- 2 garlic cloves, minced
- 1 tablespoon lime juice
- 1 tablespoon lime zest, grated
- 2 tablespoons olive oil
- A pinch of salt and black pepper
- 1 tablespoon oregano, chopped
- 2 spring onions, chopped
- 2 pounds duck breast, skinless, boneless and sliced
- 1 teaspoon turmeric powder

Directions:
1. In a large sous vide bag, mix the duck with the spring onions, turmeric and the other ingredients, seal the bag and cook in the water bath at 180 degrees F for 1 hour and 10 minutes.
2. Divide the mix between plates and serve.

Nutrition:
calories 283
fat 11
fiber 2
carbs 8
protein 15

Chicken and Cauliflower

Preparation time: 10 minutes
Cooking time: 1 hour
Servings: 4
Ingredients:
- 1 tablespoon olive oil
- A pinch of salt and black pepper
- 1 teaspoon sweet paprika
- 1 tablespoon chives, chopped

- 1 pound chicken breasts, skinless, boneless and cubed
- 1 cup cauliflower florets
- ½ cup chicken stock
- 1 red onion, sliced
- Juice of 1 lime

Directions:

1. In a large sous vide bag, mix the chicken with the cauliflower, stock and the other ingredients, seal the bag, submerge in the water bath and cook at 185 degrees F for 1 hour.
2. Divide the mix between plates and serve.

Nutrition:

calories 221

fat 12

fiber 2

carbs 5

protein 17

Chicken with Hot Red Chard

Preparation time: 10 minutes
Cooking time: 50 minutes
Servings: 4
Ingredients:

- 1 red onion, chopped
- 2 garlic cloves, minced
- 1 tablespoon lime juice
- A pinch of salt and black pepper
- ¼ cup chicken stock
- ½ tablespoon parsley, chopped
- 1 tablespoon olive oil
- 2 pounds chicken breast, skinless, boneless and sliced
- 1 teaspoon hot paprika
- 2 red chilies, minced
- 1 cup red chard, torn

Directions:

1. In a large sous vide bag, mix the chicken with the chard, chilies and the other ingredients, seal the bag, submerge in the water bath, cook at 185 degrees F for 50 minutes, divide the mix between plates and serve.

Nutrition:

calories 227

fat 12

fiber 3

carbs 7

protein 18

Creamy Chicken

Preparation time: 10 minutes
Cooking time: 50 minutes
Servings: 4
Ingredients:

- ½ teaspoon coriander, ground
- 1 yellow onion, chopped
- A pinch of salt and black pepper
- 1 tablespoon chives, chopped

- 1 pound chicken breast, skinless, boneless and cubed
- 1 tablespoon olive oil
- 1 teaspoon garam masala
- 1 cup coconut cream
- ½ teaspoon oregano, dried

Directions:

1. In a large sous vide bag, mix the chicken with the oil, cream and the other ingredients, seal the bag, cook in the water oven at 180 degrees F for 50 minutes, divide everything between plates and serve.

Nutrition:

calories 293

fat 15

fiber 4

carbs 6

protein 14

Turkey with Chickpeas

Preparation time: 10 minutes
Cooking time: 50 minutes
Servings: 4
Ingredients:

- ½ teaspoon sweet paprika
- A pinch of salt and black pepper
- 1 teaspoon chili powder
- 1 tablespoon parsley, chopped
- 1 pound turkey breasts, skinless, boneless and cubed
- 1 tablespoon olive oil
- Juice of ½ lemon
- 1 cup canned chickpeas, drained and rinsed
- ½ cup chicken stock
- 1 red onion, sliced

Directions:

1. In a large sous vide bag, mix the turkey with the oil, lemon juice and the other ingredients, seal the bag, submerge in the water bath, cook at 175 degrees F for 50 minutes, divide the mix between plates and serve.

Nutrition:

calories 223

fat 9

fiber 2

carbs 4

protein 11

Masala Turkey

Preparation time: 10 minutes
Cooking time: 1 hour
Servings: 4
Ingredients:

- 1 pound turkey breasts, skinless, boneless and roughly cubed
- 1 teaspoon garam masala
- 1 cup heavy cream
- ½ teaspoon curry powder
- 2 scallions, chopped
- 1 tablespoon olive oil

- 1 tablespoon parsley, chopped

Directions:

1. In a large sous vide bag, mix the turkey with the garam masala, cream and the other ingredients, seal the bag, submerge in the water bath, cook at 180 degrees F for 1 hour, divide the mix into bowls and serve.

Nutrition:

calories 210

fat 11

fiber 2

carbs 7

protein 14

Turkey with Pomegranate Mix

Preparation time: 10 minutes

Cooking time: 50 minutes

Servings: 4

Ingredients:

- 1 tablespoon olive oil
- 1 green chili pepper, minced
- 1 tablespoon sweet paprika
- A pinch of salt and black pepper
- 1 tablespoon chives, chopped
- 1 pound turkey breast, skinless, boneless and cut into strips
- 1 cup pomegranate seeds
- Juice of 1 lime
- 1 tablespoon soy sauce
- 4 scallions, chopped

Directions:

1. In a sous vide bag, mix the turkey with the pomegranate seeds, lime juice and the other ingredients, seal the bag, submerge in the water bath, cook at 180 degrees F for 50 minutes, divide everything into bowls and serve.

Nutrition:

calories 263

fat 8

fiber 2

carbs 7

protein 12

Chicken with Tomato and Kale

Preparation time: 10 minutes

Cooking time: 1 hour

Servings: 4

Ingredients:

- 1 cup baby kale
- 2 tablespoons olive oil
- 2 garlic cloves, minced
- 1 tablespoon oregano, chopped
- 1 pound chicken breasts, skinless, boneless and cubed
- 1 cup cherry tomatoes, halved
- 1 tablespoon balsamic vinegar
- 1 tablespoon lemon zest, grated

Directions:

1. In a sous vide bag, mix the chicken with the tomatoes, kale and the other ingredients, seal the bag, cook in the water bath at 180 degrees F for 1 hour, divide everything between plates and serve.

Nutrition:

calories 220

fat 8

fiber 2

carbs 7

protein 15

Ground Chicken and Veggies Mix

Preparation time: 10 minutes

Cooking time: 1 hour and 10 minutes

Servings: 4

Ingredients:

- 1 tablespoon balsamic vinegar
- 1 tablespoon lime zest, grated
- 1 cup roasted red peppers, cut into strips
- 1 teaspoon chili powder
- 2 tablespoon olive oil
- ¼ cup sweet chili sauce
- A pinch of salt and black pepper
- 1 tablespoon chives, chopped
- 1 pound chicken breasts, skinless, boneless and ground
- 1 zucchini, cubed
- 1 eggplant, cubed
- 1 cup cherry tomatoes, halved

Directions:

1. In a large sous vide bag, combine the ground chicken with the zucchini, eggplant and the other ingredients, toss, seal the bag, submerge in the water bath and cook at 165 degrees F for 1 hour and 10 minutes.

2. Divide everything into bowls and serve.

Nutrition:

calories 282

fat 12

fiber 2

carbs 6

protein 18

Chicken and Yogurt Sauce

Preparation time: 10 minutes

Cooking time: 1 hour

Servings: 4

Ingredients:

- 1 pound chicken breasts, skinless, boneless and sliced
- 2 cups Greek yogurt
- 2 garlic cloves, minced
- 2 tablespoons olive oil
- A pinch of salt and black pepper
- ½ teaspoon turmeric powder
- ½ teaspoon coriander, ground
- ½ teaspoon cumin, ground
- ¼ cup dill, chopped

Directions:

1.   In a large sous vide bag, mix the chicken with the yogurt, garlic and the other ingredients, seal the bag, cook in the water bath at 180 degrees F for 1 hour, divide everything into bowls and serve.
Nutrition:
calories 285
fat 16
fiber 4
carbs 8
protein 18

Duck and Plums Mix

Preparation time: 10 minutes
Cooking time: 1 hour
Servings: 4
Ingredients:
- 2 tablespoons lime juice
- 3 scallions, chopped
- 1 tablespoon olive oil
- A pinch of salt and black pepper
- 1 tablespoon chives, chopped
- 1 pound duck breasts, skinless, boneless and cubed
- 1 cup plums, stoned and halved
- 1 tablespoon balsamic vinegar
- 2 tablespoons lime zest, grated

Directions:
1.   In a sous vide bag, mix the duck with the plums, balsamic vinegar and the other ingredients, seal the bag, submerge in the water bath, cook at 180 degrees F for 1 hour, divide everything into bowls and serve.
Nutrition:
calories 292
fat 17
fiber 2
carbs 7
protein 16

Chicken Wings and Tomato Sauce

Preparation time: 10 minutes
Cooking time: 1 hour
Servings: 4
Ingredients:
- 1 pound chicken wings, halved
- 1 cup tomato sauce
- ½ teaspoon sweet paprika
- ½ teaspoon chili powder
- ½ teaspoon cumin, ground
- A pinch of salt and black pepper
- 3 scallions, chopped
- 2 tablespoons olive oil
- ¼ cup basil, chopped

Directions:
1.   In a large sous vide bag, mix the chicken wings with the tomato sauce, paprika and the other ingredients, seal the bag, submerge in the water bath, cook at 175 degrees F for 1 hour, divide everything between plates and serve.

Nutrition:
calories 224
fat 11
fiber 2
carbs 9
protein 11

Cayenne Turkey and Green Beans

Preparation time: 10 minutes
Cooking time: 1 hour and 10 minutes
Servings: 4
Ingredients:
- 1 tablespoon avocado oil
- A pinch of salt and black pepper
- 1 teaspoon cayenne pepper
- ½ cup white wine
- 1 tablespoon chives, chopped
- 2 pounds turkey breast, skinless, boneless and cubed
- 1 red onion, sliced
- 1 cup green beans, trimmed and halved
- 2 garlic cloves, minced

Directions:
1.   In a large sous vide bag, mix the turkey with the green beans, onion and the other ingredients, seal the bag, submerge into the preheated water oven and cook at 170 degrees F for 1 hour and 10 minutes.
2.   Divide everything between plates and serve.
Nutrition:
calories 22
fat 9
fiber 4
carbs 7
protein 16

Oregano Turkey

Preparation time: 10 minutes
Cooking time: 50 minutes
Servings: 4
Ingredients:
- 2 pounds turkey breast, skinless, boneless and cubed
- 2 tablespoons avocado oil
- 3 garlic cloves, minced
- 2 tablespoons oregano, chopped
- ½ cup white wine
- A pinch of salt and black pepper
- 1 teaspoon rosemary, dried

Directions:
1.   In a sous vide bag, mix the turkey with the oil, oregano and the other ingredients, seal the bag, submerge in the water oven and cook at 170 degrees F for 50 minutes.
2.   Divide the mix between plates and serve.
Nutrition:
calories 183
fat 2.5
fiber 1.2
carbs 1.5

protein 13.4

Allspice Turkey

Preparation time: 10 minutes
Cooking time: 50 minutes
Servings: 4
Ingredients:
- 2 pounds turkey breasts, skinless, boneless and cubed
- 1 red onion, chopped
- ½ teaspoon rosemary, dried
- ¼ cup red wine
- 2 tablespoons avocado oil
- 1 teaspoon allspice, ground
- 1 tablespoon chives, chopped

Directions:
1. In a large sous vide bag, combine the turkey with the onion, allspice and the other ingredients, seal the bag, cook in the water oven at 180 degrees F for 50 minutes, divide the mix between plates and serve.

Nutrition:
calories 238
fat 9.7
fiber 1
carbs 2.9
protein 33.3

Chicken with Okra

Preparation time: 10 minutes
Cooking time: 1 hour
Servings: 4
Ingredients:
- 2 tablespoons lime juice
- 1 tablespoon balsamic vinegar
- A pinch of salt and black pepper
- ½ teaspoon turmeric powder
- 1 tablespoon oregano, chopped
- 2 pounds chicken breast, skinless, boneless and cubed
- 1 red onion, chopped
- 1 cup okra, sliced
- 2 tablespoons olive oil

Directions:
1. In a large sous vide bag, mix the chicken with the onion, okra and the other ingredients, seal the bag, submerge in the water bath and cook at 180 degrees F for 1 hour.
2. Divide everything between plates and serve.

Nutrition:
calories 256
fat 12.6
fiber 0.6
carbs 1.2
protein 33.2

Cinnamon Chicken

Preparation time: 10 minutes
Cooking time: 1 hour

Servings: 4
Ingredients:
- 3 scallions, chopped
- A pinch of salt and black pepper
- 1 teaspoon chili powder
- 2 tablespoons cilantro, chopped
- 2 pounds chicken breasts, skinless, boneless and sliced
- 1 tablespoon cinnamon powder
- 2 tablespoons lemon juice
- ¼ cup chicken stock
- 2 tablespoons avocado oil

Directions:
1. In a sous vide bag, mix the chicken with the cinnamon, lemon juice, stock and the other ingredients, toss, seal the bag and cook in the water oven at 170 degrees F for 1 hour.
2. Divide the mix between plates and serve.

Nutrition:
calories 364
fat 23.2
fiber 2.3
carbs 5.1
protein 35.4

Turkey Meatballs and Sauce

Preparation time: 10 minutes
Cooking time: 55 minutes
Servings: 4
Ingredients:
- 1 pound turkey breasts, skinless, boneless and ground
- 2 eggs, whisked
- 1 red onion, sliced
- A pinch of salt and black pepper
- 1 tablespoon almond flour
- 2 tablespoons oregano, chopped
- 1 cup tomato sauce

Directions:
1. In a bowl, combine the turkey with the onion, eggs, flour salt and pepper, stir and shape medium meatballs out of this mix.
2. In a sous vide bag, mix the meatballs with the oregano and sauce, seal the bag and cook in the water bath at 170 degrees F for 55 minutes.
3. Divide the mix between plates and serve.

Nutrition:
calories 300
fat 15.8
fiber 2
carbs 5.2
protein 33.9

Bulgur and Chicken

Preparation time: 10 minutes
Cooking time: 1 hour
Servings: 4
Ingredients:

- 1 pound chicken breast, skinless, boneless and cubed
- 1 cup bulgur
- 1 cup chicken stock
- A pinch of salt and black pepper
- ½ teaspoon coriander, ground
- 1 teaspoon turmeric powder
- 1 tablespoon chives, chopped

Directions:

1.	In a sous vide bag, mix the chicken with the bulgur, stock and the other ingredients, seal the bag and cook in the water bath at 170 degrees F for 1 hour.

2.	Divide the mix between plates and serve.

Nutrition:

calories 360

fat 22.1

fiber 1.4

carbs 4.3

protein 34.5

Turkey and Tomatoes

Preparation time: 10 minutes

Cooking time: 1 hour

Servings: 4

Ingredients:

- 1 tablespoon balsamic vinegar
- 1 tablespoon avocado oil
- ½ teaspoon smoked paprika
- A pinch of salt and black pepper
- 1 tablespoon cilantro, chopped
- 2 pounds turkey breasts, skinless, boneless and cubed
- ½ pound cherry tomatoes, halved
- Juice of 1 lime

Directions:

1.	In a sous vide bag, mix the turkey with the tomatoes, lime juice and the other ingredients, seal the bag and cook in the water bath at 180 degrees F for 1 hour.

2.	Divide between plates and serve.

Nutrition:

calories 362

fat 16.1

fiber 4.4

carbs 5.4

protein 36.4

Turkey with Spinach and Kale

Preparation time: 10 minutes

Cooking time: 1 hour

Servings: 4

Ingredients:

- 2 pounds turkey breasts, skinless, boneless and cubed
- Juice of 1 lime
- ¼ cup white wine
- 4 garlic cloves, minced
- 1 tablespoon lime zest, grated

- A pinch of salt and black pepper
- 1 tablespoon parsley, chopped
- 2 tablespoons olive oil
- 1 cup baby spinach
- 1 cup baby kale

Directions:

1.	In a sous vide bag, mix the turkey with the oil, spinach and the other ingredients, seal the bag, cook in the water bath at 175 degrees F for 1 hour, divide everything between plates and serve.

Nutrition:

calories 243

fat 9

fiber 1.6

carbs 5.4

protein 34.1

Spring Onions and Turkey

Preparation time: 10 minutes

Cooking time: 50 minutes

Servings: 4

Ingredients:

- 2 pounds turkey breast, skinless, boneless and cubed
- 1 cup spring onions, chopped
- ¼ cup white wine
- ½ teaspoon sweet paprika
- ½ teaspoon chili powder
- 2 tablespoons avocado oil
- 1 tablespoon parsley, chopped
- A pinch of salt and black pepper

Directions:

1.	In a large sous vide bag, mix the turkey with the spring onions, wine and the other ingredients, seal the bag, submerge in the water bath, cook at 175 degrees F for 50 minutes, divide the mix between plates and serve.

Nutrition:

calories 222

fat 6.7

fiber 1.6

carbs 4.8

protein 34.4

Lime Red Cabbage and Chicken

Preparation time: 10 minutes

Cooking time: 1 hour

Servings: 4

Ingredients:

- 1 pound chicken breasts, skinless, boneless and cubed
- 1 cup red cabbage, shredded
- Juice of 1 lime
- Zest of 1 lime, grated
- 2 tablespoons olive oil
- 2 tablespoons balsamic vinegar
- A pinch of salt and black pepper
- 1 tablespoon chives, chopped
- 1 tablespoon rosemary, chopped

Directions:

1.   In a large sous vide bag, mix the chicken with the cabbage, lime juice and the other ingredients, seal the bag, submerge in the water bath, cook at 180 degrees F for 1 hour, divide between plates and serve.

Nutrition:

calories 264

fat 13.2

fiber 0.7

carbs 1.9

protein 33.2

SOUS VIDE MEAT RECIPES

Turmeric Pork Chops

Preparation time: 10 minutes
Cooking time: 1 hour and 30 minutes
Servings: 4
Ingredients:
- 2 tablespoons avocado oil
- ½ teaspoon turmeric powder
- 1 red onion, sliced
- Salt and black pepper to the taste
- 2 tablespoons parsley, chopped
- 2 pound pork chops
- 1 tablespoon balsamic vinegar
- ½ cup red wine

Directions:
1. In a sous vide bag, mix the pork chops with the vinegar, wine and the other ingredients, toss well, seal the bag and cook in the water oven at 186 degrees F for 1 hour and 30 minutes.
2. Divide everything between plates and serve.

Nutrition:
calories 254
fat 12
fiber 2
carbs 6
protein 16

Garlic Pork Chops

Preparation time: 10 minutes
Cooking time: 1 hour and 20 minutes
Servings: 4
Ingredients:
- 2 tablespoons avocado oil
- 1 tablespoon rosemary, chopped
- ½ teaspoon chili powder
- A pinch of salt and black pepper
- 2 pounds pork chops
- Juice of 1 lemon
- 4 garlic cloves, minced

Directions:
1. Divide the pork chops and the other ingredients into sous vide bags, seal them, cook in the water oven at 186 degrees F for 1 hour and 20 minutes, divide everything between plates and serve.

Nutrition:
calories 243
fat 15
fiber 3
carbs 6
protein 20

Creamy Pork

Preparation time: 10 minutes
Cooking time: 1 hour and 20 minutes
Servings: 4
Ingredients:
- 2 pounds pork stew meat, cubed
- 2 tablespoons avocado oil
- 1 cup heavy cream
- 4 spring onions, chopped
- ½ teaspoon garam masala
- ½ teaspoon coriander, ground
- 2 garlic cloves, minced
- A pinch of salt and black pepper

Directions:
1. In a large sous vide bag, mix the pork with the oil, cream and the other ingredients, seal the bag, submerge in the water bath and cook at 180 degrees F for 1 hour and 20 minutes.
2. Divide everything between plates and serve.

Nutrition:
calories 263
fat 14
fiber 3
carbs 6
protein 16

Italian Lamb Chops

Preparation time: 10 minutes
Cooking time: 1 hour and 20 minutes
Servings: 4
Ingredients:
- 2 pounds lamb chops
- 3 scallions, chopped
- ½ cup red wine
- 1 teaspoon Italian seasoning
- ½ teaspoon chili powder
- 2 tablespoons avocado oil
- 1 tablespoon chives, chopped
- A pinch of salt and black pepper

Directions:
1. In a large sous vide bag, mix the lamb chops with the scallions, wine and the other ingredients, seal the bag, submerge in the water bath, cook at 186 degrees F for 1 hour and 20 minutes, divide the mix between plates and serve.

Nutrition:
calories 264
fat 14
fiber 4
carbs 7
protein 15

Chives Lamb

Preparation time: 10 minutes
Cooking time: 1 hour and 20 minutes
Servings: 4
Ingredients:
- 1 tablespoon lime juice
- 2 scallions, chopped
- 2 tablespoons avocado oil
- 2 garlic cloves, minced
- A pinch of salt and black pepper
- 2 pounds lamb meat, roughly cubed

- 1 red onion, sliced
- ½ cup red wine
- 1 tablespoon chives, chopped

Directions:

1. In a large sous vide bag, mix the lamb with the onion, wine and the other ingredients, seal the bag, submerge in the water bath, cook at 180 degrees F for 1 hour and 20 minutes, divide the mix between plates and serve.

Nutrition:

calories 263
fat 12
fiber 4
carbs 6
protein 16

Oregano Pork

Preparation time: 10 minutes
Cooking time: 1 hour and 30 minutes
Servings: 4
Ingredients:

- 2 garlic cloves, minced
- 1 tablespoon avocado oil
- 1 red onion, chopped
- 1 tablespoon lime juice
- A pinch of salt and black pepper
- ½ teaspoon chili powder
- 2 pounds pork shoulder, sliced
- 1 cup red wine
- 1 tablespoon oregano, chopped

Directions:

1. In a large sous vide bag, mix the pork slices with the wine, oregano and the other ingredients, toss, seal the bag, cook in the water bath at 186 degrees F for 1 hour and 30 minutes, divide the mix between plates and serve right away.

Nutrition:

calories 263
fat 14
fiber 4
carbs 6
protein 18

Green Beans and Pork Chops

Preparation time: 10 minutes
Cooking time: 1 hour and 20 minutes
Servings: 4
Ingredients:

- 2 pounds pork chops
- 1 cup green beans, trimmed and halved
- 1 tablespoon lime zest, grated
- 1 tablespoon balsamic vinegar
- 1 tablespoon lime juice
- 1 tablespoon avocado oil
- ½ teaspoon rosemary, dried
- A pinch of salt and black pepper
- 1 tablespoon chives, chopped

Directions:

1. In a large sous vide bag, mix the pork chops with the green beans, lime zest and the other ingredients, seal the bag, submerge in the water bath, cook at 185 degrees F for 1 hour and 20 minutes, divide the mix between plates and serve.

Nutrition:

calories 264
fat 14
fiber 4
carbs 6
protein 17

Basil Lamb

Preparation time: 10 minutes
Cooking time: 1 hour and 10 minutes
Servings: 4
Ingredients:

- 1 red onion, chopped
- 2 tablespoons garlic, minced
- ¼ cup red wine
- A pinch of salt and black pepper
- 2 tablespoons avocado oil
- 2 pounds lamb chops
- 1 tablespoon basil, chopped
- 2 tablespoons soy sauce

Directions:

1. In a large sous vide bag, mix the lamb chops with the basil, oil and the other ingredients, seal the bag, cook in the water bath at 180 degrees F for 1 hour and 10 minutes, divide the mix between plates and serve.

Nutrition:

calories 263
fat 14
fiber 3
carbs 7
protein 20

Hot Beef

Preparation time: 10 minutes
Cooking time: 1 hour and 20 minutes
Servings: 4
Ingredients:

- 1 teaspoon chili powder
- ½ teaspoon red pepper flakes, crushed
- A pinch of salt and black pepper
- Juice of 1 lime
- 2 garlic cloves, minced
- A pinch of salt and black pepper
- ¼ tablespoon rosemary, chopped
- 1 tablespoon olive oil
- 2 pounds beef stew meat, cubed
- 1 red chili pepper, chopped

Directions:

1. In a large sous vide bag, mix the beef with the oil, chili pepper and the other ingredients, seal the bag, submerge in the water bath, cook at 180 degrees F for 1 hour and 20 minutes, divide the mix between plates and serve.

calories 263
fat 14
fiber 5
carbs 7
protein 15

Mint Lamb

Preparation time: 10 minutes
Cooking time: 1 hour and 20 minutes
Servings: 4
Ingredients:

- 1 red onion, chopped
- ¼ cup red wine
- ½ teaspoon chili powder
- A pinch of salt and black pepper
- 2 pounds lamb chops
- 2 tablespoons mint, chopped
- 1 tablespoon balsamic vinegar
- 1 tablespoon avocado oil

Directions:

1. In a large sous vide bag, mix the lamb chops with the mint, balsamic vinegar and the other ingredients, seal the bag, submerge in the water bath, cook at 186 degrees F for 1 hour and 20 minutes, divide everything between plates and serve.

Nutrition:
calories 253
fat 14
fiber 3
carbs 7
protein 17

Zucchini Mix and Lamb

Preparation time: 10 minutes
Cooking time: 1 hour and 10 minutes
Servings: 4
Ingredients:

- 2 tablespoons avocado oil
- 2 zucchinis, cubed
- 1 pound lamb stew meat, cubed
- 2 tablespoons lime juice
- 1 tablespoon oregano, chopped
- 2 tablespoons balsamic vinegar
- ½ teaspoon sweet paprika
- 1 red onion, chopped
- A pinch of salt and black pepper

Directions:

1. In a large sous vide bag mix the zucchinis with the lamb and the other ingredients, seal the bag, submerge in the water bath, cook at 175 degrees F for 1 hour and 10 minutes, divide the mix between plates and serve.

Nutrition:
calories 276
fat 14
fiber 3
carbs 7
protein 20

Beef and Artichokes

Preparation time: 10 minutes
Cooking time: 1 hour
Servings: 4
Ingredients:

- ¼ cup tomato passata
- 2 tablespoons avocado oil
- 1 red onion, chopped
- 2 teaspoons sweet paprika
- 1 tablespoon chives, chopped
- 2 pounds beef stew meat, cubed
- 2 cups canned artichoke hearts, drained
- Juice of ½ lemon

Directions:

1. In a large sous vide bag, mix the beef with the artichokes, lemon juice and the other ingredients, seal the bag, submerge in the water bath, cook at 180 degrees F for 1 hour, divide the mix between plates and serve.

Nutrition:
calories 287
fat 16
fiber 4
carbs 6
protein 20

Pork and Mushrooms

Preparation time: 10 minutes
Cooking time: 1 hour and 20 minutes
Servings: 4
Ingredients:

- 2 tablespoons balsamic vinegar
- 1 red onion, chopped
- 1 tablespoon lemon juice
- 1 tablespoon lemon zest, grated
- 2 tablespoon olive oil
- ½ teaspoon sweet paprika
- A pinch of salt and black pepper
- 1 tablespoon cilantro, chopped
- 2 pounds pork stew meat, cubed
- 1 cup brown mushrooms, halved
- 2 spring onions, chopped

Directions:

1. In a large sous vide bag, mix the pork with the mushrooms, spring onions and the other ingredients, seal the bag, cook in the water bath at 180 degrees F for 1 hour and 20 minutes, divide the mix between plates and serve.

Nutrition:
calories 264
fat 8
fiber 3
carbs 6
protein 17

Pork and Tomatoes

Preparation time: 10 minutes
Cooking time: 1 hour and 30 minutes
Servings: 4

Ingredients:
- 2 pounds pork stew meat, cubed
- 2 tablespoons avocado oil
- 1 pound cherry tomatoes, halved
- 3 garlic cloves, minced
- 2 spring onions, chopped
- 1 teaspoon chili powder
- Juice of 1 lime
- A pinch of salt and black pepper
- 1 tablespoon chives, chopped

Directions:
1. In a large sous vide bag, mix the pork with the oil, cherry tomatoes and the other ingredients, seal the bag, submerge in the water bath, cook at 180 degrees F for 1 hour and 30 minutes, divide between plates and serve.

Nutrition:
calories 275
fat 13
fiber 4
carbs 7
protein 20

Allspice Lamb

Preparation time: 10 minutes
Cooking time: 1 hour and 30 minutes
Servings: 4
Ingredients:
- Juice of 1 lime
- 1 yellow onion, chopped
- ½ teaspoon chili powder
- 4 garlic cloves, minced
- ¼ cup red wine
- A pinch of salt and black pepper
- 1 pound lamb stew meat , roughly cubed
- 1 teaspoon allspice, ground
- 2 tablespoons olive oil

Directions:
1. In a large sous vide bag, mix the lamb with the allspice, oil and the other ingredients, seal the bag, submerge in the water bath and cook at 187 degrees F for 1 hour and 30 minutes.
2. Divide the mix between plates and serve.

Nutrition:
calories 263
fat 12
fiber 4
carbs 7
protein 12

Pork and Fennel

Preparation time: 10 minutes
Cooking time: 1 hour and 20 minutes
Servings: 4
Ingredients:
- 1 tablespoon lemon juice
- 2 tablespoons avocado oil
- 4 garlic cloves, minced
- ¼ cup red wine

- A pinch of salt and black pepper
- 1 tablespoon chives, chopped
- 2 pounds pork stew meat, roughly cubed
- 2 fennel bulbs, sliced
- 1 tablespoon soy sauce
- 1 tablespoon brown sugar

Directions:
1. In a large sous vide bag, mix the pork with the fennel, soy sauce and the other ingredients, seal the bag, submerge in the water bath and cook at 185 degrees F for 1 hour and 20 minutes.
2. Divide the mix between plates and serve.

Nutrition:
calories 263
fat 12
fiber 3
carbs 7
protein 10

Creamy Lamb

Preparation time: 10 minutes
Cooking time: 1 hour
Servings: 4
Ingredients:
- 1 cup heavy cream
- 1 yellow onion, chopped
- A pinch of salt and black pepper
- 1 tablespoon oregano, chopped
- 2 pounds lamb chops
- 1 tablespoon lime juice
- 1 teaspoon turmeric powder
- 2 tablespoons avocado oil

Directions:
1. In a large sous vide bag, mix the lamb chops with the lime juice, cream and the other ingredients, seal the bag, submerge in the water oven, cook at 180 degrees F for 1 hour, divide the mix into bowls and serve.

Nutrition:
calories 233
fat 7
fiber 2
carbs 6
protein 12

Paprika Lamb

Preparation time: 10 minutes
Cooking time: 1 hour
Servings: 4
Ingredients:
- 2 tablespoons avocado oil
- ½ cup beef stock
- A pinch of salt and black pepper
- 2 tablespoons chives, chopped
- 2 pounds lamb chops
- 1 tablespoon sweet paprika
- ½ teaspoon rosemary, dried
- Juice of 1 lime

Directions:

1.   In a sous vide bag, mix the lamb chops with the paprika, rosemary and the other ingredients, seal the bag, submerge in the water oven and cook at 180 degrees F for 1 hour.
2.   Divide the mix between plates and serve.
Nutrition:
calories 23
fat 12
fiber 5
carbs 7
protein 10

Beef and Berries

Preparation time: 10 minutes
Cooking time: 1 hour and 20 minutes
Servings: 4
Ingredients:
- 2 pounds beef stew meat
- 1 cup blackberries, pureed
- 1 tablespoon lime juice
- ½ teaspoon chili powder
- 2 tablespoons olive oil
- 1 teaspoon sweet paprika
- 1 tablespoon chives, chopped
- A pinch of salt and black pepper

Directions:
1.   In a large sous vide bag, mix the beef stew meat with the blackberries, lime juice and the other ingredients, seal the bag, submerge in the water oven and cook at 180 degrees F for 1 hour and 20 minutes, divide the mix between plates and serve.
Nutrition:
calories 211
fat 9
fiber 2
carbs 6
protein 12

Pesto Lamb

Preparation time: 10 minutes
Cooking time: 1 hour and 10 minutes
Servings: 4
Ingredients:
- 2 pounds lamb chops
- 2 tablespoons basil pesto
- Juice of 1 lime
- 1 red onion, chopped
- 2 tablespoons olive oil
- ½ teaspoon curry powder
- A pinch of salt and black pepper
- 1 tablespoon cilantro, chopped

Directions:
1.   In a sous vide bag, combine the lamb chops with the pesto, lime juice and the other ingredients, seal the bag, submerge in the water oven and cook at 187 degrees F for 1 hour and 10 minutes.
2.   Divide everything between plates and serve.
Nutrition:
calories 254

fat 12
fiber 3
carbs 6
protein 16

Lentils Mix and Pork

Preparation time: 10 minutes
Cooking time: 1 hour and 30 minutes
Servings: 4
Ingredients:
- ½ teaspoon rosemary, dried
- ¼ cup tomato sauce
- A pinch of salt and black pepper
- 1 tablespoon parsley, chopped
- 2 pounds pork stew meat, cubed
- 1 cup canned lentils, drained and rinsed
- 2 tablespoons avocado oil
- 2 spring onions, chopped

Directions:
1.   In a large sous vide bag, mix the pork with the lentils, oil and the other ingredients, seal the bag, submerge in the water oven, cook at 180 degrees F for 1 hour and 30 minutes, divide the mix between plates and serve.
Nutrition:
calories 232
fat 10
fiber 5
carbs 7
protein 11

Lamb and Potatoes

Preparation time: 10 minutes
Cooking time: 1 hour and 30 minutes
Servings: 4
Ingredients:
- 2 pounds lamb stew meat, cubed
- 2 gold potatoes, peeled and cut into wedges
- Juice of 1 lime
- 1 teaspoon sweet paprika
- ½ teaspoon coriander, ground
- 2 tablespoons avocado oil
- 2 tablespoons chives, chopped
- 1 tablespoon balsamic vinegar
- A pinch of salt and black pepper
- ½ cup beef stock

Directions:
1.   In a large sous vide bag, mix the lamb with the potatoes, lime juice and the other ingredients, seal the bag, submerge in the water oven and cook at 180 degrees F for 1 hour and 30 minutes.
2.   Divide the mix into bowls and serve.
Nutrition:
calories 243
fat 11
fiber 4
carbs 6
protein 10

Peppers and Spiced Beef

Preparation time: 10 minutes
Cooking time: 1 hour and 30 minutes
Servings: 4
Ingredients:
- ½ teaspoon cinnamon powder
- ½ cup beef stock
- 3 garlic cloves, minced
- A pinch of salt and black pepper
- 1 tablespoon parsley, chopped
- 2 pounds beef stew meat, cubed
- 2 tablespoons avocado oil
- 2 red bell peppers, cut into strips
- Juice of ½ lemon
- ½ teaspoon nutmeg, ground

Directions:
1.   In a large sous vide bag, mix the beef with the oil, peppers and the other ingredients, seal the bag, submerge in the water oven and cook at 187 degrees F for 1 hour and 30 minutes.
2.   Divide the mix between plates and serve.

Nutrition:
calories 232
fat 12
fiber 4
carbs 6
protein 9

Rosemary Beef

Preparation time: 10 minutes
Cooking time: 1 hour and 40 minutes
Servings: 4
Ingredients:
- 2 pounds beef roast, sliced
- 2 tablespoons rosemary, chopped
- 2 tablespoons balsamic vinegar
- 2 tablespoons avocado oil
- 1 red onion, chopped
- 1 tablespoon garlic, minced
- A pinch of salt and black pepper
- 1 tablespoon chives, chopped

Directions:
1.   In a large sous vide bag, mix the beef roast with the rosemary, vinegar and the other ingredients, seal the bag, submerge in the water oven, cook at 189 degrees F for 1 hour and 40 minutes, divide the mix between plates and serve.

Nutrition:
calories 274
fat 9
fiber 5
carbs 6
protein 12

Corn and Lamb

Preparation time: 10 minutes
Cooking time: 1 hour and 30 minutes
Servings: 4
Ingredients:
- 2 scallions, chopped
- ¼ cup heavy ream
- 2 tablespoons avocado oil
- A pinch of salt and black pepper
- 1 teaspoon chili powder
- 1 tablespoon cilantro, chopped
- 4 lamb chops
- 1 cup corn
- 2 tablespoons balsamic vinegar
- 1 tablespoon lime juice

Directions:
1.   In a large sous vide bag, combine the lamb chops with the corn, vinegar and the other ingredients, seal the bag, submerge in the water oven, cook at 178 degrees F for 1 hour and 30 minutes, divide everything between plates and serve.

Nutrition:
calories 23
fat 9
fiber 3
carbs 6
protein 10

Sage Beef

Preparation time: 10 minutes
Cooking time: 1 hour and 20 minutes
Servings: 4
Ingredients:
- ¼ cup red wine
- 2 tablespoons olive oil
- 1 red onion, sliced
- ½ teaspoon chili powder
- A pinch of salt and black pepper
- 2 pounds beef roast, sliced
- 2 tablespoons soy sauce
- 1 tablespoon sage, chopped

Directions:
1.   In a large sous vide bag, combine the roast with the soy sauce, sage and the other ingredients, seal the bag, submerge in the water oven, cook at 180 degrees F for 1 hour and 20 minutes, divide between plates and serve with a side salad.

Nutrition:
calories 200
fat 11
fiber 3
carbs 6
protein 15

Peas and Lemon Chops

Preparation time: 10 minutes
Cooking time: 1 hour and 20 minutes
Servings: 4
Ingredients:
- 2 pounds pork chops
- 1 cup fresh peas
- Juice of ½ lemon
- Zest of 1 lemon, grated
- 2 tablespoons olive oil

- ½ cup beef stock
- A pinch of salt and black pepper
- 1 tablespoon chives, chopped

Directions:

1. In a large sous vide bag, mix the pork chops with the peas, lemon juice and the other ingredients, seal the bag, submerge in the water bath, cook at 180 degrees F for 1 hour and 20 minutes, divide everything between plates and serve.

Nutrition:

calories 210

fat 5

fiber 3

carbs 8

protein 12

Parsley Pork

Preparation time: 10 minutes

Cooking time: 1 hour and 30 minutes

Servings: 4

Ingredients:

- ½ cup white wine
- 2 scallions, chopped
- Juice of 1 lime
- ½ teaspoon coriander, ground
- Salt and black pepper to the taste
- 2 pounds pork stew meat, roughly cubed
- 2 tablespoons olive oil
- 2 tablespoons parsley, chopped

Directions:

1. In a large sous vide bag, mix the pork with the oil, parsley and the other ingredients, seal the bag, submerge in the water oven and cook at 180 degrees F for 1 hour and 30 minutes.

2. Divide the mix between plates and serve right away.

Nutrition:

calories 248

fat 11

fiber 3

carbs 6

protein 15

Beef and Sprouts

Preparation time: 10 minutes

Cooking time: 1 hour and 20 minutes

Servings: 4

Ingredients:

- 1 cup Brussels sprouts, trimmed and halved
- ½ teaspoon chili powder
- A pinch of salt and black pepper
- 1 tablespoon cilantro, chopped
- 2 pounds beef stew meat
- 2 tablespoons avocado oil
- 2 tablespoons balsamic vinegar

Directions:

1. In a sous vide bag, mix the beef with the oil, vinegar and the other ingredients, seal the bag,

submerge in the water oven and cook at 180 degrees F for 1 hour and 20 minutes.

2. Divide everything between plates and serve.

Nutrition:

calories 233

fat 9

fiber 3

carbs 7

protein 14

Avocado Mix and Lamb

Preparation time: 10 minutes

Cooking time: 1 hour and 10 minutes

Servings: 4

Ingredients:

- 1 tablespoon chives, chopped
- 2 scallions, chopped
- ½ teaspoon coriander, ground
- 1 teaspoon chili powder
- A pinch of salt and black pepper
- 2 pounds lamb stew, roughly cubed
- 2 tablespoons avocado oil
- 1 cup avocado, peeled, pitted and cubed

Directions:

1. In a large sous vide bag, mix the lamb with the avocado, oil and the other ingredients, seal the bag, submerge in the water oven, cook at 180 degrees F for 1 hour and 10 minutes, divide the mix between plates and serve.

Nutrition:

calories 227

fat 14

fiber 4

carbs 6

protein 16

Beef and Corn

Preparation time: 10 minutes

Cooking time: 1 hour and 30 minutes

Servings: 4

Ingredients:

- 1 tablespoon balsamic vinegar
- 1 tablespoon lime juice
- 1 tablespoon olive oil
- 1 teaspoon hot paprika
- 1 tablespoon chives, chopped
- 2 pounds beef stew meat, cubed
- 2 cups corn
- 1 red onion, chopped

Directions:

1. In a sous vide bag, mix the beef with the corn, onion and the other ingredients, seal the bag, submerge in the water bath and cook at 180 degrees F for 1 hour and 30 minutes.

2. Divide the mix between plates and serve.

Nutrition:

calories 236

fat 12

fiber 2

carbs 7
protein 15

Pork and Olives

Preparation time: 10 minutes
Cooking time: 1 hour and 30 minutes
Servings: 4
Ingredients:
- 1 cup black olives, pitted and halved
- 2 tablespoons lemon juice
- 2 tablespoons olive oil
- A pinch of salt and black pepper
- 2 pounds pork stew meat, roughly cubed
- 1 teaspoon coriander, ground
- ½ teaspoon turmeric powder
- ¼ cup red wine

Directions:
1. In a large sous vide bag, mix the pork with the coriander, turmeric and the other ingredients, seal the bag, submerge in the water oven and cook at 186 degrees F for 1 hour and 30 minutes.
2. Divide the mix between plates and serve.

Nutrition:
calories 273
fat 12
fiber 4
carbs 7
protein 17

Cucumber Mix and Lamb

Preparation time: 10 minutes
Cooking time: 1 hour and 30 minutes
Servings: 4
Ingredients:
- ¼ cup beef stock
- 4 garlic cloves, minced
- A pinch of salt and black pepper
- 1 tablespoon cilantro, chopped
- 2 pounds lamb stew meat, roughly cubed
- 2 tablespoons olive oil
- 1 cup cucumbers, cubed
- 1 teaspoon cumin, ground

Directions:
1. In a large sous vide bag mix the lamb with the oil, cucumber and the other ingredients, seal the bag, cook in the water oven at 180 degrees F for 1 hour and 30 minutes, divide the mix between plates and serve.

Nutrition:
calories 244
fat 12
fiber 2
carbs 5
protein 16

Carrots Mix and Ground Lamb

Preparation time: 10 minutes
Cooking time: 1 hour
Servings: 4
Ingredients:
- 2 tablespoons olive oil
- 3 carrots, peeled and grated
- 1 parsnip, peeled and sliced
- ¼ cup red wine
- 1 tablespoon chives, chopped
- A pinch of salt and black pepper
- 2 pounds lamb stew meat, ground
- 1 tablespoon balsamic vinegar
- 1 red onion, sliced

Directions:
1. In a large sous vide bag, mix the lamb with the vinegar, onion and the other ingredients, seal the bag, submerge in the water oven, cook at 175 degrees F for 1 hour, divide the mix into bowls and serve.

Nutrition:
calories 254
fat 14
fiber 3
carbs 6
protein 17

Lamb and Capers

Preparation time: 10 minutes
Cooking time: 1 hour and 10 minutes
Servings: 4
Ingredients:
- 2 pounds lamb stew meat, cubed
- 1 red onion, sliced
- 2 tablespoons capers, drained
- Juice of 1 lemon
- ½ teaspoon chili pepper
- 1 green bell pepper, cut into strips
- 2 tablespoons olive oil
- ½ teaspoon red pepper flakes, crushed
- A pinch of salt and black pepper
- 1 tablespoon cilantro, chopped

Directions:
1. In a large sous vide bag, mix the lamb with the onion, capers and the other ingredients, seal the bag, submerge in the water bath, cook at 180 degrees F for 1 hour and 10 minutes, divide the mix between plate sand serve.

Nutrition:
calories 263
fat 14
fiber 3
carbs 6
protein 20

Beef and Spicy Zucchinis

Preparation time: 10 minutes
Cooking time: 1 hour and 10 minutes
Servings: 4
Ingredients:
- ½ teaspoon hot paprika
- 1 red onion, sliced
- 2 tablespoons avocado oil

- ¼ cup beef stock
- A pinch of salt and black pepper
- 1 teaspoon cayenne pepper
- 1 tablespoon chives, chopped
- 2 pounds beef stew meat, cubed
- 2 zucchinis, cubed
- 1 teaspoon chili powder

Directions:

1. In a large sous vide bag, mix the beef with the zucchinis, chili powder and the other ingredients, seal the bag, cook in the water bath at 175 degrees F for 1 hour and 10 minutes, divide mix between plates and serve.

Nutrition:

calories 283

fat 13

fiber 4

carbs 6

protein 16

Pork with Tomatoes and Potatoes

Preparation time: 10 minutes
Cooking time: 1 hour and 40 minutes
Servings: 4
Ingredients:

- Juice of 1 lime
- 1 red onion, chopped
- 2 tablespoons avocado oil
- 3 garlic cloves, minced
- 1 tablespoon chives, chopped
- 2 pounds pork stew meat, roughly cubed
- 1 cup cherry tomatoes, halved
- ½ pound gold potatoes, peeled and cut into wedges
- 1 teaspoon sweet paprika

Directions:

1. In a large sous vide bag, mix the pork with the tomatoes, potatoes and the other ingredients, seal the bag, submerge in the water bath, cook at 180 degrees F for 1 hour and 40 minutes, divide the mix between plates and serve.

Nutrition:

calories 253

fat 14

fiber 2

carbs 6

protein 18

Savoy Cabbage Mix and Lamb

Preparation time: 10 minutes
Cooking time: 1 hour and 20 minutes
Servings: 4
Ingredients:

- 2 pounds lamb shoulder, cubed
- 2 tablespoons olive oil
- 1 cup Savoy cabbage, shredded
- 1 tablespoon balsamic vinegar
- 2 spring onions, chopped
- 1 tablespoon balsamic vinegar

- A pinch of salt and black pepper
- Juice of 1 lime
- 1 tablespoon chives, chopped

Directions:

1. In a large sous vide bag, mix the lamb with the cabbage, oil and the other ingredients, seal the bag, submerge in the water bath, cook at 180 degrees F for 1 hour and 20 minutes, divide everything between plates and serve.

Nutrition:

calories 264

fat 14

fiber 3

carbs 6

protein 17

Carrots and Cabbage with Beef

Preparation time: 10 minutes
Cooking time: 1 hour and 30 minutes
Servings: 4
Ingredients:

- 2 tablespoons balsamic vinegar
- 2 pounds beef stew meat, roughly cubed
- 1 red onion, chopped
- A pinch of salt and black pepper
- ½ teaspoon cumin, ground
- 1 tablespoon chives, chopped
- 2 tablespoons olive oil
- 2 carrots, peeled and sliced
- 1 cup red cabbage, shredded
- Juice of 1 lime

Directions:

1. In a sous vide bag, mix the beef with the oil, carrots and the other ingredients, seal the bag, submerge in the water oven and cook at 186 degrees F for 1 hour and 30 minutes.
2. Divide the mix into bowls and serve.

Nutrition:

calories 273

fat 13

fiber 2

carbs 6

protein 15

Orange Lamb

Preparation time: 10 minutes
Cooking time: 1 hour
Servings: 4
Ingredients:

- 2 pounds lamb chops
- 2 tablespoons olive oil
- Juice of 2 oranges
- 2 tablespoons orange zest, grated
- ½ teaspoon turmeric powder
- A pinch of salt and black pepper
- 1 tablespoon chives, chopped

Directions:

1. In a large sous vide bag, mix the lamb chops with the oil, orange juice and the other ingredients,

seal the bag, submerge in the water bath, cook at 180 degrees F for 1 hour, divide between plates and serve.
Nutrition:
calories 274
fat 14
fiber 2
carbs 6
protein 16

Ginger Pork

Preparation time: 10 minutes
Cooking time: 1 hour and 10 minutes
Servings: 4
Ingredients:
- ½ teaspoon chili powder
- ½ teaspoon coriander, ground
- A pinch of salt and black pepper
- ¼ cup beef stock
- 1 tablespoon cilantro, chopped
- 2 pounds pork shoulder, boneless and cubed
- 2 spring onions, chopped
- 1 tablespoon ginger, grated

Directions:
1. In a sous vide bag, mix the pork with the ginger, spring onions and the other ingredients, seal the bag, submerge in the water bath, cook at 175 degrees F for 1 hour and 10 minutes, divide the mix between plates and serve with a side salad.
Nutrition:
calories 264
fat 14
fiber 2
carbs 8
protein 12

Swiss Chard and Beef

Preparation time: 10 minutes
Cooking time: 1 hour and 10 minutes
Servings: 4
Ingredients:
- 2 pounds beef stew meat, roughly cubed
- 2 scallions, chopped
- 1 cup red chard, torn
- Juice of 1 lime
- 1 tablespoon olive oil
- 1 teaspoon hot paprika
- ½ teaspoon turmeric powder
- 1 tablespoon chives, chopped
- A pinch of salt and black pepper

Directions:
1. In a large sous vide bag, mix the beef with the scallions, chard and the other ingredients, seal the bag, submerge in the water bath, cook at 176 degrees F for 1 hour and 10 minutes, divide the mix between plates and serve with a side salad.
Nutrition:
calories 200
fat 9

fiber 2
carbs 6
protein 12

Nutmeg Pork Roast

Preparation time: 10 minutes
Cooking time: 1 hour and 40 minutes
Servings: 4
Ingredients:
- 2 pounds pork roast, sliced
- 1 teaspoon nutmeg, ground
- Juice of ½ lemon
- ½ tablespoon lemon zest, grated
- 2 tablespoons olive oil
- A pinch of salt and black pepper
- ½ cup red wine
- 1 tablespoon chives, chopped

Directions:
1. In a large sous vide bag, mix the pork roast with the nutmeg, lemon juice and the other ingredients, seal the bag, submerge in the water bath, cook at 180 degrees F for 1 hour and 40 minutes, divide roast between plates and serve with a side salad.
Nutrition:
calories 234
fat 11
fiber 3
carbs 7
protein 15

Ginger Artichokes with Lamb

Preparation time: 10 minutes
Cooking time: 1 hour and 10 minutes
Servings: 4
Ingredients:
- ½ teaspoon chili powder
- ½ teaspoon turmeric powder
- 1 cup beef stock
- 2 tablespoons olive oil
- 1 tablespoon parsley, chopped
- 2 pounds lamb meat, cubed
- 1 cup canned artichoke hearts, drained and quartered
- 1 tablespoon ginger, grated
- 1 red onion, sliced
- Juice of ½ lime

Directions:
1. In a large sous vide bag, mix the lamb with the artichokes, ginger, and the other ingredients, seal the bag, submerge in the water bath, cook at 180 degrees F for 1 hour and 10 minutes, divide the mix between plates and serve.
Nutrition:
calories 273
fat 14
fiber 2
carbs 6
protein 15

Balsamic Pork Chops

Preparation time: 10 minutes
Cooking time: 1 hour and 20 minutes
Servings: 4
Ingredients:
- 1 pound pork chops
- 2 tablespoons balsamic vinegar
- 1 tablespoon olive oil
- 4 garlic cloves, minced
- ¼ cup red wine
- A pinch of salt and black pepper
- 1 tablespoon chives, chopped

Directions:
1. In a large sous vide bag, mix the pork chops with the vinegar, oil and the other ingredients, seal the bag, submerge in the water bath, cook at 184 degrees F for 1 hour and 20 minutes, divide everything between plates and serve.

Nutrition:
calories 292
fat 12
fiber 3
carbs 7
protein 16

Creamy Scallions Sauce and Pork

Preparation time: 10 minutes
Cooking time: 1 hour and 20 minutes
Servings: 4
Ingredients:
- ½ teaspoon garam masala
- 2 tablespoons olive oil
- 1 tablespoon chives, chopped
- A pinch of salt and black pepper
- 2 pounds pork stew meat, cubed
- 1 cup heavy cream
- ½ cup scallions, chopped
- Juice of 1 lime
- 1 teaspoon turmeric powder

Directions:
1. In a large sous vide bag, mix the pork with the cream, scallions, lime juice and the other ingredients, seal the bag, submerge in the water bath, cook at 180 degrees F for 1 hour and 20 minutes, divide everything into bowls and serve.

Nutrition:
calories 277
fat 14
fiber 3
carbs 7
protein 17

Almond Beef

Preparation time: 10 minutes
Cooking time: 1 hour and 15 minutes
Servings: 4
Ingredients:
- ½ cup beef stock
- ½ teaspoon rosemary, dried
- A pinch of salt and black pepper
- 1 tablespoon chives, chopped
- 2 pounds beef stew meat, cubed
- 2 tablespoons avocado oil
- 1 tablespoon almond butter
- 1 tablespoon almonds, chopped

Directions:
1. In a large sous vide bag, mix the beef with the oil, almond butter and the other ingredients, seal the bag, submerge in the water bath, cook at 180 degrees F for 1 hour and 15 minutes, divide everything between plates and serve.

Nutrition:
calories 274
fat 12
fiber 4
carbs 7
protein 16

Pork, Capers and Green Beans

Preparation time: 10 minutes
Cooking time: 1 hour and 10 minutes
Servings: 4
Ingredients:
- 2 pounds pork chops
- 1 tablespoon capers, drained
- 1 cup green beans, halved
- Juice of ½ lemon
- 2 tablespoons olive oil
- 2 garlic cloves, minced
- 2 scallions, chopped
- A pinch of salt and black pepper
- 1 tablespoon chives, chopped

Directions:
1. In a large sous vide bag, mix the pork chops with the capers, green beans and the other ingredients, seal the bag, submerge in the water bath, cook at 187 degrees F for 1 hour and 10 minutes, divide the mix between plates and serve.

Nutrition:
calories 269
fat 12
fiber 3
carbs 5
protein 16

Beef and Beets

Preparation time: 10 minutes
Cooking time: 1 hour and 35 minutes
Servings: 4
Ingredients:
- 2 tablespoons olive oil
- 2 garlic cloves, minced
- A pinch of salt and black pepper
- ½ teaspoon chili powder
- 1 tablespoon cilantro, chopped
- 2 pounds beef stew meat, cubed
- 2 beets, peeled and cut into wedges
- 1 red onion, chopped

- 2 tablespoons balsamic vinegar

Directions:

1. In a large sous vide bag, mix the beef with the beets, onion and the other ingredients, seal the bag, submerge in the water bath, cook at 180 degrees F for 1 hour and 35 minutes, divide everything between plates and serve.

Nutrition:

calories 293

fat 14

fiber 4

carbs 6

protein 18

Lamb and Broccoli

Preparation time: 10 minutes

Cooking time: 1 hour and 30 minutes

Servings: 4

Ingredients:

- 2 spring onions, chopped
- 2 pounds lamb chops
- 1 cup broccoli florets
- 2 tablespoons olive oil
- 2 tablespoons lime zest, grated
- Juice of ½ lime
- 1 tablespoon chives, chopped
- A pinch of salt and black pepper
- 1 tablespoon cilantro, chopped

Directions:

1. In a large sous vide bag, mix the lamb chops with the spring onions, broccoli and the other ingredients, seal the bag, cook in the water bath at 175 degrees F for 1 hour and 30 minutes, divide the mix between plates and serve.

Nutrition:

calories 263

fat 12

fiber 3

carbs 6

protein 13

Radish Mix and Lamb

Preparation time: 10 minutes

Cooking time: 1 hour and 30 minutes

Servings: 4

Ingredients:

- 2 spring onions, chopped
- ½ teaspoon rosemary, dried
- ¼ cup beef stock
- 2 garlic cloves, minced
- Salt and black pepper to the taste
- 2 pounds lamb shoulder, cubed
- 1 cup radishes, halved
- 2 tablespoons avocado oil
- 1 tablespoon lemon juice
- 1 tablespoon lemon zest, grated

Directions:

1. In a large sous vide bag, mix the lamb with the radishes, oil and the other ingredients, seal the

bag, cook in the water oven at 175 degrees F for 1 hour and 30 minutes, divide everything between plates and serve.

Nutrition:

calories 454

fat 26.5

fiber 0.3

carbs 1.1

protein 35.6

Citrus Lamb Mix

Preparation time: 10 minutes

Cooking time: 1 hour and 30 minutes

Servings: 6

Ingredients:

- 2 pounds lamb chops
- Juice of 1 orange
- Juice of 1 lime
- Zest of 1 orange, grated
- 1 teaspoon nutmeg, ground
- 2 spring onions, chopped
- ½ teaspoon chili powder
- 1 tablespoon olive oil
- 2 garlic cloves, minced
- A pinch of salt and black pepper
- 1 tablespoon chives, chopped

Directions:

1. In a large sous vide bag, mix the lamb chops with the orange juice, lime juice and the other ingredients, seal the bag, submerge in the water bath, cook at 180 degrees F for 1 hour and 30 minutes, divide between plates and serve with a side salad.

Nutrition:

calories 352

fat 26.5

fiber 0.3

carbs 0.7

protein 26.5

Red Onions Mix and Pork

Preparation time: 10 minutes

Cooking time: 1 hour and 30 minutes

Servings: 4

Ingredients:

- 1 teaspoon chili powder
- 2 tablespoons chives, chopped
- 2 garlic cloves, minced
- ½ cup beef stock
- A pinch of salt and black pepper
- 2 pounds pork shoulder, cubed
- 2 tablespoons olive oil
- 2 big red onions, sliced
- 2 tablespoons balsamic vinegar

Directions:

1. In a large sous vide bag, mix the pork with the oil, onions and the other ingredients, seal the bag, submerge in the water bath, cook at 180 degrees F for 1 hour and 30 minutes, divide everything between plates and serve right away.

Nutrition:
calories 373
fat 25
fiber 1.6
carbs 6.9
protein 28.8

Pork and Walnuts Mix

Preparation time: 10 minutes
Cooking time: 1 hour and 20 minutes
Servings: 4
Ingredients:
- 2 pound pork stew meat, cubed
- 2 tablespoons olive oil
- 2 tablespoons balsamic vinegar
- 1 tablespoon walnuts, chopped
- 2 tablespoons cilantro, chopped
- 1 tablespoon lime juice
- 2 garlic cloves, minced
- A pinch of salt and black pepper

Directions:
1. In a large sous vide bag, mix the pork with the oil, vinegar, and the other ingredients, seal the bag, submerge in the water bath, cook at 180 degrees F for 1 hour and 20 minutes, divide the mix between plates and serve.

Nutrition:
calories 285
fat 14.6
fiber 0.6
carbs 3.1
protein 33.9

Pumpkin Mix and Pork

Preparation time: 10 minutes
Cooking time: 1 hour and 20 minutes
Servings: 4
Ingredients:
- ½ teaspoon cumin, ground
- 2 scallions, chopped
- A pinch of salt and black pepper
- ½ cup beef stock
- 1 tablespoon cilantro, chopped
- 2 pounds pork stew meat, cubed
- 1 tablespoon olive oil
- 1 cup pumpkin, peeled and roughly cubed
- Juice of 1 lime
- ½ teaspoons garlic powder
- ½ teaspoon chili powder

Directions:
1. In a large sous vide bag, mix the pork with the oil, pumpkin and the other ingredients, seal the bag, submerge in the water bath, cook at 180 degrees F for 1 hour and 20 minutes, divide the mix between plates and serve.

Nutrition:
calories 353
fat 17.4
fiber 0.4

carbs 1.2
protein 34.2

Peppers and Avocado with Pork

Preparation time: 10 minutes
Cooking time: 1 hour and 20 minutes
Servings: 4
Ingredients:
- 1 cup beef stock
- ½ teaspoon sweet paprika
- ½ teaspoon chili powder
- 1 tablespoon avocado oil
- A pinch of salt and black pepper
- 1 tablespoon cilantro, chopped
- 2 pounds pork shoulder, cubed
- 2 spring onions, chopped
- 2 red bell peppers, cut into strips
- 1 cup avocado, peeled, pitted and halved
- ½ pound baby spinach

Directions:
1. In a large sous vide bag, mix the pork with the onions, bell peppers and the other ingredients, seal the bag, submerge in the water bath, cook at 180 degrees F for 1 hour and 20 minutes, divide the mix between plates and serve.

Nutrition:
calories 384
fat 26.5
fiber 1.8
carbs 5
protein 28.4

Beets and Radishes with Ground Beef

Preparation time: 10 minutes
Cooking time: 1 hour
Servings: 4
Ingredients:
- 2 pounds beef stew meat, ground
- 2 beets, peeled and cubed
- 1 cup radishes, sliced
- 1 teaspoon sweet paprika
- ½ teaspoon chili powder
- ½ tablespoon lemon zest, grated
- Juice of ½ lemon
- 1 tablespoon avocado oil
- A pinch of salt and black pepper
- 2 garlic cloves, minced
- 1 tablespoons chives, chopped

Directions:
1. In a sous vide bag, mix the beef with the beets, radishes and the other ingredients, seal the bag, submerge in the water bath, cook at 180 degrees F for 1 hour, divide the mix into bowls and serve.

Nutrition:
calories 367
fat 24.5
fiber 1.3
carbs 6.8
protein 28.2

Orange Pork and Veggies

Preparation time: 10 minutes
Cooking time: 1 hour and 20 minutes
Servings: 4
Ingredients:
- 1 eggplants, cubed
- 1 carrot, peeled and sliced
- 1 cup green beans, trimmed and halved
- ½ cup orange juice
- 2 tablespoons oregano, chopped
- A pinch of salt and black pepper
- 2 tablespoons avocado oil
- 2 pounds pork chops
- 1 orange, peeled and cut into segments
- 1 zucchini, cubed

Directions:
1.   In a large sous vide bag, mix the pork chops with the oil, orange and the other ingredients, seal the bag, submerge in the water bath, cook at 180 degrees F for 1 hour and 20 minutes, divide the mix between plates and serve.

Nutrition:
calories 272
fat 14.5
fiber 0.1
carbs 0.3
protein 33.3

Oregano and Chili Lamb

Preparation time: 10 minutes
Cooking time: 1 hour and 20 minutes
Servings: 4
Ingredients:
- 1 pound lamb chops
- 2 red chilies, minced
- 2 tablespoons oregano, chopped
- 2 tablespoons balsamic vinegar
- 2 tablespoons olive oil
- 1 cup beef stock
- ½ teaspoon chili powder
- 2 tablespoons chives, chopped
- A pinch of salt and black pepper

Directions:
1.   In a large sous vide bag, mix the lamb chops with the oregano, chilies and the other ingredients, seal the bag, submerge in the water bath, cook at 175 degrees F for 1 hour and 20 minutes, divide the mix between plates and serve.

Nutrition:
calories 393
fat 13
fiber 0.1
carbs 0.2
protein 27.2

Pork and Pears Mix

Preparation time: 10 minutes
Cooking time: 1 hour and 20 minutes
Servings: 4
Ingredients:
- 1 tablespoon avocado oil
- ½ teaspoon coriander, ground
- A pinch of red pepper flakes, crushed
- 1 tablespoon chives, chopped
- 1 tablespoon cilantro, chopped
- A pinch of salt and black pepper
- 2 pounds pork shoulder, cubed
- 2 pears, cored and cut into wedges
- 2 tablespoons balsamic vinegar
- ¼ cup red wine

Directions:
1.   In a large sous vide bag, mix the pork with the pears, vinegar and the other ingredients, seal the bag submerge in the water oven and cook at 178 degrees F for 1 hour and 20 minutes.
2.   Divide everything between plates and serve.

Nutrition:
calories 396
fat 26.4
fiber 2.3
carbs 5.5
protein 28.5

SOUS VIDE VEGETABLE RECIPES

Lime Artichokes

Preparation time: 5 minutes
Cooking time: 35 minutes
Servings: 4
Ingredients:
- 4 artichokes, trimmed and halved
- 1 tablespoon lime juice
- 2 tablespoons balsamic vinegar
- ½ teaspoon coriander, ground
- A pinch of salt and black pepper

Directions:
1.   In a large sous vide bag, mix the artichokes with the lime juice and the other ingredients, seal the bag, submerge in the water bath, cook at 160 degrees F for 35 minutes, divide between plates and serve.

Nutrition:
calories 56
fat 1.8
fiber 0.4
carbs 0.5
protein 5.6

Basil Green Beans

Preparation time: 10 minutes
Cooking time: 35 minutes
Servings: 4
Ingredients:
- 1 pound green beans, trimmed
- 1 tablespoon soy sauce
- 1 tablespoon butter, melted
- Juice of ½ lime
- 2 tablespoons basil, chopped
- A pinch of salt and black pepper
- A pinch of red pepper flakes
- A pinch of salt and black pepper

Directions:
1.   In a sous vide bag, mix the green beans with the soy sauce, butter and the other ingredients, seal the bag, submerge in the water bath, cook at 174 degrees F for 35 minutes, divide the between plates and serve.

Nutrition:
calories 10
fat 1.1
fiber 0.8
carbs 1.6
protein 0.6

Buttery Leeks

Preparation time: 5 minutes
Cooking time: 25 minutes
Servings: 4
Ingredients:
- 2 leeks, sliced
- 2 tablespoons lime juice
- 2 tablespoons butter, melted
- 1 tablespoon dill, chopped
- ½ teaspoon coriander, ground
- A pinch of salt and black pepper

Directions:
1.   In a sous vide bag, mix the leeks with the melted butter and the other ingredients, seal the bag, submerge in the water oven, cook at 170 degrees F for 25 minutes, divide the mix between plates and serve.

Nutrition:
calories 148
fat 7.8
fiber 2.9
carbs 5.4
protein 5.5

Green Beans and Capers

Preparation time: 5 minutes
Cooking time: 30 minutes
Servings: 4
Ingredients:
- 1 tablespoon capers, drained
- 1 tablespoon sweet paprika
- 1 tablespoon basil, chopped
- 2 garlic cloves, chopped
- 1 pound green beans, trimmed and halved
- 1 tablespoon balsamic vinegar
- ½ teaspoon chili powder
- Juice of ½ lemon

Directions:
1.   In a sous vide bag, mix the green beans with the capers, vinegar and the other ingredients, seal the bag, submerge in the water bath, cook at 164 degrees F for 30 minutes, divide the mix between plates, and serve.

Nutrition:
calories 106
fat 1.9
fiber 0.2
carbs 0.5
protein 7.8

Balsamic Tomatoes

Preparation time: 5 minutes
Cooking time: 30 minutes
Servings: 4
Ingredients:
- 1 pound cherry tomatoes, halved
- 2 tablespoons balsamic vinegar
- 2 tablespoons avocado oil
- 1 tablespoon basil, chopped
- ½ teaspoon chili powder
- ½ teaspoon sweet paprika
- A pinch of salt and black pepper
- 1 tablespoon chives, chopped

Directions:

1.   In a sous vide bag, mix the tomatoes with the vinegar, oil and the other ingredients, seal the bag, submerge in the water bath, cook at 167 degrees F for 30 minutes, divide mix between plates and serve.

Nutrition:
calories 42
fat 1.2
fiber 0.7
carbs 1
protein 3.5

Mustard Asparagus

Preparation time: 5 minutes
Cooking time: 30 minutes
Servings: 4
Ingredients:
- 1 pound asparagus, trimmed
- 2 tablespoons avocado oil
- 2 tablespoons mustard
- 2 tablespoons lime juice
- A pinch of salt and black pepper
- 1 teaspoon garlic powder
- 1 tablespoon basil, chopped

Directions:
1.   In a sous vide bag, mix the asparagus with the oil, mustard and the other ingredients, seal the bag, submerge in the water bath, cook at 170 degrees F for 30 minutes, divide between plates and serve.

Nutrition:
calories 102
fat 7.5
fiber 3
carbs 6.1
protein 3.4

Corn and Green Beans

Preparation time: 5 minutes
Cooking time: 30 minutes
Servings: 4
Ingredients:
- 1 tablespoon balsamic vinegar
- Juice of ½ lime
- 2 tablespoons oregano, chopped
- A pinch of salt and black pepper
- ½ cup chicken stock
- 1 pound green beans, trimmed and halved
- 1 cup corn

Directions:
1.   In a sous vide bag, mix the green beans with the corn, vinegar and the other ingredients, seal the bag, cook in the water bath at 165 degrees F for 30 minutes, divide everything between plates and serve.

Nutrition:
calories 121
fat 11.5
fiber 1.8
carbs 4.1
protein 1.9

Balsamic Radishes

Preparation time: 5 minutes
Cooking time: 30 minutes
Servings: 4
Ingredients:
- 1 pound radishes, halved
- 2 tablespoons balsamic vinegar
- ½ teaspoon garam masala
- ½ cup chicken stock
- 1 tablespoon chives, chopped
- 1 teaspoon chili powder

Directions:
1.   In a sous vide bag, mix the radishes with the vinegar, masala and the other ingredients, seal the bag, submerge in the water bath, cook at 165 degrees F for 30 minutes, divide the mix between plates and serve.

Nutrition:
calories 45
fat 0.6
fiber 0.1
carbs 0.4
protein 2

Parsley Artichokes

Preparation time: 5 minutes
Cooking time: 30 minutes
Servings: 4
Ingredients:
- 1 teaspoon chili powder
- A pinch of salt and black pepper
- 1 tablespoon parsley, chopped
- 4 artichokes, trimmed and halved
- 2 teaspoons lemon zest, grated
- 1 tablespoon lemon juice

Directions:
1.   In a sous vide bag, mix the artichokes with the lemon juice and the other ingredients, seal the bag, submerge in the water bath, cook at 170 degrees F for 30 minutes, divide the mix between plates, and serve.

Nutrition:
calories 82
fat 2.5
fiber 1.9
carbs 2.1
protein 5.6

Balsamic Zucchini Mix

Preparation time: 10 minutes
Cooking time: 30 minutes
Servings: 4
Ingredients:
- 2 garlic cloves, minced
- 1 tablespoon dill, chopped
- ½ teaspoon chili powder
- 1 pound zucchinis, roughly cubed
- 2 tablespoons balsamic vinegar
- 1 tablespoon capers, drained

* A pinch of salt and black pepper

Directions:
1. In a sous vide bag, mix the zucchinis with the vinegar and the other ingredients, seal the bag, cook in the water bath at 165 degrees F for 30 minutes, divide everything between plates and serve.

Nutrition:
calories 46
fat 1.7
fiber 0.1
carbs 0.6
protein 2.7

Garlic Brussels Sprouts

Preparation time: 10 minutes
Cooking time: 35 minutes
Servings: 4
Ingredients:
* 1 pound Brussels sprouts, trimmed and halved
* Juice of 1 lemon
* 3 garlic cloves, minced
* ½ teaspoon coriander, ground
* ½ teaspoon sweet paprika
* A pinch of salt and black pepper
* 1 tablespoon rosemary, chopped

Directions:
1. In a sous vide bag, mix the sprouts with the lemon juice, garlic and the other ingredients, seal the bag, cook in the water bath at 167 degrees F for 35 minutes, divide the mix between plates and serve.

Nutrition:
calories 71
fat 2.1
fiber 1.1
carbs 1.3
protein 4.4

Creamy Bell Peppers

Preparation time: 10 minutes
Cooking time: 30 minutes
Servings: 4
Ingredients:
* ½ teaspoon coriander, ground
* 1 tablespoon lime juice
* 1 tablespoon chives, chopped
* 1 pound red bell peppers, cut into wedges
* 1 cup heavy cream
* 1 teaspoon turmeric powder

Directions:
1. In a sous vide bag, mix the peppers with the cream, turmeric and the other ingredients, seal the bag, submerge in the water bath, cook at 180 degrees F fro 30 minutes, divide the mix between plates and serve.

Nutrition:
calories 70
fat 1.8
fiber 1.1

carbs 1.4
protein 0.6

Cayenne Broccoli

Preparation time: 5 minutes
Cooking time: 25 minutes
Servings: 4
Ingredients:
* 1 pound broccoli florets
* ½ cup chicken stock
* Juice of 1 lime
* A pinch of cayenne pepper
* A pinch of salt and black pepper
* 1 tablespoon chives, chopped

Directions:
1. In a sous vide bag, mix the broccoli with the lime juice, cayenne and the other ingredients, seal the bag, submerge in the water bath, cook at 165 degrees F for 25 minutes, divide the mix between plates and serve.

Nutrition:
calories 63
fat 5.7
fiber 0.4
carbs 2.8
protein 0.7

Nutmeg Brussels Sprouts

Preparation time: 5 minutes
Cooking time: 35 minutes
Servings: 4
Ingredients:
* 1 pound Brussels sprouts, halved
* 2 tablespoons balsamic vinegar
* 2 tablespoons olive oil
* 1 teaspoon nutmeg, ground
* 1 tablespoon chives, chopped

Directions:
1. In a sous vide bag, mix the sprouts with the oil and the other ingredients, seal the bag, cook in the water oven at 165 degrees F for 35 minutes, divide the mix between plates and serve.

Nutrition:
calories 68
fat 4.2
fiber 2.3
carbs 3.4
protein 2.4

Garlic Kale

Preparation time: 5 minutes
Cooking time: 20 minutes
Servings: 4
Ingredients:
* 1 pound baby kale
* A pinch of salt and black pepper
* 1 teaspoon sweet paprika
* 1 teaspoon chives, chopped
* 3 garlic cloves, minced

- 2 tablespoons olive oil

Directions:
1. In a sous vide bag, mix the kale with the garlic, oil and the other ingredients, seal the bag, submerge in the water oven, cook at 160 degrees F for 20 minutes, divide the mix between plates and serve.

Nutrition:
calories 32
fat 3.4
fiber 2.3
carbs 2.9
protein 2.3

Chives Radish

Preparation time: 10 minutes
Cooking time: 25 minutes
Servings: 4
Ingredients:
- 1 pound radishes, sliced
- 1 tablespoon olive oil
- 1 tablespoon lime juice
- 1 teaspoon chili powder
- A pinch of salt and black pepper
- 1 tablespoon chives, minced

Directions:
1. In a sous vide bag, mix the radishes with the oil, lime juice and the other ingredients, seal the bag, cook in the water oven at 165 degrees F for 25 minutes, divide mix between plates and serve.

Nutrition:
calories 38
fat 1.5
fiber 0.2
carbs 0.4
protein 2.5

Dill Tomatoes

Preparation time: 10 minutes
Cooking time: 20 minutes
Servings: 4
Ingredients:
- 2 pounds tomatoes, cut into wedges
- 1 tablespoon lemon zest, grated
- A pinch of salt and black pepper
- 1 tablespoon dill, chopped
- 1 teaspoon rosemary, dried
- 1 teaspoon chili powder

Directions:
1. In a sous vide bag, mix the tomatoes with the lemon zest and the other ingredients, seal the bag, submerge in the water oven, cook at 170 degrees F for 20 minutes, divide the mix between plates and serve.

Nutrition:
calories 161
fat 10.1
fiber 3.1
carbs 4.5

protein 9.6

Green Beans Sauté

Preparation time: 10 minutes
Cooking time: 25 minutes
Servings: 4
Ingredients:
- ½ teaspoon coriander, ground
- A pinch of salt and black pepper
- 2 tablespoons garlic, minced
- 1 tablespoon dill, chopped
- 1 pound green beans, trimmed
- 1 tablespoon soy sauce
- 2 tablespoons olive oil
- 2 spring onions, chopped

Directions:
1. In a sous vide bag, mix the green beans with the soy sauce, oil and the other ingredients, seal the bag, cook in the water oven at 165 degrees F for 25 minutes, divide the mix between plates and serve.

Nutrition:
calories 165
fat 14.5
fiber 2.8
carbs 6.4
protein 2.7

Garlic Spinach

Preparation time: 10 minutes
Cooking time: 15 minutes
Servings: 4
Ingredients:
- 1 pound baby spinach
- Juice of 1 lime
- 1 tablespoon olive oil
- 4 garlic cloves, minced
- A pinch of salt and black pepper
- 1 teaspoon chili powder

Directions:
1. In a sous vide bag, mix the spinach with the lime juice and the other ingredients, seal the bag, cook in the water bath at 160 degrees F for 15 minutes, divide the mix between plates and serve.

Nutrition:
calories 95
fat 3.7
fiber 1.9
carbs 2.4
protein 3.8

Creamy Zucchini

Preparation time: 10 minutes
Cooking time: 25 minutes
Servings: 4
Ingredients:
- A pinch of salt and black pepper
- 1 cup heavy cream
- ½ teaspoon rosemary, dried
- 1 tablespoon dill, chopped

- 2 tablespoons rosemary, chopped
- 1 pound zucchinis, cut into wedges
- 2 tablespoons lime juice
- 1 tablespoon olive oil

Directions:

1. In a sous vide bag, mix the zucchinis with the rosemary and the other ingredients, seal the bag, submerge in the water bath, cook at 160 degrees F for 25 minutes, divide the mix between plates and serve.

Nutrition:

calories 181

fat 11.8

fiber 4.2

carbs 5.9

protein 3.6

Spicy Eggplant

Preparation time: 10 minutes

Cooking time: 25 minutes

Servings: 4

Ingredients:

- 1 pound eggplants, sliced
- ¼ cup lemon juice
- 2 tablespoons olive oil
- ½ teaspoon hot paprika
- 1 red chili pepper, minced
- 1 tablespoon chili powder
- A pinch of salt and black pepper

Directions:

1. In a large sous vide bag, mix the eggplants with the lemon juice, oil and the other ingredients, seal the bag, submerge in the water bath, cook at 170 degrees F for 25 minutes, divide the mix between plates and serve.

Nutrition:

calories 65

fat 1.5

fiber 0.3

carbs 0.9

protein 2.8

Pesto Tomato Mix

Preparation time: 10 minutes

Cooking time: 20 minutes

Servings: 4

Ingredients:

- 1 pound cherry tomatoes, halved
- 2 tablespoons olive oil
- 2 tablespoons basil pesto
- ½ teaspoon sweet paprika
- 1 teaspoon garlic, minced
- A pinch of salt and black pepper
- 1 tablespoon chives, chopped

Directions:

1. In a sous vide bag, mix the tomatoes with the pesto, oil and the other ingredients, seal the bag, cook in the water bath at 167 degrees F for 20 minutes, divide the mix between plates and serve.

Nutrition:

calories 25

fat 1.9

fiber 0.5

carbs 1.4

protein 1.4

Cabbage Sauté

Preparation time: 10 minutes

Cooking time: 25 minutes

Servings: 4

Ingredients:

- 2 tablespoons olive oil
- 1 teaspoon sweet paprika
- A pinch of salt and black pepper
- ¼ cup chicken stock
- 1 tablespoon dill, chopped
- 1 pound red cabbage, shredded
- 1 tablespoon lime juice

Directions:

1. In a sous vide bag, mix the cabbage with the lime juice, oil and the other ingredients, seal the bag, cook in the water bath at 170 degrees F for 25 minutes, divide the mix between plates and serve.

Nutrition:

calories 36

fat 1.4

fiber 0.2

carbs 0.4

protein 2

Tomato Mix and Zucchini

Preparation time: 10 minutes

Cooking time: 30 minutes

Servings: 4

Ingredients:

- 2 tablespoons balsamic vinegar
- A pinch of salt and black pepper
- 2 tablespoons parsley, chopped
- 2 cups zucchinis, sliced
- 1 cup cherry tomatoes, halved
- 2 tablespoons olive oil

Directions:

1. In a sous vide bag, mix the zucchinis with the tomatoes and the other ingredients, seal the bag, submerge in the water bath, cook at 160 degrees F for 30 minutes, divide the mix between plates and serve.

Nutrition:

calories 41

fat 1.2

fiber 0.2

carbs 0.6

protein 2.4

Paprika Okra

Preparation time: 10 minutes

Cooking time: 25 minutes

Servings: 4

Ingredients:
- 1 tablespoon lemon juice
- A pinch of salt and black pepper
- 1 tablespoon balsamic vinegar
- 1 tablespoon chives, chopped
- 2 cups okra
- 1 teaspoon sweet paprika
- 1 tablespoon olive oil

Directions:
1. In a sous vide bag, mix the okra with the lemon juice, paprika and the other ingredients, seal the bag, cook in the water bath at 160 degrees F for 25 minutes, divide the mix between plates and serve.

Nutrition:
calories 26
fat 1.2
fiber 0.2
carbs 0.7
protein 1.4

Chili Collard Greens

Preparation time: 10 minutes
Cooking time: 20 minutes
Servings: 4
Ingredients:
- 1 red chili pepper, minced
- 2 tablespoons olive oil
- 1 tablespoon sweet paprika
- A pinch of salt and black pepper
- 1 tablespoon cilantro, chopped
- 1 pound collard greens, trimmed
- 2 tablespoons balsamic vinegar
- ½ teaspoon chili powder

Directions:
1. In a sous vide bag, mix the collard greens with the vinegar, chili powder and the other ingredients, seal the bag, cook in the water bath at 160 degrees F for 20 minutes, divide the mix between plates and serve.

Nutrition:
calories 151
fat 12.2
fiber 4.3
carbs 6.8
protein 4

Radish Mix and Beet

Preparation time: 10 minutes
Cooking time: 35 minutes
Servings: 4
Ingredients:
- 1 pound radishes, halved
- ½ pound beets, peeled and cut into wedges
- 2 tablespoons olive oil
- 2 tablespoons balsamic vinegar
- 1 tablespoon chives, chopped
- A pinch of salt and black pepper

Directions:
1. In a sous vide bag, mix the radishes with the beets, oil and the rest of the ingredients, seal the bag, cook in the water oven at 167 degrees F for 35 minutes, divide the mix between plates and serve.

Nutrition:
calories 61
fat 1.3
fiber 0.8
carbs 1
protein 3.2

Cilantro Hot Artichokes

Preparation time: 10 minutes
Cooking time: 30 minutes
Servings: 4
Ingredients:
- 2 tablespoons olive oil
- 2 tablespoons balsamic vinegar
- A pinch of red pepper flakes, crushed
- A pinch of salt and black pepper
- ½ cup canned artichoke hearts, drained and chopped
- 2 red chilies, minced
- ½ teaspoon hot paprika
- 1 tablespoon cilantro, chopped

Directions:
1. In a large sous vide bag, mix the artichoke hearts with the chilies and the other ingredients, seal the bag, cook in the water bath at 170 degrees F for 30 minutes, divide the mix between plates and serve.

Nutrition:
calories 141
fat 1.5
fiber 0.2
carbs 1.2
protein 7.3

Dill Endives

Preparation time: 10 minutes
Cooking time: 25 minutes
Servings: 4
Ingredients:
- A pinch of salt and black pepper
- 1 tablespoon dill, chopped
- ½ teaspoon cumin, ground
- ½ teaspoon coriander, ground
- 2 endives, halved
- 2 tablespoons olive oil
- 2 tablespoons lime juice

Directions:
1. In a sous vide bag, mix the endives with the oil, lime juice and the other ingredients, seal the bag, cook in the water bath at 170 degrees F for 25 minutes, divide the mix between plates and serve.

Nutrition:
calories 96
fat 1.4
fiber 0.8
carbs 1

protein 5.6

Lime Fennel

Preparation time: 10 minutes
Cooking time: 25 minutes
Servings: 4
Ingredients:
- A pinch of salt and black pepper
- 1 teaspoon chili powder
- 1 tablespoon rosemary, chopped
- 2 fennel bulbs, sliced
- Juice of 1 lime
- 1 tablespoon lime zest, grated
- 2 tablespoons avocado oil
- ½ teaspoon coriander, ground

Directions:
1.   In a sous vide bag, mix the fennel with the lime juice, zest and the other ingredients, seal the bag, cook in the water bath at 167 degrees F for 25 minutes, divide the mix between plates and serve.

Nutrition:
calories 41
fat 1.4
fiber 0.1
carbs 0.5
protein 2.3

Paprika Olives Mix

Preparation time: 10 minutes
Cooking time: 15 minutes
Servings: 4
Ingredients:
- 2 cups kalamata olives, pitted
- A pinch of salt and black pepper
- 2 tablespoons olive oil
- ½ teaspoon sweet paprika
- ½ teaspoon rosemary, dried
- Juice of 1 lime
- 2 tablespoons parsley, chopped

Directions:
1.   In a sous vide bag, mix the olives with the oil, paprika and the other ingredients, seal the bag, cook in the water bath at 165 degrees F for 15 minutes, divide the mix between plates and serve.

Nutrition:
calories 64
fat 4
fiber 2.8
carbs 3
protein 1.4

Olives and Tomatoes

Preparation time: 10 minutes
Cooking time: 30 minutes
Servings: 4
Ingredients:
- 2 tablespoons avocado oil
- 1 tablespoon lemon juice
- 2 spring onions, chopped

- A pinch of salt and black pepper
- 1 tablespoon chives, chopped
- 1 cup black olives, pitted and halved
- 1 cup green olives, pitted and halved
- 1 pound cherry tomatoes, halved

Directions:
1.   In a sous vide bag, mix the olives with the tomatoes, oil and the other ingredients, seal the bag, cook in the water bath at 165 degrees F for 30 minutes, divide the mix between plates and serve.

Nutrition:
calories 99
fat 3.7
fiber 2.3
carbs 3
protein 4

Eggplant and Okra Mix

Preparation time: 5 minutes
Cooking time: 25 minutes
Servings: 4
Ingredients:
- Juice of ½ lemon
- 2 garlic cloves, minced
- A pinch of salt and black pepper
- 1 tablespoon chives, chopped
- 1 teaspoon cumin, ground
- 1 pound eggplants, peeled and cubed
- 1 cup okra, sliced
- 2 tablespoons avocado oil
- ½ teaspoon turmeric powder
- ½ teaspoon sweet paprika

Directions:
1.   In a sous vide bag, mix the eggplant with the okra, oil and the other ingredients, seal the bag, cook in the water bath at 165 degrees F for 25 minutes, divide the mix between plates and serve.

Nutrition:
calories 94
fat 1.5
fiber 0.4
carbs 1
protein 4.5

Beets and Olives

Preparation time: 10 minutes
Cooking time: 35 minutes
Servings: 4
Ingredients:
- 1 pound beets, peeled and cubed
- 1 cup kalamata olives, pitted and halved
- 1 cup black olives, pitted and halved
- 1 teaspoon coriander, ground
- ½ teaspoon hot paprika
- 1 tablespoon avocado oil
- 1 shallot, minced
- A pinch of salt and black pepper
- ¼ cup chicken stock

Directions:

1.	In a sous vide bag, mix the beets with the olives, coriander and the other ingredients, seal the bag, cook in the water bath at 170 degrees F for 35 minutes, divide the mix between plates and serve.

Nutrition:
calories 83
fat 4.4
fiber 2.3
carbs 3.4
protein 2

Lemon Bok Choy

Preparation time: 10 minutes
Cooking time: 20 minutes
Servings: 4
Ingredients:
- ½ teaspoon sweet paprika
- A pinch of salt and black pepper
- ¼ cup lemon juice
- 1 tablespoon chives, chopped
- 1 pound bok choy, roughly torn
- 2 tablespoons balsamic vinegar
- 1 tablespoon olive oil

Directions:
1.	In a sous vide bag, mix the bok choy with the vinegar, oil and the other ingredients, seal the bag, cook in the water bath at 170 degrees F for 20 minutes, divide the mix between plates and serve.

Nutrition:
calories 34
fat 1
fiber 0.2
carbs 0.5
protein 1.3

Ginger Bok Choy Mix

Preparation time: 10 minutes
Cooking time: 20 minutes
Servings: 4
Ingredients:
- 2 tablespoons olive oil
- 1 tablespoon ginger, grated
- 1 tablespoon chives, chopped
- 1 pound bok choy, torn
- 1 cup cherry tomatoes, halved
- 2 tablespoons lime juice

Directions:
1.	In a sous vide bag, mix the bok choy with the tomatoes and the other ingredients, seal the bag, cook in the water bath at 160 degrees F for 20 minutes, divide the mix between plates and serve.

Nutrition:
calories 62
fat 4.1
fiber 2.3
carbs 3
protein 2.5

Spicy Cabbage with Kale

Preparation time: 10 minutes
Cooking time: 30 minutes
Servings: 4
Ingredients:
- ½ teaspoon hot paprika
- ½ teaspoon chili powder
- 2 garlic cloves, chopped
- 1 tablespoon olive oil
- 1 tablespoon cilantro, chopped
- 1 pound red cabbage, shredded
- 2 cups baby kale
- Juice of 1 lime

Directions:
1.	In a sous vide bag, mix the cabbage with the kale, lime juice and the other ingredients, seal the bag, cook in the water bath at 165 degrees F for 30 minutes,, divide the mix between plates and serve.

Nutrition:
calories 63
fat 3.5
fiber 2
carbs 3.1
protein 2

Mint Eggplant

Preparation time: 10 minutes
Cooking time: 20 minutes
Servings: 4
Ingredients:
- Juice of 1 lime
- 1 tablespoon mint, chopped
- 2 spring onions, chopped
- A pinch of salt and black pepper
- 1 pound eggplants, roughly cubed
- 2 tablespoons olive oil
- ½ teaspoon sweet paprika

Directions:
1.	In a sous vide bag, mix the eggplants with the mint, oil and the other ingredients, seal the bag, cook in the water bath at 175 degrees F for 20 minutes, divide the mix into bowls and serve.

Nutrition:
calories 76
fat 3.7
fiber 0.5
carbs 1.2
protein 0.5

Broccoli and Tomatoes

Preparation time: 10 minutes
Cooking time: 30 minutes
Servings: 4
Ingredients:
- 1 pound broccoli florets
- ½ pound cherry tomatoes, halved
- 1 teaspoon sweet paprika
- 1 tablespoon olive oil
- 2 shallots, chopped
- A pinch of salt and black pepper

Directions:
1.   In a sous vide bag, mix the broccoli with the tomatoes and the other ingredients, seal the bag, coo in the water oven at 164 degrees F for 30 minutes, divide between plates and serve.
Nutrition:
calories 81
fat 4.2
fiber 2.3
carbs 3.5
protein 3.8

Balsamic Pearl Onions

Preparation time: 10 minutes
Cooking time: 20 minutes
Servings: 4
Ingredients:
- 1 pound pearl onions, peeled
- 1 tablespoon balsamic vinegar
- A pinch of salt and black pepper
- ¼ teaspoon red pepper flakes
- 1 tablespoon chives, chopped
- 4 garlic cloves, chopped
- Juice of ½ lime

Directions:
1.   In a sous vide bag, mix the pearl onions with the garlic, lime juice and the other ingredients, seal the bag, cook in the water oven at 165 degrees F for 20 minutes, divide the mix between plates and serve.
Nutrition:
calories 34
fat 1.2
fiber 0.4
carbs 0.4
protein 2.5

Coconut Cabbage

Preparation time: 10 minutes
Cooking time: 30 minutes
Servings: 4
Ingredients:
- 1 teaspoon rosemary, dried
- A pinch of salt and black pepper
- 2 tablespoons cilantro, chopped
- ½ cup coconut cream
- Juice of ½ lime
- 1 pound red cabbage, cut into wedges
- 2 tablespoons balsamic vinegar

Directions:
1.   In a large sous vide bag, mix the cabbage with the cream, lime juice and the other ingredients, seal the bag, cook in the water oven at 170 degrees F for 30 minutes, divide the mix between plates and serve.
Nutrition:
calories 118
fat 6.8
fiber 2.9

carbs 5.1
protein 1.5

Turmeric Brussels Sprouts

Preparation time: 10 minutes
Cooking time: 30 minutes
Servings: 4
Ingredients:
- ½ cup chicken stock
- A pinch of salt and black pepper
- 2 tablespoons ghee, melted
- 2 tablespoons chives, chopped
- 2 pounds Brussels sprouts, halved
- 1 teaspoon turmeric powder
- Zest of 1 lime, grated

Directions:
1.   In a sous vide bag, mix the sprouts with the turmeric, lime zest and the other ingredients, seal the bag, cook in the water bath at 170 degrees F for 30 minutes, divide between plates and serve.
Nutrition:
calories 166
fat 7.3
fiber 3.4
carbs 4.4
protein 7.8

Lemon Cauliflower

Preparation time: 5 minutes
Cooking time: 30 minutes
Servings: 4
Ingredients:
- 2 pounds cauliflower florets
- 2 tablespoons soy sauce
- 1 tablespoon olive oil
- 1 tablespoon lemon juice
- 1 tablespoon lemon zest, grated
- ½ cup chicken stock
- A pinch of salt and black pepper

Directions:
1.   In a large sous vide bag, mix the cauliflower with the soy sauce, oil and the other ingredients, seal the bag, cook in the water bath at 170 degrees F for 30 minutes, divide the mix between plates and serve.
Nutrition:
calories 81
fat 1.2
fiber 0.5
carbs 1
protein 6.5

Bok Choy and Cauliflower Mix

Preparation time: 5 minutes
Cooking time: 35 minutes
Servings: 4
Ingredients:
- ½ teaspoon cumin, ground
- ½ teaspoon garlic powder
- ½ teaspoon sweet paprika

- ½ cup chicken stock
- 2 tablespoons chives, chopped
- 1 tablespoon tomato sauce
- 2 cups bok choy, torn
- 2 cups cauliflower florets
- 1 tablespoon olive oil

Directions:

1.	In a sous vide bag, mix the bok choy with the cauliflower, oil and the other ingredients, seal the bag, submerge in the water bath, cook at 174 degrees F for 35 minutes, divide the mix between plates and serve.

Nutrition:
calories 24
fat 1.6
fiber 0.6
carbs 1
protein 2.5

Nutmeg Fennel and Tomatoes

Preparation time: 5 minutes
Cooking time: 35 minutes
Servings: 4
Ingredients:

- 2 tablespoons olive oil
- 1 tablespoon soy sauce
- 2 tablespoons lemon juice
- ¼ cup veggie stock
- A pinch of salt and black pepper
- 2 fennel bulbs, sliced
- 1 pound cherry tomatoes, halved
- ½ teaspoon nutmeg, ground

Directions:

1.	In a sous vide bag, mix the fennel with the cherry tomatoes, nutmeg and the other ingredients, seal the bag, cook in the water oven at 170 degrees F for 35 minutes, divide the mix between plates and serve.

Nutrition:
calories 243
fat 20.4
fiber 4.3
carbs 5.7
protein 4.2

Avocado Mix and Green Beans

Preparation time: 10 minutes
Cooking time: 25 minutes
Servings: 4
Ingredients:

- 1 pound green beans, trimmed
- 1 cup avocado, peeled, pitted and cubed
- 1 tablespoon olive oil
- Juice of 1 lime
- 1 green onion, sliced
- 1 tablespoon mint, chopped
- A pinch of salt and black pepper
- 1 tablespoon chives, chopped

Directions:

1.	In a sous vide bag, mix the green beans with the avocado, oil and the other ingredients, seal the bag, submerge in the water oven and cook at 170 degrees F for 25 minutes.
2.	Divide the mix between plates and serve.

Nutrition:
calories 40
fat 1.2
fiber 0.4
carbs 0.6
protein 2.4

Green Beans and Pine Nuts Mix

Preparation time: 10 minutes
Cooking time: 25 minutes
Servings: 4
Ingredients:

- 2 tablespoons olive oil
- A pinch of salt and black pepper
- 2 tablespoons almonds, chopped
- 1 tablespoon chives, chopped
- ¼ cup chicken stock
- 1 pound green beans, trimmed
- 2 tablespoons pine nuts, toasted
- 1 tablespoon balsamic vinegar

Directions:

1.	In a sous vide bag, mix the green beans with the pine nuts, vinegar and the other ingredients, seal the bag, submerge in the water bath, cook at 170 degrees F for 25 minutes, divide the mix between plates and serve.

Nutrition:
calories 56
fat 1.7
fiber 0.5
carbs 1
protein 2.9

Mustard Roasted Peppers

Preparation time: 10 minutes
Cooking time: 30 minutes
Servings: 4
Ingredients:

- 2 tablespoons olive oil
- 1 tablespoon balsamic vinegar
- 2 garlic cloves, minced
- A pinch of salt and black pepper
- ¼ cup chicken stock
- 1 bunch parsley, chopped
- 2 cups roasted red peppers, cut into strips
- 2 tablespoons mustard

Directions:

1.	In a large sous vide bag, mix the peppers with the mustard, oil and the other ingredients, seal the bag, cook in the water bath at 166 degrees F for 30 minutes, divide the mix between plates and serve.

Nutrition:
calories 25
fat 1

fiber 0.1
carbs 0.5
protein 1

Green Beans and Peppers

Preparation time: 10 minutes
Cooking time: 35 minutes
Servings: 4
Ingredients:
- 2 red bell peppers, cut into wedges
- 1 pound green beans, trimmed and halved
- 2 tablespoons soy sauce
- Juice of ½ lime
- A pinch of salt and black pepper
- 2 garlic cloves, minced
- 1 cup black olives, pitted and halved

Directions:
1. In a sous vide bag, mix the peppers with the green beans, soy sauce and the other ingredients, seal the bag, submerge in the water bath, cook at 180 degrees F for 35 minutes, divide the mix between plates and serve.

Nutrition:
calories 70
fat 3.9
fiber 2.8
carbs 3.2
protein 1.6

Lemon Okra

Preparation time: 10 minutes
Cooking time: 35 minutes
Servings: 4
Ingredients:
- 1 tablespoon olive oil
- A pinch of salt and black pepper
- 1 cup canned tomatoes, crushed
- 1 bunch parsley, chopped
- 2 garlic cloves, crushed
- 2 cups okra
- Juice of 1 lemon
- 2 tablespoons balsamic vinegar

Directions:
1. In a sous vide bag, mix the okra with the lemon juice, vinegar and the other ingredients, seal the bag, cook in the water oven at 160 degrees F for 35 minutes, divide the mix between plates and serve.

Nutrition:
calories 94
fat 1.4
fiber 0.2
carbs 0.6
protein 5.3

Spring Onions and Ginger Radish

Preparation time: 10 minutes
Cooking time: 30 minutes
Servings: 4
Ingredients:
- 1 pound radishes, halved
- 4 spring onions, chopped
- 2 tablespoons balsamic vinegar
- Juice of ½ lime
- 3 garlic cloves, minced
- 1 tablespoon olive oil
- ½ inch ginger, grated
- 1 tablespoon chives, chopped

Directions:
1. In a large sous vide bag, mix the radishes with the spring onions, vinegar and the other ingredients, seal the bag, submerge in the water bath, cook at 165 degrees F for 30 minutes, divide the mix between plates and serve as a side dish.

Nutrition:
calories 83
fat 4.4
fiber 2.1
carbs 3.3
protein 2.6

Broccoli and Zucchini Mix

Preparation time: 10 minutes
Cooking time: 30 minutes
Servings: 4
Ingredients:
- 1 pound zucchinis, roughly cubed
- ½ teaspoon sweet paprika
- ¼ cup chicken stock
- A pinch of salt and black pepper
- 2 tablespoons olive oil
- 1 tablespoon chives, chopped
- 2 cups broccoli florets
- 2 tablespoons balsamic vinegar

Directions:
1. Divide the zucchinis, broccoli, vinegar and the other ingredients, into sous vide bags, seal them, submerge in the preheated water bath, cook at 170 degrees F for 30 minutes, divide the mix between plates and serve.

Nutrition:
calories 112,
fat 7.5
fiber 2.4
carbs 4.5
protein 4

Broccoli and Rice

Preparation time: 10 minutes
Cooking time: 45 minutes
Servings: 4
Ingredients:
- 1 tablespoon olive oil
- ½ teaspoon sweet paprika
- ½ teaspoon rosemary, dried
- Juice of ½ lime
- 2 shallots, chopped
- A pinch of salt and black pepper
- 1 tablespoon cilantro, chopped

- 1 cup wild rice
- 1 cup chicken stock
- 1 cup broccoli florets

Directions:

1. In a large sous vide bag, mix the rice with the stock and the other ingredients, seal the bag, submerge in the water bath, cook at 170 degrees F for 45 minutes, divide the mix between plates and serve.

Nutrition:
calories 149
fat 12.1
fiber 3
carbs 7.8
protein 5.2

Coconut Broccoli Mix

Preparation time: 10 minutes
Cooking time: 35 minutes
Servings: 4
Ingredients:

- 2 tablespoons avocado oil
- 1 pound broccoli florets
- 3 garlic cloves, minced
- ½ cup coconut cream
- Zest of 1 lime, grated
- 1 tablespoon dill, chopped
- A pinch of salt and black pepper

Directions:

1. In a sous vide bag, mix the broccoli with the oil, garlic and the other ingredients, seal the bag, cook in the water bath at 170 degrees F for 35 minutes, divide the mix between plates and serve.

Nutrition:
calories 170
fat 14
fiber 3.8
carbs 6.5
protein 4.3

Balsamic Mushroom Mix

Preparation time: 10 minutes
Cooking time: 30 minutes
Servings: 4
Ingredients:

- 1 tablespoon lime juice
- ½ teaspoon rosemary, dried
- ½ teaspoon garam masala
- A pinch of salt and black pepper
- ¼ cup chicken stock
- 1 tablespoon dill, chopped
- 2 tablespoons olive oil
- 1 pound brown mushrooms, halved
- 1 tablespoon soy sauce

Directions:

1. In a large sous vide bag, mix the mushrooms with the oil, soy sauce and the other ingredients, seal the bag, cook in the water bath at

175 degrees F for 30 minutes, divide the mix between plates and serve.

Nutrition:
calories 41
fat 4.3
fiber 1.9
carbs 3.5
protein 3.9

Tomatoes Sauté and Mushroom

Preparation time: 10 minutes
Cooking time: 35 minutes
Servings: 4
Ingredients:

- ½ teaspoon chili powder
- 2 spring onions, chopped
- A pinch of salt and black pepper
- 1 tablespoon chives, chopped
- 2 tablespoons olive oil
- 1 pound cherry tomatoes, halved
- ½ pound mushrooms, halved
- ¼ cup red wine
- ½ teaspoon rosemary, dried
- ½ teaspoon coriander, ground

Directions:

1. In a sous vide bag, mix the tomatoes with the mushrooms, oil and the other ingredients, seal the bag, submerge in the water bath, cook at 170 degrees F for 35 minutes, divide the mix between plates and serve.

Nutrition:
calories 60
fat 4.6
fiber 1.4
carbs 3.2
protein 3.6

Radish Mix and Balsamic Walnuts

Preparation time: 5 minutes
Cooking time: 35 minutes
Servings: 4
Ingredients:

- ½ teaspoon sweet paprika
- A pinch of salt and black pepper
- 1 tablespoon balsamic vinegar
- 1 tablespoon chives, chopped
- ¼ cup walnuts
- 1 pound radishes, halved
- 2 tablespoons olive oil

Directions:

1. In a sous vide bag, mix the radishes with the walnuts, oil and the other ingredients, seal the bag, submerge in the water bath, cook at 170 degrees F for 35 minutes, divide the mix between plates and serve.

Nutrition:
calories 13
fat 1.2
fiber 0.2

carbs 0.3
protein 0.5

Mushrooms and Paprika Avocado

Preparation time: 10 minutes
Cooking time: 30 minutes
Servings: 4
Ingredients:
- 1 pound white mushrooms, halved
- 1 cup avocado, peeled, pitted and cubed
- ½ cup black olives, pitted and halved
- Juice of 1 lime
- ½ teaspoon sweet paprika
- A pinch of salt and black pepper
- ¼ cup veggie stock
- 1 tablespoon rosemary, chopped
- 1 tablespoon avocado oil

Directions:
1. In a sous vide bag, mix the mushrooms with the avocado, olives and the other ingredients, seal the bag, submerge in the water bath, cook at 170 degrees F for 30 minutes, divide the mix between plates and serve.

Nutrition:
calories 14
fat 2.3
fiber 1.3
carbs 2.1
protein 0.5

Coconut Tomatoes and Spinach

Preparation time: 10 minutes
Cooking time: 30 minutes
Servings: 4
Ingredients:
- 1 tablespoon avocado oil
- ¼ cup coconut cream
- 1 teaspoon chili powder
- A pinch of salt and black pepper
- 1 tablespoon chives, chopped
- 1 pound baby spinach
- ½ pound cherry tomatoes, halved
- ½ cup coconut flesh, unsweetened and shredded

Directions:
1. In a sous vide bag, mix the spinach with the tomatoes, coconut and the other ingredients, seal the bag, cook in the water bath at 165 degrees F for 30 minutes, divide the mix between plates and serve.

Nutrition:
calories 41
fat 3.9
fiber 1
carbs 1.9
protein 0.6

Radishes and Chili Okra

Preparation time: 10 minutes
Cooking time: 30 minutes
Servings: 4
Ingredients:
- 2 tablespoons balsamic vinegar
- 2 tablespoons avocado oil
- 2 teaspoons chili paste
- 1 tablespoon cilantro, chopped
- 1 pound radishes, halved
- 2 cups okra, sliced
- 1 cup cherry tomatoes, halved

Directions:
1. In a large sous vide bag, mix the radishes with the okra, tomatoes and the other ingredients, seal the bag, submerge in the water bath, cook at 175 degrees F for 30 minutes, divide everything between plates and serve.

Nutrition:
calories 84
fat 2.4
fiber 2
carbs 6
protein 4.2

SOUS VIDE DESSERT RECIPES

Coffee Cream

Preparation time: 2 hours
Cooking time: 20 minutes
Servings: 6
Ingredients:
- 4 eggs, whisked
- Zest of 1 lime, grated
- 2 tablespoons coffee powder
- 3 tablespoons brown sugar
- 2 cups coconut cream

Directions:
1. In a blender, combine the eggs with the lime zest and the other ingredients, pulse well, pour this into a sous vide bag, seal, submerge in the preheated water oven and cook at 140 degrees F for 20 minutes.
2. Transfer this mix to a container and cool down for 2 hours before serving.

Nutrition:
calories 172
fat 2
fiber 1
carbs 4
protein 2

Turmeric and Lime Crème Brule

Preparation time: 1 hour
Cooking time: 1 hour and 10 minutes
Servings: 4
Ingredients:
- 1-quart heavy cream
- 4 tablespoons brown sugar
- ½ teaspoon turmeric powder
- ½ tablespoon lime zest, grated
- 8 egg yolks

Directions:
1. Heat up a pan with the cream over medium heat, add the lime zest and turmeric, cook for 10 minutes, take off the heat and cool down for 1 hour.
2. Heat up the pot with the cream over medium-high heat and take it off heat again.
3. In a bowl, mix the egg yolks with the sugar and the turmeric cream, whisk well, pour this into a large sous vide bag, seal the bag, introduce it in the preheated water oven and cook at 185 degrees F for 1 hour.
4. Divide into bowls and serve cold.

Nutrition:
calories 232
fat 4
fiber 5
carbs 8
protein 4

Walnuts Pudding

Preparation time: 10 minutes
Cooking time: 40 minutes
Servings: 4
Ingredients:
- 3 tablespoons brown sugar
- ½ cup walnuts, chopped
- ¼ cup lemon juice
- 1/3 cup coconut milk
- ¼ cup coconut flour
- 1 teaspoon butter, melted
- 2 eggs, whisked

Directions:
1. In a bowl, mix the eggs with the sugar, and the other ingredients except the butter and whisk well..
2. Grease 4 ramekins with the butter, divide the pudding mix in each and cover the ramekins with some tin foil.
3. Place ramekins in your sous vide machine, fill it with water until it reaches halfway up the side of the ramekins, cook at 185 degrees F for 40 minutes and serve cold.

Nutrition:
calories 192
fat 3
fiber 6
carbs 9
protein 6

Cinnamon Apples

Preparation time: 10 minutes
Cooking time: 40 minutes
Servings: 4
Ingredients:
- 1 pound apples, cored and cut into wedges
- 1 teaspoon cinnamon powder
- ½ teaspoon nutmeg, ground
- 3 tablespoons sugar

Directions:
1. In a sous vide bag, combine the apples with the cinnamon and the other ingredients, seal the bag, submerge it in the preheated water oven and cook at 176 degrees F for 40 minutes.
2. Divide the mix into bowls and serve them as a dessert.

Nutrition:
calories 177
fat 3
fiber 7
carbs 8
protein 3

Vanilla Pudding

Preparation time: 10 minutes
Cooking time: 30 minutes
Servings: 4
Ingredients:
- 1 cup heavy cream
- 1/3 cup milk
- 1 tablespoon sugar

- 3 eggs, whisked
- ½ teaspoon nutmeg, ground
- ¼ teaspoon vanilla extract

Directions:

1.	In a bowl, mix the cream with the milk and the other ingredients, whisk and divide the pudding into 4 ramekins.

2.	Put the ramekins in your water oven, fill the oven with water halfway up the sides of the ramekins, cook at 180 degrees F for 30 minutes and serve the puddings cold.

Nutrition:

calories 200

fat 2

fiber 5

carbs 7

protein 5

Grapes Bowls

Preparation time: 10 minutes

Cooking time: 40 minutes

Servings: 4

Ingredients:

- 2 cups grapes
- ½ cup heavy cream
- 2 tablespoons sugar
- 1 teaspoon nutmeg, ground

Directions:

1.	In a sous vide bag, combine the grapes with the cream and the other ingredients, seal the bag, submerge in the preheated water oven and cook at 176 degrees F for 40 minutes.

2.	Divide into bowls and serve.

Nutrition:

calories 162

fat 3

fiber 3

carbs 5

protein 3

Rice Pudding and Grapes

Preparation time: 10 minutes

Cooking time: 1 hour and 30 minutes

Servings: 4

Ingredients:

- 1 cup white rice
- 2 cups almond milk
- 1 cup grapes, halved
- 3 tablespoons sugar
- 1 tablespoon vanilla extract

Directions:

1.	In a sous vide bag, combine the rice with the milk and the other ingredients, seal the bag, submerge in the preheated water oven and cook at 180 degrees F for 1 hour and 30 minutes.

2.	Divide into bowls and serve.

Nutrition:

calories 162

fat 4

fiber 6

carbs 8

protein 4

Raisins Pudding

Preparation time: 10 minutes

Cooking time: 1 hour

Servings: 4

Ingredients:

- 2 cups almond milk
- 2 tablespoons almonds, chopped
- 1 teaspoon cardamom powder
- 2 tablespoons ghee, melted
- 3 tablespoons sugar
- 1 cup raisins
- ½ cup white rice

Directions:

1.	In a sous vide bag, combine the rice with the raisins, milk and the other ingredients, seal the bag, submerge in the water bath, cook at 174 degrees F for 1 hour, divide into bowls and serve as a dessert.

Nutrition:

calories 172

fat 4

fiber 2

carbs 6

protein 5

Orange Bowls

Preparation time: 10 minutes

Cooking time: 25 minutes

Servings: 2

Ingredients:

- ½ cup grapes, halved
- Juice of 1 orange
- 1 tablespoon dried lavender buds
- 2 tablespoons sugar
- 2 oranges, peeled and cut into wedges
- 1 teaspoon vanilla extract

Directions:

1.	In a sous vide bag, combine the oranges with the grapes and the other ingredients, seal the bag, submerge in the preheated water oven and cook at 185 degrees F for 25 minutes.

2.	Divide into bowls and serve cold.

Nutrition:

calories 181

fat 2

fiber 2

carbs 5

protein 4

Almond Cheesecake

Preparation time: 10 minutes

Cooking time: 1 hour and 30 minutes

Servings: 4

Ingredients:

- Cooking spray

For the filling:

- 12 ounces cream cheese
- 3 tablespoon sugar
- ½ cup almonds, chopped
- ¼ cup coconut cream
- 2 eggs, whisked
- Zest of 1 lime, grated
- 2 tablespoons lime juice
- 2 tablespoons butter, melted
- ¼ cup graham crackers, crushed
- ½ tablespoon brown sugar

Directions:
1. In a bowl, combine the butter with the crackers and brown sugar and stir well.
2. Grease 4 ramekins with the cooking spray and press the crackers layer on the bottom of each.
3. In a bowl, mix the cream cheese with the almonds and the other ingredients for the filling and blend using your mixer.
4. Divide this in each ramekin, cover them with tin foil, place them in your water oven, add water to cover the ramekins halfway and cook at 175 degrees F for 1 hour and 30 minutes.
5. Serve cold.

Nutrition:
calories 192
fat 2
fiber 5
carbs 7
protein 3

Cocoa Strawberries Cream

Preparation time: 10 minutes
Cooking time: 25 minutes
Servings: 6
Ingredients:
- 2 tablespoons sugar
- 4 eggs, whisked
- 1 cup strawberries, halved
- 1/3 cup cocoa powder
- ¼ cup heavy cream

Directions:
1. In a blender, mix the eggs with the berries and the other ingredients, pulse well, pour into a sous vide bag, seal, submerge in the water oven and cook at 165 degrees F for 25 minutes.
2. Divide this into dessert bowls and serve.

Nutrition:
calories 161
fat 2
fiber 3
carbs 6
protein 3

Caramel Apples Mix

Preparation time: 10 minutes
Cooking time: 50 minutes
Servings: 4
Ingredients:
- 1 teaspoon cinnamon powder
- 1 cup heavy cream
- ½ cup caramel syrup
- 2 tablespoons butter, melted
- 4 apples, cored and halved

Directions:
1. In a sous vide bag, mix the apples with the butter and the other ingredients, seal the bag, submerge in the preheated water oven and cook at 175 degrees F for 50 minutes.
2. Divide into bowls and serve warm,

Nutrition:
calories 200
fat 3
fiber 5
carbs 7
protein 2

Strawberries Bowls and Avocado

Preparation time: 10 minutes
Cooking time: 20 minutes
Servings: 2
Ingredients:
- 1 cup coconut cream
- ½ teaspoon vanilla extract
- 2 tablespoons sugar
- 2 cups strawberries, halved
- 1 cup avocado, peeled, pitted and halved

Directions:
1. In a sous vide bag, combine the berries with the avocado, cream and the other ingredients, seal the bag, submerge it in the preheated water oven and cook at 170 degrees F for 20 minutes.
2. Divide into bowls and serve.

Nutrition:
calories 155
fat 2
fiber 5
carbs 8
protein 4

Blackberries Cream

Preparation time: 10 minutes
Cooking time: 40 minutes
Servings: 4
Ingredients:
- 1 tablespoon sugar
- ½ teaspoon vanilla extract
- ¼ teaspoon cinnamon powder
- 2 cups blackberries
- 3 eggs, whisked
- 2 tablespoons butter, melted

Directions:
1. In a blender, mix the berries with the eggs and the other ingredients, pulse well, transfer to a sous vide bag, seal, submerge it in the preheated water oven and cook at 185 degrees F for 40 minutes.
2. Divide into bowls and serve really cold.

Nutrition:
calories 162

fat 4
fiber 4
carbs 5
protein 5

Lemon Compote

Preparation time: 10 minutes
Cooking time: 45 minutes
Servings: 6
Ingredients:
- ½ cup sugar
- Juice of 2 lemons
- Zest of 2 lemons, grated
- 1 cup water
- 1 lemon, peeled and chopped
- ½ teaspoon vanilla extract

Directions:
1. In a sous vide bag, combine the lemon juice with the sugar and the other ingredients, seal the bag, , submerge it in the preheated water oven and cook at 180 degrees F for 45 minutes
2. Divide into bowls and serve for dessert.

Nutrition:
calories 132
fat 2
fiber 3
carbs 4
protein 3

Apple Compote

Preparation time: 10 minutes
Cooking time: 40 minutes
Servings: 4
Ingredients:
- 1 tablespoon lemon zest, grated
- ½ teaspoon vanilla extract
- 2 teaspoons lemon juice
- ½ pound apples, cored and cut into wedges
- 4 tablespoons sugar
- 1 cup water

Directions:
1. In a sous vide bag, mix the apples with the sugar water and the other ingredients, seal the bag, submerge in the preheated water oven and cook at 183 degrees F for 40 minutes.
2. Divide into bowls and serve.

Nutrition:
calories 161
fat 2
fiber 5
carbs 5
protein 3

Orange Jam

Preparation time: 15 minutes
Cooking time: 40 minutes
Servings: 8
Ingredients:
- 3 cups oranges, peeled and cut into wedges
- ½ teaspoon vanilla powder
- ¼ cup sugar
- Zest of 1 orange, grated
- 1 cup water

Directions:
1. In a sous vide bag, mix the oranges with the sugar and the other ingredients, seal the bag, submerge it in the preheated water oven and cook at 140 degrees F for 40 minutes.
2. Transfer the jam to jars, seal and serve.

Nutrition:
calories 100
fat 1
fiber 1
carbs 2
protein 4

Avocado Cream

Preparation time: 2 hours
Cooking time: 20 minutes
Servings: 6
Ingredients:
- 2 tablespoons water
- ½ tablespoon lemon juice
- 2 tablespoons sugar
- ½ cup heavy cream
- 1 teaspoon gelatin
- 8 ounces cream cheese
- 1 cup avocado, peeled, pitted and mashed

Directions:
1. In a blender, combine the cream cheese with the avocado and the other ingredients and pulse well.
2. Divide this into 6 ramekins, cover with tin foil. introduce them all in your water oven, add water to cover the ramekins halfway and cook the pie at 183 degrees F for 20 minutes
3. Keep the cream in the fridge for 2 hours before serving.

Nutrition:
calories 234
fat 3
fiber 2
carbs 6
protein 7

Chocolate Cream Cheese Ramekins

Preparation time: 3 hours
Cooking time: 30 minutes
Servings: 4
Ingredients:
- 4 tablespoons heavy cream
- 2 cups cream cheese
- ½ cup sugar
- 1 teaspoon vanilla extract
- Cooking spray
- 1 tablespoon vanilla extract
- 4 tablespoons butter, melted
- 1 cup dark chocolate, melted

Directions:
1.	Grease 4 ramekins with the cooking spray.
2.	In a bowl, mix the melted butter with the chocolate and the other ingredients, whisk and divide into the ramekins.
3.	Cover the ramekins with tin foil, add water to the oven halfway to the sides of the ramekins and cook at 160 degrees F for 30 minutes.
4.	Keep the cream into the fridge for 3 hours before serving.
Nutrition:
calories 210
fat 43
fiber 3
carbs 7
protein 7

Coconut Raspberry Bowls

Preparation time: 10 minutes
Cooking time: 30 minutes
Servings: 6
Ingredients:
- 3 tablespoons sugar
- ½ teaspoon vanilla extract
- ½ teaspoon ginger, powder
- 1 cup raspberries
- ½ cup coconut butter, melted
- 1 cup coconut cream

Directions:
1.	In a sous vide bag, mix the cream with the raspberries, butter and the other ingredients, seal the bag, submerge in the preheated water oven and cook at 185 degrees F for 30 minutes.
2.	Divide into bowls and serve cold.
Nutrition:
calories 234
fat 22
fiber 2
carbs 7
protein 2

Plums Cream and Mascarpone

Preparation time: 10 minutes
Cooking time: 30 minutes
Servings: 4
Ingredients:
- 1 cup heavy cream
- 2 tablespoons sugar
- 1 cup plums, chopped
- 2 tablespoons lemon juice
- 8 ounces mascarpone cheese

Directions:
1.	In a bowl, mix the cream with the mascarpone and the other ingredients, whisk, transfer to a sous vide bag, seal, it, submerge in the preheated water oven and cook at 180 degrees F for 30 minutes.
2.	Divide into bowls and keep in the fridge until you serve.

Nutrition:
calories 265
fat 7
fiber 6
carbs 12
protein 4

Maple and Plums Pudding

Preparation time: 10 minutes
Cooking time: 40 minutes
Servings: 2
Ingredients:
- 2 tablespoons sugar
- 1 cup plums, stones removed and chopped
- 2 tablespoons cocoa powder
- 1 cup coconut milk
- ½ cup heavy cream
- 2 tablespoons water
- 1 tablespoon gelatin
- 3 tablespoons maple syrup

Directions:
1.	In a bowl, mix the gelatin with the water, maple syrup and the other ingredients, whisk well, divide into 2 ramekins, put them in your water oven, add water to cover the ramekins halfway and cook them at 180 degrees F for 40 minutes.
2.	Serve cold.
Nutrition:
calories 140
fat 2
fiber 2
carbs 4
protein 4

Almond Blueberries Ramekins

Preparation time: 10 minutes
Cooking time: 20 minutes
Servings: 4
Ingredients:
- 2 cups almond milk
- 1 teaspoon vanilla extract
- ½ teaspoon nutmeg, ground
- 2 tablespoons sugar
- 2 cups blueberries
- 2 tablespoons walnuts, chopped

Directions:
1.	In a bowl, mix the milk with the blueberries and the other ingredients, whisk well, divide into ramekins, put them in the water bath, add water to cover the ramekins halfway and cook at 170 degrees F for 20 minutes.
2.	Cool the mix down before serving.
Nutrition:
calories 210
fat 3
fiber 4
carbs 6
protein 7

Rice Pudding and Carrot

Preparation time: 10 minutes
Cooking time: 45 minutes
Servings: 4
Ingredients:
- 1 cup white rice
- ½ cup carrots, peeled and grated
- 3 egg yolks
- ½ teaspoon vanilla extract
- 2 cups coconut milk
- 2 tablespoons sugar

Directions:
1. In a sous vide bag, mix the rice with the milk and the other ingredients, seal the bag, submerge into your water oven, cook at 1 degrees F for 45 minutes, divide into bowls and serve.

Nutrition:
calories 140
fat 2
fiber 3
carbs 6
protein 2

Cardamom Pudding

Preparation time: 10 minutes
Cooking time: 30 minutes
Servings: 2
Ingredients:
- 3 tablespoons sugar
- 1 cup rice
- 2 cups coconut milk
- ½ teaspoon cardamom, ground

Directions:
1. In a sous vide bag, mix the rice with the milk and the other ingredients, seal the bag, submerge in the water oven and cook at 170 degrees F for 30 minutes.
2. Serve the rice pudding cold.

Nutrition:
calories 150
fat 1
fiber 2
carbs 5
protein 6

Nuts Custard

Preparation time: 10 minutes
Cooking time: 35 minutes
Servings: 6
Ingredients:
- 4 tablespoons lemon zest, grated
- 4 eggs, whisked
- 2 tablespoons sugar
- 2 tablespoons lemon juice
- 2 cups almond milk
- 2 tablespoons walnuts, chopped
- 2 tablespoons macadamia nuts, chopped

Directions:

1. In a blender, mix the walnuts with the macadamia nuts, milk and the other ingredients, pulse well, pour into ramekins and place them in your water oven.
2. Add water to cover the ramekins halfway and cook at 180 degrees F for 35 minutes.
3. Leave the custard to cool down before serving.

Nutrition:
calories 120
fat 6
fiber 2
carbs 5
protein 7

Creamy Berries Bowls

Preparation time: 10 minutes
Cooking time: 30 minutes
Servings: 4
Ingredients:
- ½ cup blackberries
- ½ cup blueberries
- ½ cup raspberries
- 2 tablespoons sugar
- 3 tablespoons walnuts, chopped
- 2 cups heavy cream

Directions:
1. In a sous vide bag, mix the berries with the cream and the other ingredients, seal the bag, submerge in the water bath and cook at 160 degrees F for 30 minutes.
2. Divide into bowls and serve.

Nutrition:
calories 135
fat 34
fiber 2
carbs 6
protein 2

Sweet Coconut Mix

Preparation time: 10 minutes
Cooking time: 40 minutes
Servings: 4
Ingredients:
- 2 cups coconut cream
- 1 cup coconut flesh, shredded
- 2 tablespoons sugar
- 1 apple, cored and cubed
- 1 cup strawberries

Directions:
1. In a sous vide bag, mix the coconut with the cream and the other ingredients, seal the bag, submerge it in the preheated water oven and cook at 170 degrees F for 40 minutes.
2. Divide this mix into bowls and serve cold.

Nutrition:
calories 162
fat 4
fiber 1

carbs 5
protein 4

Carrot Custard

Preparation time: 10 minutes
Cooking time: 40 minutes
Servings: 4
Ingredients:
- 1 cup carrots, peeled and grated
- ½ teaspoon vanilla extract
- 1 teaspoon cinnamon powder
- 3 tablespoons sugar
- 1 tablespoon gelatin
- ¼ cup warm water
- 1 cup heavy cream
- 1 cup coconut cream

Directions:
1. In a bowl, mix the cream with the gelatin, water and the other ingredients, whisk really well, divide custard into ramekins, cover them with tin foil, place them in your water oven, add water to cover the ramekins halfway and cook at 167 degrees F for 40 minutes.
2. Serve the custard cold.

Nutrition:
calories 200
fat 2
fiber 1
carbs 3
protein 5

Pears Jam

Preparation time: 10 minutes
Cooking time: 1 hour
Servings: 8
Ingredients:
- 2 pounds pears, cored and roughly cubed
- 1 cup water
- 3 tablespoons sugar
- ½ teaspoon nutmeg, ground
- ½ teaspoon vanilla extract
- 1 tablespoon cinnamon powder

Directions:
1. In a sous vide bag, combine the pears with the water, sugar and the other ingredients, toss, seal the bag, submerge in the preheated water oven and cook at 183 degrees F for 1 hour.
2. Transfer the jam to a large bowl, blend it a bit using an immersion blender, divide into smaller bowls and serve cold.

Nutrition:
calories 140
fat 0
fiber 2
carbs 7
protein 4

Strawberries Compote

Preparation time: 10 minutes

Cooking time: 30 minutes
Servings: 4
Ingredients:
- Zest of 1 lime, grated
- 3 tablespoons sugar
- 1 cup water
- 2 cups strawberries, chopped
- Juice of 1 lime

Directions:
1. In a sous vide bag, mix the berries with the water and the other ingredients, seal the bag, submerge it in the preheated water oven and cook at 183 degrees F for 30 minutes.
2. Divide into cups and serve cold.

Nutrition:
calories 200
fat 1
fiber 3
carbs 12
protein 3

Cinnamon Nectarines Bowls

Preparation time: 10 minutes
Cooking time: 40 minutes
Servings: 4
Ingredients:
- 1 pound nectarines, stones removed and halved
- 2 tablespoons sugar
- 1 cup almond milk
- ½ teaspoon vanilla extract
- ½ teaspoon cinnamon powder
- 1 teaspoon almond extract

Directions:
1. In a sous vide bag, mix the nectarines with the milk, sugar and the other ingredients, seal the bag, submerge in the preheated water oven and cook at 183 degrees F for 40 minutes.
2. Divide into bowls and serve them cold.

Nutrition:
calories 152
fat 2
fiber 2
carbs 4
protein 3

Rhubarb Compote

Preparation time: 10 minutes
Cooking time: 35 minutes
Servings: 4
Ingredients:
- 1 teaspoon cinnamon powder
- 1 teaspoon vanilla extract
- 1 cup water
- 2 cups rhubarb, roughly sliced
- 2 tablespoons sugar

Directions:
1. In a sous vide bag, mix the rhubarb with the sugar and the other ingredients, seal the bag,

submerge in the preheated water oven and cook at 183 degrees F for 35 minutes
2.   Divide into bowls and serve cold.
Nutrition:
calories 120
fat 2
fiber 2
carbs 6
protein 2

Berries Compote and Apples

Preparation time: 10 minutes
Cooking time: 40 minutes
Servings: 4
Ingredients:
- 1 cup strawberries
- 3 tablespoon sugar
- 1 teaspoon cinnamon powder
- 4 apples, cored and roughly chopped
- 2 cups water

Directions:
1.   In a sous vide bag, mix the apples with the berries and the other ingredients, seal the bag, submerge in the preheated water oven and cook at 170 degrees F for 40 minutes.
2.   Divide into bowls and serve cold.
Nutrition:
calories 142
fat 2
fiber 2
carbs 6
protein 2

Minty Apples Compote

Preparation time: 10 minutes
Cooking time: 30 minutes
Servings: 4
Ingredients:
- 4 apples, cored and cut into wedges
- 3 tablespoon sugar
- ½ teaspoon vanilla extract
- ½ cup water
- 1 tablespoon mint, chopped

Directions:
1.   In a sous vide bag, combine the apples with the sugar and the other ingredients, seal, submerge in the preheated water oven and cook at 180 degrees F for 30 minutes.
2.   Divide into bowls and serve cold.
Nutrition:
calories 101
fat 1
fiber 1
carbs 8
protein 1

Figs and Grapes Compote

Preparation time: 10 minutes
Cooking time: 30 minutes

Servings: 4
Ingredients:
- 1 pound figs
- ½ cup water
- 4 tablespoons sugar
- 1 cup apple juice
- 1 cup grapes, halved

Directions:
1.   In a sous vide bag, combine the apple juice with the grapes and the other ingredients, seal the bag, submerge it in the preheated water oven and cook at 170 degrees F for 30 minutes.
2.   Divide this into bowls and serve cold.
Nutrition:
calories 130
fat 0
fiber 1
carbs 9
protein 1

Sweet Pumpkin Bowls

Preparation time: 10 minutes
Cooking time: 40 minutes
Servings: 4
Ingredients:
- 1 tablespoon sugar
- 2 cups pumpkin, peeled and roughly cubed
- 1 tablespoon butter, melted
- ½ teaspoon cinnamon powder
- ½ cup coconut cream

Directions:
1.   In a sous vide bag, mix the pumpkin with the sugar, butter and the other ingredients, toss, seal the bag, submerge it in the preheated water oven and cook at 182 degrees F for 40 minutes.
2.   Divide into bowls and serve warm.
Nutrition:
calories 120
fat 1
fiber 1
carbs 2
protein 2

Pecan Plums Bowls

Preparation time: 10 minutes
Cooking time: 35 minutes
Servings: 4
Ingredients:
- ½ teaspoon vanilla extract
- Juice of 1 lime
- 2 tablespoons sugar
- ½ teaspoon cinnamon powder
- 1 pound plums, stoned and halved
- ½ cups pecans, chopped
- 1 cup heavy cream

Directions:
1.   In a sous vide bag, mix the plums with the pecans, cream and the other ingredients, toss, seal

the bag, submerge in the preheated water oven and cook at 183 degrees F for 35 minutes.
2.   Divide into bowls and serve.
Nutrition:
calories 152
fat 2
fiber 2
carbs 8
protein 7

Rhubarb Jam and Blackberry

Preparation time: 10 minutes
Cooking time: 50 minutes
Servings: 4
Ingredients:
- 1 pound blackberries
- 2 cups rhubarb, chopped
- 2 cups water
- Juice of 1 lime
- 1 cup sugar

Directions:
1.   In a sous vide bag, mix the berries with the rhubarb and the other ingredients, whisk, seal the bag, submerge it in the preheated water oven and cook at 185 degrees F for 1 hour.
2.   Divide into cups and serve cold.
Nutrition:
calories 100
fat 2
fiber 3
carbs 8
protein 3

Black Currant Marmalade

Preparation time: 2 hours
Cooking time: 1 hour
Servings: 8
Ingredients:
- Juice of 1 lemon
- Zest of 1 lemon, grated
- 2 tablespoon water
- ½ pound blueberries
- 4 ounces black currant
- 2 cups sugar

Directions:
1.   In a sous vide bag, mix the berries with the currant and the other ingredients, whisk, seal the bag, submerge it in the preheated water oven and cook at 180 degrees F for 1 hour.
2.   Divide into bowls and keep in the fridge for 2 hours before serving.
Nutrition:
calories 100
fat 2
fiber 3
carbs 7
protein 3

Lime Jam

Preparation time: 10 minutes
Cooking time: 45 minutes
Servings: 8
Ingredients:
- 2 tablespoons lime zest, grated
- 2 tablespoons lime juice
- 1 cup sugar
- 1 cup water
- 1 tablespoon ginger, grated

Directions:
1.   In a sous vide bag, mix the lime juice with the sugar and the other ingredients, seal the bag, submerge it in the preheated water oven and cook at 160 degrees F for 45 minutes.
2.   Divide into bowls and serve cold.
Nutrition:
calories 162
fat 2
fiber 3
carbs 8
protein 4

Creamy Pears

Preparation time: 10 minutes
Cooking time: 50 minutes
Servings: 6
Ingredients:
- 1 pound, cored and cut into quarters
- 1 cup heavy cream
- ¼ cup apple juice
- 1 teaspoon cinnamon powder
- ½ teaspoon nutmeg, ground

Directions:
1.   In a sous vide bag, mix the pears with the cream and the other ingredients, seal the bag, submerge it in the preheated water oven and cook at 180 degrees F for 50 minutes.
2.   Divide into bowls and serve cold.
Nutrition:
calories 100
fat 2
fiber 2
carbs 6
protein 4

Peaches Bowls

Preparation time: 10 minutes
Cooking time: 30 minutes
Servings: 6
Ingredients:
- ½ teaspoon cinnamon powder
- 1 teaspoon vanilla extract
- 1 cup heavy cream
- 6 peaches, cored and cut into quarters
- 3 tablespoons sugar

Directions:
1.   In a sous vide bag, mix the peaches with the sugar and the other ingredients, seal the bag,

submerge it in the preheated water bath and cook at 183 degrees F for 30 minutes.

2.   Divide into bowls and serve.

Nutrition:

calories 125

fat 3

fiber 5

carbs 6

protein 4

Figs Bowls and Avocado

Preparation time: 10 minutes

Cooking time: 40 minutes

Servings: 4

Ingredients:

- ½ cup coconut milk
- ½ cup sugar
- ½ teaspoon ginger, ground
- 1 cup heavy cream
- 1 cup avocado, peeled, pitted and cubed
- 1 pound figs, halved

Directions:

1.   In a sous vide bag, mix the avocado with the figs and the other ingredients, toss, seal the bag, submerge it in the preheated water oven and cook at 170 degrees F for 40 minutes.

2.   Divide into bowls and serve cold.

Nutrition:

calories 121

fat 2

fiber 2

carbs 6

protein 4

Peach Jelly

Preparation time: 10 minutes

Cooking time: 40 minutes

Servings: 4

Ingredients:

- 4 pears, cored and cubed
- Juice of 1 lemon
- 2 cups currant jelly
- 3 tablespoons sugar
- ½ teaspoon almond extract
- ½ teaspoon vanilla extract

Directions:

1.   In a sous vide bag, mix the pears with the jelly and the other ingredients, seal the bag, shake it a bit, submerge it in the preheated water oven and cook at 180 degrees F for 40 minutes.

2.   Divide everything into dessert bowls and serve cold.

Nutrition:

calories 182

fat 3

fiber 1

carbs 2

protein 3

Cocoa Berries Cream

Preparation time: 5 minutes

Cooking time: 35 minutes

Servings: 4

Ingredients:

- 1 cup dark chocolate, chopped
- 1 cup coconut milk
- 2 tablespoons sugar
- 1 tablespoon cocoa powder
- 1 cup blackberries

Directions:

1.   In a blender, mix the chocolate with the milk, berries and the other ingredients, pulse well, divide into 4 ramekins, place the ramekins in your water oven, fill the oven with water halfway up the sides of the ramekins, cover the ramekins with tin foil and cook at 180 degrees F for 35 minutes.

2.   Serve warm.

Nutrition:

calories 110

fat 3

fiber 2

carbs 4

protein 2

Cauliflower Rice Pudding and Dates

Preparation time: 5 minutes

Cooking time: 45 minutes

Servings: 4

Ingredients:

- ½ cup dates, chopped
- 1 cup cauliflower rice
- 2 cups almond milk
- 2 tablespoons sugar
- ½ teaspoon cinnamon powder
- ½ teaspoon vanilla extract

Directions:

1.   In a sous vide bag, mix the cauliflower with the dates and the other ingredients, seal the bag, submerge in the water oven, and cook at 180 degrees F for 45 minutes.

2.   Divide into bowls and serve warm.

Nutrition:

calories 174

fat 1

fiber 3

carbs 6

protein 7

Pumpkin Curd and Berry

Preparation time: 10 minutes

Cooking time: 25 minutes

Servings: 4

Ingredients:

- 3 tablespoons sugar
- 1 cup raspberries
- 1 cup pumpkin, peeled and chopped
- 2 egg yolks, whisked
- 2 tablespoons lemon juice

- 2 tablespoons butter, melted

Directions:
1. In a blender, combine the berries with the pumpkin and the other ingredients and pulse well.
2. Pour this into a sous vide bag, seal it, submerge in the preheated water oven and cook at 180 degrees F for 25 minutes.
3. Transfer the mix to a container and serve cold.

Nutrition:
calories 132
fat 1
fiber 5
carbs 7
protein 4

Peach Compote

Preparation time: 10 minutes
Cooking time: 30 minutes
Servings: 4
Ingredients:
- Juice of 1 lime
- Zest of 1 lime, grated
- 3 tablespoons sugar
- 1 pound peaches, stones removed and halved
- 2 cups water

Directions:
1. In a sous vide bag, combine the peaches with the water and the other ingredients, seal the bag, submerge it in the preheated water oven and cook at 180 degrees F for 30 minutes.
2. Divide into bowls and serve cold.

Nutrition:
calories 105
fat 2
fiber 0
carbs 2
protein 2

Tomato Jam

Preparation time: 10 minutes
Cooking time: 25 minutes
Servings: 6
Ingredients:
- 2 pounds tomatoes, peeled and cubed
- 3 tablespoons sugar
- 1 cup water
- ½ teaspoon ginger powder
- 1 tablespoon vinegar

Directions:
3. In a sous vide bag, mix the tomatoes with the sugar and the other ingredients, seal, submerge in the preheated water oven and cook at 180 degrees F for 25 minutes.
4. Transfer to a blender, pulse a bit, divide into bowls and serve cold.

Nutrition:
calories 102

fat 2
fiber 1
carbs 2
protein 6

Dates Espresso Cream

Preparation time: 10 minutes
Cooking time: 30 minutes
Servings: 4
Ingredients:
- 2 tablespoons espresso powder
- 1 cup heavy cream
- 2 eggs, whisked
- Cooking spray
- 2 cups dates, chopped
- 2 tablespoons brown sugar

Directions:
1. In a blender, combine the espresso powder with the dates and the other ingredients and pulse well..
2. Grease 4 ramekins with the cooking spray, divide the mix in each and cover them with tin foil.
3. Put the ramekins in the water bath, fill it with water halfway and cook at 180 degrees F for 30 minutes.
4. Serve the cream cold.

Nutrition:
calories 152
fat 5
fiber 2
carbs 6
protein 3

Mango Bowls

Preparation time: 10 minutes
Cooking time: 20 minutes
Servings: 4
Ingredients:
- 1 tablespoon almonds, chopped
- 1 cup mango, peeled and roughly cubed
- 1 cup heavy cream
- 1 teaspoon almond extract
- 1 tablespoon brown sugar

Directions:
1. In a sous vide bag, mix the mango with the cream and the other ingredients, seal the bag, submerge in the water oven, cook at 170 degrees F for 20 minutes, divide the mix into bowls and serve.

Nutrition:
calories 220
fat 4
fiber 2
carbs 4
protein 6

Fruit Salad

Preparation time: 10 minutes
Cooking time: 20 minutes
Servings: 4

Ingredients:
- 2 tablespoons brown sugar
- 1 cup avocado, peeled, pitted and cubed
- ½ cup mango, peeled and cubed
- 1 cup heavy cream
- 1 cup blackberries
- 1 cup strawberries

Directions:
1. In a sous vide bag, mix the avocado with the mango and the other ingredients, seal the bag, cook in the water oven and cook at 170 degrees F for 20 minutes.
2. Divide the mix into bowls and serve.

Nutrition:
calories 262
fat 7
fiber 2
carbs 5
protein 8

Apples Bowls and Nuts

Preparation time: 10 minutes
Cooking time: 20 minutes
Servings: 4
Ingredients:
- 4 apples, cored and halved
- 1 tablespoon brown sugar
- ½ cup heavy cream
- 2 tablespoons almonds, chopped
- 1 tablespoon pecans, chopped
- 1 tablespoon walnuts, chopped

Directions:
1. In a sous vide bag, mix the apples with the sugar, cream and the other ingredients, seal the bag, submerge in the water bath, cook at 180 degrees F for 20 minutes, divide the mix into bowls and serve.

Nutrition:
calories 120
fat 2
fiber 2
carbs 4
protein 3

Peaches Bowls and Plums

Preparation time: 10 minutes
Cooking time: 15 minutes
Servings: 4
Ingredients:
- ½ teaspoon vanilla extract
- 3 tablespoons sugar
- 1 teaspoon ginger powder
- 2 cups plums, pitted and halved
- 1 cup peaches, stones removed and cubed
- 1 cup heavy cream

Directions:
1. In a sous vide bag, mix the plums with the peaches, cream and the other ingredients, seal the bag, submerge in the water bath, cook at 170 degrees F for 15 minutes, divide the mix into bowls and serve.

Nutrition:
calories 162
fat 2
fiber 2
carbs 4
protein 5

Berries Pudding and Yogurt

Preparation time: 5 minutes
Cooking time: 25 minutes
Servings: 4
Ingredients:
- 1 cup Greek yogurt
- 1 cup raspberries
- 3 tablespoons sugar
- ½ teaspoon cinnamon powder
- 1 cup heavy cream
- 2 eggs, whisked
- ½ teaspoon baking soda

Directions:
1. In a blender, combine the cream with the eggs, yogurt and the other ingredients, pulse well, transfer to a sous vide bag, submerge in the water oven, cook at 180 degrees F for 25 minutes, divide into bowls and serve.

Nutrition:
calories 172
fat 2
fiber 3
carbs 4
protein 5

Ginger Cream and Strawberries

Preparation time: 10 minutes
Cooking time: 30 minutes
Servings: 4
Ingredients:
- 1 tablespoon ginger, grated
- ½ teaspoon vanilla extract
- ½ teaspoon almond extract
- 1 cup heavy cream
- 1 cup strawberries, chopped
- 1 cup Greek yogurt
- 2 tablespoons brown sugar

Directions:
1. In a blender, combine the berries with the yogurt, sugar and the other ingredients, pulse well and divide into 4 ramekins.
2. Cover the ramekins with tin foil, put them in the water oven, fill it halfway with water, cook at 170 degrees F for 30 minutes and serve cold.

Nutrition:
calories 200
fat 5
fiber 3
carbs 4
protein 5

Cinnamon Cream

Preparation time: 10 minutes
Cooking time: 25 minutes
Serving: 4
Ingredients:

- 1 tablespoon cinnamon powder
- 1 cup heavy cream
- ½ teaspoon pumpkin pie spice
- 2 eggs, whisked
- 1 cup Greek yogurt
- 2 tablespoons brown sugar

Directions:

1. In a bowl, mix the cream with the eggs, cinnamon and the other ingredients, whisk well, transfer to a sous vide bag, seal it, submerge in the water bath, cook at 170 degrees F for 25 minutes, divide into bowls, cool down and serve.

Nutrition:
calories 200
fat 5
fiber 2
carbs 5
protein 6

Quinoa Pudding

Preparation time: 10 minutes
Cooking time: 20 minutes
Servings: 4
Ingredients:

- 2 tablespoons honey
- ½ teaspoon ginger powder
- 1 teaspoon cinnamon powder
- 1 cup quinoa
- 2 cups almond milk
- 2 tablespoons sugar

Directions:

1. In a sous vide bag, mix the quinoa with the sugar, honey and the other ingredients, seal the bag, submerge in the water bath, cook at 180 degree F for 20 minutes divide the pudding into bowls and serve.

Nutrition:
calories 172
fat 4
fiber 2
carbs 4
protein 5

Quinoa Bowls and Avocado

Preparation time: 10 minutes
Cooking time: 30 minutes
Servings: 4
Ingredients:

- 1 cup avocado, peeled, pitted and roughly cubed
- 1 cup quinoa
- 2 cups coconut milk
- 2 tablespoons sugar
- ½ teaspoon almond extract

Directions:

1. In a sous vide bag, mix the quinoa with the milk and the other ingredients, seal the bag, submerge in the water bath, cook at 180 degrees F for 30 minutes, divide into bowls and serve warm.

Nutrition:
calories 172
fat 2
fiber 2
carbs 4
protein 6

APPENDIX : RECIPES INDEX

Chicken Dip 61
Chicken Salad 60
Chicken Soup 29
Chicken Wings and Tomato Sauce 92
Chicken with Brussels Sprouts Mix 85
Chicken with Endives 85
Chicken with Hot Red Chard 90
Chicken with Okra 93
Chicken with Tomato and Kale 91
Chickpeas Breakfast Spread 21
Chickpeas Spread 64
Chickpeas Stew 36
Chili Chicken 29
Chili Chicken 83
Chili Cod 71
Chili Collard Greens 115
Chili Mussels and Lime 72
Chili Tuna 67
Chinese Beef Bites 62
Chives Avocado Quinoa 20
Chives Cod 72
Chives Lamb 96
Chives Potatoes 51
Chives Radish 113
Chives Shrimp Mix 69
Chocolate Cream Cheese Ramekins 126
Cilantro Hot Artichokes 115
Cinnamon Apples 123
Cinnamon Chicken 93
Cinnamon Cream 134
Cinnamon Eggs 13
Cinnamon Nectarines Bowls 129
Cinnamon Rice Pudding 9
Cinnamon Toast 7
Citrus Lamb Mix 107
Clam Bowls 58
Clams and Wine Sauce 78
Cocoa Berries Cream 132
Cocoa Strawberries Cream 125
Coconut Berry Mix 8
Coconut Broccoli Mix 121
Coconut Cabbage 118
Coconut Cheese Dip 52
Coconut Cod 74
Coconut Dip 65
Coconut Eggs 9
Coconut Endives and Radish 45
Coconut Leeks Mix 12
Coconut Pork Chops and Curry 33
Coconut Raspberry Bowls 127
Coconut Tomatoes and Spinach 122
Coconut Turkey 87
Cod and Carrots 71
Cod and Green Beans 68

Cod Salsa 23
Cod Salsa 58
Cod, Olives and Zucchinis 76
Coffee Cream 123
Coriander Leg of Lamb 27
Coriander Shrimp Mix 75
Coriander Tomato and Spinach Mix 43
Corn and Green Beans 111
Corn and Lamb 101
Crab Dip 54
Cranberry Beef 31
Cream Cheese and Spinach Eggs 10
Creamy Bell Peppers 112
Creamy Berries Bowls 128
Creamy Calamari 23
Creamy Chicken 90
Creamy Cod and Zucchinis 79
Creamy Corn 49
Creamy Corn Dip 60
Creamy Garlic Spinach and Corn 47
Creamy Lamb 99
Creamy Pears 131
Creamy Pork 96
Creamy Radish and Corn Mix 49
Creamy Salmon Mix 77
Creamy Scallions Sauce and Pork 106
Creamy Spinach 41
Creamy Tomatoes 50
Creamy Zucchini 113
Creole Calamari 77
Cucumber Mix and Lamb 103
Cucumber Salad and Shrimp 57
Cumin Okra 42
Cumin Turkey 87
Curry Chicken Thighs 28
Curry Sea Bass 75
Curry Shrimp 69
Curry Trout and Green Beans 75

D

Dates Espresso Cream 133
Dill Eggplant 50
Dill Endives 115
Dill Peas 51
Dill Tomatoes 113
Duck and Plums Mix 92
Duck and Spinach Salad 61
Duck and Tomatoes 82

E

Eggplant and Okra Mix 116
Eggplant and Pearl Onion Mix 44
Eggplant Bowls 18
Eggplant Dip 64
Eggplant Stew 35
Eggs and Asparagus 15

Printed by Libri Plureos GmbH in Hamburg, Germany